SURINAM

Marxist Regimes Series

Series editor: Bogdan Szajkowski,
Department of Sociology, University College,
Cardiff

Further Titles

SURINAM

Politics, Economics and Society

Henk E. Chin and Hans Buddingh'

 Frances Pinter (Publishers),
London and New York

First published in Great Britain in 1987 by
Frances Pinter (Publishers) Limited
25 Floral Street, London WC2E 9DS

British Library Cataloguing in Publication Data
Chin, Henk E.
    Surinam: politics, economics and society.
    —(Marxist regimes series).
    1. Surinam—Social conditions
    I. Title   II. Buddingh', Hans   III. Series
    988'.303   HN330.5.A8
ISBN   0-86187-516-8
ISBN   0-86187-517-6 Pbk

Typeset by Joshua Associates Limited, Oxford
Printed by SRP Ltd, Exeter

Editor's Preface

This, the first study in the English language of Surinam's politics, economics and society, comes out at the time of renewed interest in the country's future. Torn by increasingly debilitating internal strife, which may result in outside intervention, Surinam is at the crossroads, as is the future of the Marxist groups which weald unprecedented power in the country's politics.

This volume also offers a unique insight into the role played by Marxist groups in the development of a Third World polity faced by enormous social, political and economic problems, and, as such, must be seen as an important contribution to the wider discussion of options available to Marxist regimes in the first stages of their establishment.

The study of Marxist regimes has commonly been equated with the study of communist political systems. There were several historical and methodological reasons for this. For many years it was not difficult to distinguish the eight regimes in Eastern Europe and four in Asia which resoundingly claimed adherence to the tenets of Marxism and more particularly to their Soviet interpretation—Marxism–Leninism. These regimes, variously called 'People's Republic', 'People's Democratic Republic', or 'Democratic Republic', claimed to have derived their inspiration from the Soviet Union to which, indeed, in the overwhelming number of cases they owed their establishment.

To many scholars and analysts these regimes represented a multiplication of and geographical extension of the 'Soviet model' and consequently of the Soviet sphere of influence. Although there were clearly substantial similarities between the Soviet Union and the people's democracies, especially in the initial phases of their development, these were often overstressed at the expense of noticing the differences between these political systems.

It took a few years for scholars to realize that generalizing the particular, i.e., applying the Soviet experience to other states ruled by elites which claimed to be guided by 'scientific socialism', was not good enough. The relative simplicity of the assumption of a cohesive communist bloc was questioned after the expulsion of Yugoslavia from the Communist Information Bureau in 1948 and in particular after the workers' riots in Poznań in 1956 and the Hungarian revolution of the same year. By the mid-1960s, the totalitarian model of communist politics, which until then had been very much in force, began to crumble. As some of these regimes articulated demands for a distinctive path of socialist development, many specialists studying these systems began to notice that the cohesiveness of the communist bloc was less apparent than had been claimed before.

Also by the mid-1960s, in the newly independent African states 'democratic' multi-party states were turning into one-party states or military dictatorships, thus questioning the inherent superiority of liberal democracy, capitalism and the values that went with it. Scholars now began to ponder on the simple contrast between multi-party democracy and a one-party totalitarian rule that had satisfied an earlier generation.

More importantly, however, by the beginning of that decade Cuba had a revolution without Soviet help, a revolution which subsequently became to many political elites in the Third World not only an inspiration but a clear military, political and ideological example to follow. Apart from its romantic appeal, to many nationalist movements the Cuban revolution also demonstrated a novel way of conducting and winning a nationalist, anti-imperialist war and accepting Marxism as the state ideology without a vanguard communist party. The Cuban precedent was subsequently followed in one respect or another by scores of Third World regimes, which used the adoption of 'scientific socialism' tied to the tradition of Marxist thought as a form of mobilization, legitimation or association with the prestigious symbols and powerful high-status regimes such as the Soviet Union, China, Cuba and Vietnam.

Despite all these changes the study of Marxist regimes remains in its infancy and continues to be hampered by constant and not always pertinent comparison with the Soviet Union, thus somewhat blurring the important underlying common theme—the 'scientific theory' of the laws of development of human society and human history. This doctrine is claimed by the leadership of these regimes to consist of the discovery of objective causal relationships; it is used to analyse the contradictions which arise between goals and actuality in the pursuit of a common destiny. Thus the political elites of these countries have been and continue to be influenced in both their ideology and their political practice by Marxism more than any other current of social thought and political practice.

The growth in the number and global significance, as well as the ideological political and economic impact, of Marxist regimes has presented scholars and students with an increasing challenge. In meeting this challenge, social scientists on both sides of the political divide have put forward a dazzling profusion of terms, models, programmes and varieties of interpretation. It is against the background of this profusion that the present comprehensive series on Marxist regimes is offered.

This collection of monographs is envisaged as a series of multi-disciplinary textbooks on the governments, politics, economics and society of these countries. Each of the monographs was prepared by a specialist on the country concerned. Thus, over fifty scholars from all over the world have contributed monographs which were based on first-hand knowledge. The geographical diversity of the authors, combined with the fact that as a group they represent many disciplines of social science, gives their individual analyses and the series as a whole an additional dimension.

Each of the scholars who contributed to this series was asked to analyse such topics as the political culture, the governmental structure, the ruling party, other mass organizations, party-state relations, the policy process, the economy, domestic and foreign relations together with any features peculiar to the country under discussion.

This series does not aim at assigning authenticity or authority to any single one of the political systems included in it. It shows that, depending on a variety of historical, cultural, ethnic and political factors, the pursuit of goals derived from the tenets of Marxism has produced different political forms at different times and in different places. It also illustrates the rich diversity among these societies, where attempts to achieve a synthesis between goals derived from Marxism on the one hand, and national realities on the other, have often meant distinctive approaches and solutions to the problems of social, political and economic development.

University College   *Bogdan Szajkowski*
Cardiff

Contents

List of Tables

Preface and Acknowledgements

World attention has focused on Surinam several times in recent years: first in February 1980, when sixteen meagrely armed sergeants seized power. The new military regime promised to dismantle the old system of injustice, corruption and social inequality. The revolution, it said, would mark the dawn of a new age for the country and its people.

Two small Marxist groups, which had provided political support for the military immediately after the coup, have tried with varying degrees of success to expand their influence. This was the first time in the country's history that Marxist groups were able to play a role at the centre of political power.

Surinam made world news again in December 1982, when fifteen prominent critics of the regime were gunned down while in military custody. Since then, several foreign powers (most notably the United States and neighbouring Brazil) have expressed deep concern with the strong Cuban presence in Surinam, particularly in 1982 and 1983.

This tiny country recently regained international attention and prompted French concern when reports were made of an apparent Libyan presence in the country, the massacre of several hundred civilians by the National Army in its war with the 'Jungle Commando' and the ensuing stream of refugees to French Guyana.

This book provides an historical overview of Surinam's economic, political and social developments from the country's earliest history to the present day. Greatest emphasis, however, has been placed on the rule of the current military regime, during which Marxist groups have played an unprecedentedly major role in national politics. At the time the book was completed, the country's immediate future was quite uncertain. The concluding remarks therefore include the authors' (brief) reflections on what they consider the most probable short-term turns of events.

The authors would like to thank Bogdan Szajkowski for providing them with the opportunity to add to this series their observations and ideas about Surinam, the birthplace of one of the authors and a country which has won the heart of the other author during his frequent visits.

We are grateful to Silvia W. de Groot and Hans Brandsma, both of the University of Amsterdam, for their constructive contributions to some specific parts of this book.

Further thanks to Rudi Kross and Frans van Klaveren, both experts in the field of Surinamese affairs, for reading and commenting on sections of the manuscript, and to our typist, Cynthia Pools.

Finally, we would like to thank Sam Garrett for his competent translation of the manuscript.

Amsterdam, April 1987
Henk E. Chin
Hans Buddingh'

Basic Data

Official name	Republic of Surinam (Republiek Suriname)
Capital	Paramaribo
Land	Area 163,820 sq. km.
Population	405,000 (end 1986)
Population growth (% p.a.)	1.6 (1980–6)
Total labour force	130,000 (1986)
Ethnic groups (%)	East Indians 35.0; Coloureds 32.0; Indonesians 15.0; Bushnegros 10.5; Amerindians 2.5; Chinese 2.0; Europeans 1.5; Others 1.5
Official language	Dutch
Other significant languages	Sranan and other Creole languages, Sarnami (originated from Hindi and Urdu), Javanese (Indonesian language), Amerindian dialects
Administrative division	10 districts
Political structure	
Constitution	Suspended since 13 August 1980
Highest legislative body	Government (Military Authority, Supreme Council ('Top Beraad') and Cabinet) and National Assembly (not generally elected)
Highest executive body	Supreme Council
Military leader	Desi Bouterse
Prime minister	Jules Wijdenbosch
President	F. Ramdat Misier (acting)
Leader of the government	Desi Bouterse

Economy
   GNP (factor cost)   US$1,090m. (1984)
   GNP per capita   US$2,770 (1984)
   GNP by %   Agriculture & Forestry 9; Mining &
                                   Processing 17; Industry 17;
                                   Government 24; Other Services 33
                                   (1984)

   Average annual growth
   of GNP   1970–9 4.7%; 1979–85 −2.3%
   State budget   Expenditure US$472m.
                                     Revenue US$268m. (1985)

Defence expenditure % of
   state budget   10–25 (1981–6)

Monetary unit   Surinam Guilder (US$1 − SG 1.785)

Main natural resources   Bauxite, timber, fishing, agriculture
Main crops   Rice, bananas, palm kernel, shrimps
Land tenure   Freehold, leasehold and state farms

Trade and balance of payments

	1980	*1982*	*1985*
Exports US$m.	514	429	332
Imports US$m.	504	516	304

Main exports   Bauxite, alumina, aluminium, rice,
                                   shrimps, bananas, palm oil, wood and
                                   wood products

Main imports   Capital goods, fuel and chemicals, raw
                                     materials, consumer goods, arms

Destination of exports
(1983, % of total exports)   Netherlands 26; USA 17; FRG 13;
                                   Norway 12; other countries 32

Origin of imports
(1983, % of total imports)   USA 33; Trinidad & Tobago 23;
                                   Netherlands 10; Japan 6; Brazil 5; other
                                   countries 23

Main trading partners
(1984)   USA, Netherlands, Other EC, Norway,
                                   Trinidad & Tobago, Brazil, Japan

Foreign debt	US$150m. (early 1987)
Foreign aid	Netherlands US$106m. (1982); (suspended after December 1982); USA US$1m. (1982) (suspended after December 1982); EC Development Fund US$3.1m. (1984)
Armed forces	Surinam National Defence Force, regular army of 2,000; People's Militia, of 900

Education and health

Adult literacy	84 (1984)
Primary	299 schools; 71,460 pupils (1985)
Secondary	1,761 schools; 21,470 students (1985)
Technical	58 schools and colleges; 11,800 students (1985)
Teacher training	3 colleges; 1,330 students (1985)
University	1, opened in 1968
Life expectancy	68 (1984)
Infant death rate (per 1000)	29.4 (1982)
Population per hospital bed	119 (1982)
Population per physician	859 (1982)

Main religions	Roman Catholic, Evangelical Brethren Community of Surinam (formerly the Moravian Brethren of Hernhutt), other Reformed churches, Methodism, Baptism and other Christian churches, Hinduism, Islamism, Judaism, Buddhism, Bushnegro (Afro-American) and (Amer) Indian tribal religions
Foreign relations	Diplomatic and consular relations with 41 countries, of which 23 have representatives in Paramaribo

Membership of international organizations	IBA (International Bauxite Association), 1984
	UN, 1975
	ECLA (Economic Commission for Latin America), 1976
	ACP (Africa, Caribbean and Pacific Group of countries associated with the European Community), 1976
	OAS (Organization of American States), 1977
	IMF (International Monetary Fund) and World Bank, 1978
	Non-Aligned Movement, 1979
	IADB (Inter-American Development Bank), 1980

Population Forecasting

The following data are projections produced by Poptran, University College Cardiff Population Centre, from United Nations Assessment Data published in 1980, and are reproduced here to provide some basis of comparison with other countries covered by the Marxist Regimes Series.

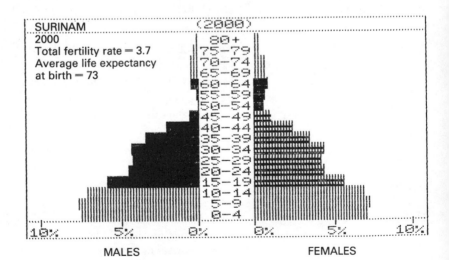

SURINAM   (2000)
2000
Total fertility rate = 3.7
Average life expectancy
at birth = 73

MALES   FEMALES

Projected Data for Surinam 2000

Total population ('000)	698
Males ('000)	341
Females ('000)	357
Total fertility rate	3.69
Life expectancy (male)	69.8
Life expectancy (female)	75.0
Crude birth rate	31.8
Crude death rate	3.9
Annual growth rate	2.79%
Under 15s	43.78%
Over 65s	3.59%
Women aged 15–49	25.37%
Doubling time	25 years
Population density	4 per sq. km.
Urban population	54.1%

List of Abbreviations

ACP	Africa, Caribbean and Pacific Group of countries associated with the European Community
ALCOA	Aluminum Company of America
ASFA	Association of Surinamese Manufacturers
CCK	Committee of Christian Churches
DVF	Democratic People's Front
EBG	Evangelical Brethren Community
ECLA	Economic Commission for Latin America
IADB	Inter-American Development Bank
IBA	International Bauxite Association
IMF	International Monetary Fund
KPS	Communist Party of Surinam
KTPI	Indonesian Joint Peasants' Party
MDP	Multi-Annual Development Programme
NBS	Surinam Nationalist Movement
NMR	National Military Council
NPS	National Party Surinam
OAS	Organization of American States
OC	Organization Committee
OSAV	Organization of Cooperative Autonomous Trade Unions
PAG	Political Advisory Group
PALU	Progressive Union of Workers and Peasants
PNR	Nationalist Republican Party
PSV	Surinam Progressive People's Party
PWO	Progressive Employees' Organization
RVP	Revolutionary People's Party
SNLA	Surinamese National Liberation Army
SSU	Surinamese Socialist Union
UNCHR	United Nations Commission on Human Rights
VFB	25 February Movement
VHP	United Hindu Party (Now: Progressive Reformational Party)
VP	People's Party
VSB	United Surinamese Trade and Industry

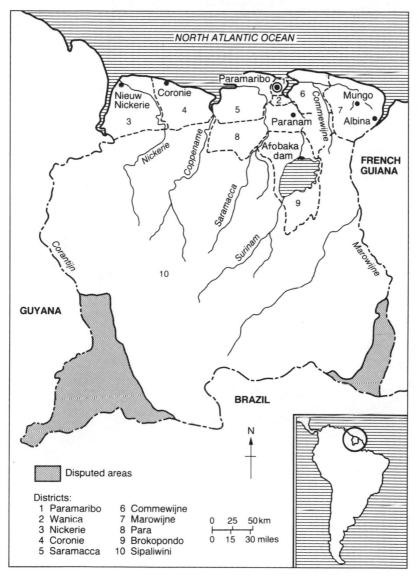

NORTH ATLANTIC OCEAN

Paramaribo

Nieuw Nickerie
Coronie
Mungo
Albina

Paranam

Afobaka dam

FRENCH GUIANA

GUYANA

BRAZIL

N

Disputed areas

Districts:
1 Paramaribo   6 Commewijne
2 Wanica   7 Marowijne
3 Nickerie   8 Para
4 Coronie   9 Brokopondo
5 Saramacca   10 Sipaliwini

0   25   50 km
0   15   30 miles

Surinam: Provincial Boundaries

1 History and Political Traditions

Geographical and Historical Setting

Geographical Setting

Surinam lies on the northern coast of the South American continent, between 2 and 6° latitude and 54 and 58° longitude. The country covers 163,820 sq. kms, including two disputed territories in the south-west and south-east bordering on Guyana and French Guyana respectively. Surinam is one of the smallest South American nations, and is approximately five times as large as The Netherlands and roughly equal in size to Bangladesh. Surinam is bordered to the north by the Atlantic Ocean, to the west by Guyana, to the east by French Guyana and to the south by Brazil.

Surinam has a tropical climate, with a rainy season and regional differences in precipitation. A rain forest climate prevails along the coast and along the southern border with Guyana, with monthly precipitation of more than 60mm. The majority of the country, and particularly the south, has a monsoon climate, with several months showing less than 60mm. of rain but the remainder of the year considerably more. The populated area—the north, with the exception of a small coastal area—constitutes just over one-tenth of the entire country and has an alternating wet/dry climate, with one or more months in which there is less than 60mm. of precipitation. Average annual precipitation in the capital city of Paramaribo totals some 2,200mm.

Four seasons can be distinguished, namely: the minor rainy season, from early December to early February; the minor dry season, from early February to late April; the major rainy season, from late April to mid-August; the major dry season, from mid-August to early December.

The average annual midday temperature in the capital is around 27°C. The range between minimum and maximum midday temperatures is 8°C. In the hinterland, temperature extremes can vary by as much as 11°C. The range in average temperatures between the warmest month, September, and the coldest month, January, is only 2°C. Surinam is not subject to extremely high temperatures. Tropical cyclones and earthquakes do not occur.

In geological terms, Surinam—with the exception of several intrusive Mesozoic rock formations—is part of the 'Guyana Shell', one of the earth's oldest Pre-Cambrian massifs, covered in the north by sedimentary rock. The landscape rises to the south of this sedimentary belt. Surinam's many large rivers therefore run from south to north. Several smaller rivers, however, have not broken through the ridges paralleling the coastline, and bend in a westerly direction at the coast. These rivers serve as important waterways, but at the edge of the Guyana Shell, some 60 to 100 kms from the coast, rapids (*soelas*) hinder upstream navigation by larger ships.

The country can be divided into a number of zones with regard to topographies and soil types. The narrow coastal zone—some 350 kms long—consists of many sandbanks and mudbanks, deposited by the southern equatorial currents from the area surrounding the mouth of the Amazon. Owing to the prevailing winds, these banks are continually moving westward at the rate of several kilometres per year. Partly because of the lack of suitable sandy beaches, the development of beach tourism has no place here. Salt marsh vegetation is found in those parts of the narrow coastal region where the mud deposits are fairly high.

Behind the mudbanks begins the New Coastal Plain, formed during the Weichsel Ice Age from sand and clay from the Demerara formation, also originating from the mouth of the Amazon. This coastal plain, totalling some 17,000 sq. kms, consists largely of clay in which a great deal of peat has formed. This marshy area is intersected by the above-mentioned ridges, which run parallel to the coast. These ridges consist largely of leached quartz sand, most of which comes from the local rivers. The New Coastal Plain has traditionally been the country's primary agricultural area, particularly in those parts where sufficient peat deposits have been formed in the swamps and fertile soil has been created which remains dry throughout most of the year.

Moving to the south, the New Coastal Plain is followed by the Old Coastal Plain, a swathe of both swamps and dry ground with a surface area of some 4,000 sq. km. The Old Coastal Plain has an irregular topographical pattern, and consists largely of fine clays and sands from the Coropina formation, formed during the Eem interglacial period between the last two Ice Ages. Various topographies, including swamps, old ridges and clay flats, can be found in this coastal plain. Various crops are grown here, depending on the type of landscape and the possibilities for drainage and irrigation. The New and Old Coastal Plains in fact constitute Surinam's populated region.

South of the Old Coastal Plain is an irregular belt of savannas, referred to as the Zanderij formation, dating from the Pliocene era. This formation rests on bleached sand sediment, rich in quartz and belonging to the Coesewijn Series from the Guyana system. Although savannas are found in this landscape of rolling hills, most of the region is covered in tropical rain forest.

In addition, swamp formation still takes place in the lower-lying areas—the creekbeds that intersect the landscape—and here one finds the country's southernmost swamps.

Further to the south is an area belonging to the Guyana Shell. This area, which covers some 80 per cent of the entire country, consists largely of a central mountain range with various branches off. Hilly areas are found between and around these branches. Close to the Brazilian border is the Sipaliwini Plain, a savanna-like landscape. This region is almost entirely covered in heavy jungle. The Guyana Shell began its formation from the original—primarily granite and igneous—rock some 1.9 billion years ago. Ores, the most important of which are bauxite and lateristic iron ore, were formed by erosion.

Surinam's high country is extensive but moderate in elevation. At 1,280 metres, Juliana Peak, in the Wilhelmina Range, is Surinam's highest summit.

Historical Setting

Surinam is part of the Guyana region, the existence of which was first noted in 1498 by Christopher Columbus. The coast of Guyana was discovered by Alonzo de Ojeda and Juan de la Cosa in 1499. The region was also visited in 1500 by Vincente Yanez Pinzon, the discoverer of the Amazon River. Various expeditions from Europe to this region followed, as part of the fruitless search for El Dorado.

Various abortive attempts at settlement were made by the Spanish, British, Dutch and French during the first half of the seventeenth century. The failure of these attempts was due in part to the resistance posed by the native Indian inhabitants. In 1650, Lord Francis Willoughby, Earl of Parham and colonial governor of the then flourishing but overcrowded British sugar island of Barbados, sent an expedition to Surinam to investigate the possibility of establishing a new colony. This expedition led to a permanent settlement by a group of experienced British planters and their slaves. This group was soon reinforced by a group of Portuguese Jews, who were fleeing the Inquisition after Spain's annexation of Portugal. In 1662, Charles II of England granted ownership of the settled land to Lord Willoughby and Laurens Hide, Earl of Clarendon. This group of colonists, which first settled in Torarica, had moved to the present site of Paramaribo as early as 1665.

Under British rule, a successful start was made with production for export, particularly the production of sugar. Surinam fell into Dutch hands in 1667. Early in that year, a Dutch fleet commanded by Admiral Abraham Crynssen seized this region from the British. Although the British Admiral Harmon recaptured the region almost immediately, the country was ultimately awarded to Holland in that same year under the Treaty of Breda. With the exception of the period 1804–16, when Surinam was once again under British rule, the country remained part of The Netherlands until its independence. After an initial period during which Surinam was governed by the Provincial Council of Zealand, the colony was sold to the Dutch West India Company in 1682. In 1683, Surinam came under the administrative rule of the Geoctroyeerde Societeit van Suriname. This company was created when the City of Amsterdam and the Aarssens van Sommelsdijck family each purchased one-third of the shares in the new colony. The Dutch Parliament awarded the ruling charter upon condition that the Societeit would administer Surinam under Parliament's own sovereign authority. The Aarssens van Sommelsdijck family's shares were sold to the City of Amsterdam in 1770, but the charter remained valid until 1795, when the Societeit was dissolved and replaced by the Committé tot de Zaken van de Kolonien en bezittingen op de kust van Guinea en in Amerika (Administrative Committee for the Colonies and Possessions on the Coasts of Guinea and in America). Following the polity of 1798, the Committé was replaced by a Raad voor het Bestuur van de West-Indische Bezittingen en Kolonien in Amerika en op de Kust van Guinea (Administrative Council for the West Indian Possessions and Colonies in America and the Coast of Guinea). In 1814, authority over the colony's administration was granted to the Dutch royal house. Policy was implemented by the Minister of Colonies, who became directly responsible to the Dutch Parliament in 1848.

Cornelis van Aarssens van Sommelsdijck was appointed first colonial governor of Surinam by the Dutch West India Companay, with the endorsement of the Dutch Parliament and the Prince of Orange. The colony of Surinam was administered by the governor, aided by a Political Council which was divided into two courts: a Police Council and a Criminal Law Council. Another council was also set up: the Council of Civil Law. All council members were chosen by the governor, following nomination by the colonists and, more specifically, by the plantation owners. This arrangement remained in force until 1816, although the governor during the interim British government was, of course, British-appointed. A new administrative system was used after 1816; its most significant change was the governor's appointment by royal decree. Power was shifted even further onto the shoulders of the mother country in 1828, the year in which the administration of Surinam was placed in the hands of the Colonial Office. The administration of all Dutch West India colonies was centralized under one Governor-General, posted in Surinam. But a round of decentralization once again took place in 1832, resulting in the colonists regaining a greater say in government matters.

The British introduced plantation production to Surinam in the early seventeenth century. Plantation agriculture, which originated in Roman times and reached its zenith during the fifteenth and sixteenth centuries on Spain and Portugal's Atlantic island colonies, was brought to Brazil and the Spanish possessions in the Americas in the early sixteenth century. Plantation farming in Surinam received an additional stimulus in 1664 with the arrival of a group of Jewish plantation owners. But Surinam's development into a blooming plantation colony began largely after the country came into Dutch hands and after Dutch planters, driven out of Brazil as from 1648 at the insistence of the British, had settled *en masse* in the area. At first the plantations were established further inland, but the planters from Zealand introduced the polder system of land reclamation and so turned the low-lying coastal plain into Surinam's most important production area. It should be noted in this regard that a mass migration of British planters to other British colonies in the Caribbean took place immediately after the Dutch acquisition of Surinam via the Treaty of Breda. Due in part to the resulting raids on plantations carried out by runaway slaves (the so-called Marrons or Maroons), production suffered a temporary but substantial setback. But the new Dutch colonial governor, Cornelis van Aarssens van Sommelsdijck, suppressed the Maroon uprisings with an iron hand, and production came once again into full swing under the Dutch planters.

Sugar production was the major activity, with coffee and cacao production gaining rapidly in importance from the early eighteenth century. The production of cotton also became more significant during the eighteenth century, and a considerable number of indigo and wood plantations were established as well.

Until the end of the eighteenth century, Surinam remained a classic plantation colony. The vast majority of the population lived on the many plantations. In 1791, the population totalled some 49,000, of which only 9,650 lived in Paramaribo. There were no more than 3,360 whites in the country (Van Lier, 1977, pp. 22 ff.). Furthermore, this small group of whites consisted of a great variety of nationalities. After the Dutch, the Jews (accounting for one-third of the total white population) were the largest group. In addition to the Dutch and Jewish populations, there were also a number of British stragglers and a striking number of French and Germans. Owing to Indian raids in French Guyana during the British period, a number of French settlers had moved to Surinam. During the governorship of Cornelis van Aarssens van Sommelsdijck (himself married to a French noblewoman), a number of French craftsmen, a group of 'Labadistes' (followers of the former Jesuit priest Jean de Labadie), a communal sect and a number of predominantly wealthy Huguenots settled in Surinam. The German settlers were mostly mercenaries, who remained in the country after their military activities, and farmers in search of a livelihood. There was also a very specific group of German settlers: the Moravian Brethren from Herrnhut, who began arriving as missionaries in Surinam in 1735. This group was to lay the foundation for one of Surinam's major Protestant communities.

The first slaves were brought to Surinam by the British and the Portuguese Jews, after it became clear that forced labour crews from Europe could not be used for plantation work in the tropics and that the Indians were too few in number and physically unsuited to heavy agricultural labour in the plantation-production system. The African slaves brought to Surinam came from a large number of tribes and a variety of regions along Africa's western coast, from Senegal to Angola (Van Lier, 1977, pp. 88 ff.). The slave trade in Dutch territories was abolished in 1814. Until 1824, however, slaves were still being smuggled into Surinam. An estimated 300,000 to 350,000 African slaves were brought to Surinam before this time.

From the time the British introduced the plantation system in Surinam with the use of African slaves, an increasing number of these slaves fled into the up-country forests. These Marrons settled in a number of separate tribes and established stable communities along the big rivers, particularly the Marowijne, the Suriname and the Saramacca. The Marrons were in a state of perpetual warfare with the plantation owners and the colonial rulers. Peace settlements were made with the whites during the 1760s, and the Marrons were accorded autonomy. Yet this peace merely marked the formation of a new group of runaway slaves, the 'Bonis', and guerrilla warfare against the white colonists was resumed at fever pitch. The vast majority of Bonis were ultimately killed or driven into French Guyana. A treaty signed in 1791 placed the remaining Bonis—who had settled along the Marowijne River— under the supervision of the Djukas, a group of runaway slaves that lived along the same river and with whom the whites had made peace.

Slavery in the British colonies was abolished in 1834, and France followed suit in 1848. But abolition did not take place in Surinam until 1863. According to the Emancipation Decree, all of the some 33,000 slaves in Surinam were free agents as from 1 July 1863; this same decree, however, placed these former slaves under special government supervision for a period of no longer than ten years, in order that they should be available to perform paid labour under contract.

As early as 1853, ten years before emancipation, a number of Chinese and

Madeiran contract labourers had been recruited to work on the plantations. These workers usually failed to extend their (five-year) contracts, and instead became small-scale merchants. As from 1858, a total of some 5,000 Chinese contract labourers were recruited on a larger scale to work on the plantations. But China's closure of its ports to foreign pressgangs and the failure of the Chinese labourers to extend their contracts (they chose instead to either leave the country or change jobs) quickly underscored the need to find other means to meet the demand for plantation labourers (Dew, 1978, p. 26).

The arrival of contract labourers from India, still a British colony at the time, began in 1873: one decade after emancipation and the very year in which the former slaves were finally free to leave the plantations. From 1873 to 1916, some 34,000 East Indians were recruited to work in Surinam. Approximately 82 per cent of these workers were Hindu; the rest were Moslem. About one-third of this group returned to India after their contracts had expired; some of them later came back to Surinam. The net immigration of East Indians during the above-mentioned period has been estimated at around 22,000 (Dew, 1978, p. 26).

As from 1890, contract labourers began coming to Surinam from what was then the Dutch colony of Nederlands-Indie (Indonesia). During the period until 1939, the year in which the last group of Indonesian contract labourers entered the country, more than 33,000 Indonesians settled in Surinam. In 1947, 8,440 Indonesians were repatriated (Panday, 1959, p. 158).

Despite efforts to preserve plantation production after emancipation, Surinam's international importance as an agricultural supplier continued to wane. The international economic significance of sugar—Surinam's main export product during this period—decreased with time. Furthermore, the competitive position of Surinamese cane sugar had been severely undermined by the advent of sugar beet. Sugar beet production was heavily promoted during the Napoleonic wars, particularly in Western Europe. By the second half of the nineteenth century, this had become the principal form of sugar. The opening of the Suez Canal in 1869, which served to greatly reduce the prices of Asian products on the European market, also dealt a heavy blow to the competitive position of Surinamese products on the international market.

Attempts to boost the production of other important agricultural products, such as cotton, cacao and coffee, met with only temporary success. Plantation production therefore dwindled rapidly from the late nineteenth century, while small-scale agricultural production increased. Although this small-scale farming did show a certain degree of development, its significance for export during this period was very limited.

In 1873, the search for production alternatives led to gold prospecting in south-eastern Surinam's Lawa region, along the banks of the Marowijne River. Profitable gold deposits had already been struck and extracted on the French side of this river. A substantial quantity of gold was finally struck in the Lawa region in 1875, and the first foreign mining companies, primarily the Amsterdamse Gouddelving Maatschappij Suriname, began operating there in 1876. Sundry large and small ventures soon followed.

The most significant prospecting contract signed was that with the Nederlandse Maatschappij Suriname, which was granted the concession for 500,000 hectares of the most promising stakes. In return, this company was to build a railway within four years between Paramaribo and the Lawa region.

The Nederlandse Maatschappij Suriname failed to live up to its part of the bargain. The high costs of the railway, which was never actually built according to plan and never ran profitably, were assumed by the colonial government. To cover these costs, Surinam was forced to take out a DG. 8m. loan, albeit under Dutch state credit guarantee. Furthermore, the Dutch government had no choice but to first buy out Nederlandse Maatschappij Suriname's concession, to the tune of DG. 535,250 (Heilbron & Willemsen, 1980, p. 31). The Lawa project, which ultimately cost a total of Dfl. 12m., was launched as a multi-purpose project. In addition to serving the goldmines, the prospects presented for the railway included benefits for the region's agricultural production, the harvesting of balata—a kind of natural rubber—and wood production. Gold remained one of Surinam's major export products until 1918. During the period 1904 to 1908, it came second only to sugar as Surinam's chief export, accounting for some 30 per cent of the country's total exports in value terms (Willemsen, 1980, p. 334). After this period, the production and export of gold decreased drastically.

As from the late 1910s, the production of balata assumed vital importance for Surinam's economy. Balata had been harvested on a small scale in Surinam from as early as 1882. But large-scale production only began in 1889, after the British Garnett & Winter firm (already active in this field in British Guyana) received an important concession. Such concessions were soon awarded to a number of Dutch and American firms as well.

From the late 1910s to the mid-1920s, balata harvesting was second only to sugar production as Surinam's major export-oriented economic activity. In fact, during the period 1909 to 1913, balata was the country's number-one export product, accounting for an average of some 40 per cent of the country's total exports (Willemsen, 1980, p. 304). The decline of balata production after the mid-1920s can be attributed to overcropping by the various firms and the rise of other, primarily Asian, rubber-producing countries.

The scale of the economic activities related to the production of gold and balata was not sufficient to compensate for the decline of plantation production. Surinam became an impoverished colony, able to operate only with the financial aid of the mother country. Between emancipation and the beginning of the Second World War, the gaps in the colonial budget had consistently to be bridged with (Dutch) government subsidies. In some budgetary years these subsidies accounted for almost 40 per cent of the colony's total government spending (Willemsen, 1980, pp. 325 ff.).

The growth of the bauxite industry, however, resulted in a dramatic improvement in Surinam's economic situation from the early 1940s. Demand for aluminium (for use in the arms and aircraft industries) blossomed during the Second World War. The presence of bauxite reserves in Surinam had been confirmed in the early years of this century. Until 1915, however, the American firm Norton—which had commercial ties with the ALCOA concern—was the country's sole bauxite operator and exported only a small quantity of this ore for use in the chemical industry. In 1916, ALCOA officially began operations in Surinam with the setting-up of its SURALCO (Surinam Aluminum Company) subsidiary. The significance for the national economy of bauxite-production and export grew considerably as from 1922; in the wake of the Second World War, activities in the bauxite sector came to dominate Surinam's economy.

The abolition of slavery led to far-reaching changes in society. A new polity was introduced to Surinam in 1865. This Surinaamse Regeringsreglement (Surinamese Government Order) which came into force on 1 January 1866, led to the establishment of a representative body, the Koloniale Staten, later referred to as the Staten van Suriname. Van Lier (1977, p. 224) states that, in imposing this order, the Dutch legislature was looking for a constitutional form which would leave as many matters as possible in the hands of Surinamese legislators, without producing a full-blown parliamentary system in the colony. For those matters dealt with by local bodies in Surinam, the condition of regulation by colonial statute was applied; the authority of the Dutch ruler did not pertain to such statutes. The King did, however, have the right to nullify such statutes. The Regeringsreglement granted the colony the right to approve its own budget, but went on to make a number of major exceptions. The order stated that the Surinamese budget was to be drawn up in The Netherlands if one or more of the following three conditions were present: if Dutch government subsidy was needed to supplement the colony's funds, if the Dutch ruler withheld approval of the budget submitted by the Surinamese Staten, or if the Staten failed to submit the budget within the period of time stated in the government order. It also stipulated that the colonial governor was to promptly heed the Dutch ruler's orders when carrying out his official duties, and be answerable to the King for his actions.

The Koloniale Staten's members were elected by a small group of citizens in accordance with the system of poll-tax suffrage, whereby the right to vote was reserved for those who paid more than a given minimum sum in direct taxes. The assembly consisted of thirteen members, nine elected and four appointed by the colonial governor.

In 1901, the Government Order was altered to effectively renege on a substantial portion of the political rights granted to the colony. The Dutch ruler was once again given authority in all matters for regulation by local bodies, with the exception of drafting the closing section of the colonial budget, establishing tax rates and issuing crown lands.

The Dutch Government felt the Koloniale Staten had ambitions to become an all-too-independent body. The main reason behind this suspicion was the conflict between the Staten and the progressive colonial governor De Savornin Lohman (1889–91), who hoped to transform Surinam into a prosperous colony with a modern production apparatus. During De Savornin Lohman's brief term of office, the central sugar factory at Marienburg was fitted out and substantial modernizations were introduced in goldmining. The governor also submitted a draft bill to the Koloniale Staten which would have lowered the poll tax and so doubled the colony's number of eligible voters. The bill was defeated, however, by an 11-to-1 vote in the assembly. The governor's desire to modernize was totally at odds with the interests of the established planters' class. Furthermore, De Savornin Lohman (a reputedly headstrong and arrogant man) saw little reason to pay heed to the Koloniale Staten, an attitude which resulted in a series of conflicts and wider social unrest.

The clash between the governor and the Staten reached its pitch when massive unrest and the threat of armed resistance arose in the district of Para, where many former slaves had settled. The widespread insubordination in the district was a protest against an 1886 hike in property taxes and capital levies. By 1889, when Lohman was appointed, these back taxes were still in arrears. The Staten accused the governor of extreme laxity in his dealings with the protesters and of generating class tension. The assembly also accused him of 'unlawful dealings' which made it impossible for him to continue in his post. Although De Savornin Lohman's friends in the Dutch Parliament came to his defence, criticism continued to mount and the governor stepped down in April 1891.

Amendments to the Government Order of 1901 put an end to the appointment of Staten members by the colonial governor. It was argued that such appointments undermined rather than strengthened the governor's influence and position and prompted the elected members to redouble their efforts to avoid any hint of partiality towards the colonial government. The order also included a clause granting suffrage to all persons paying taxes on an annual income of at least SG. 1,400. But the considerable size of even this reduced sum meant that Surinam's voting population remained quite small.

Before 1906, members of the Koloniale Staten were elected without any prior nomination. In general, therefore, only marginal interest was shown in these elections. But after the introduction of preliminary nominations in late 1905, the general interest in politics grew. This resulted in 1908 in the setting-up of two electoral associations: the Algemeene Kiesvereniging (Popular Electoral Association), representing largely the upper classes, and Eendracht maakt Macht (Unity grants Power), led by representatives of the middle classes who presented themselves as the champions of the lower-middle classes and the common people.

The Algemeene Kiesvereniging soon faded out of the picture. But in 1918 Eendracht maakt Macht once again met a challenger: the Surinaamsche Kiesvereniging (Surinamese Electoral Association), set up by planters' groups worried about their rapidly dwindling influence. After suffering several defeats, the Surinaamsche Kiesvereniging also quit the political arena, in 1924. Eendracht maakt Macht was itself finally disbanded in 1936 owing to bitter internal dissension.

The conflict between the Dutch Government in The Hague and the local government of Surinam deepened between 1901 and the start of the Second World War. This was not only due to the rescinding of powers once granted to the local bodies, but even more to the perennial increase in Surinam's subsidy requirements during this period. Provisional budgets submitted by the colonial governor and the Staten were first amended at will by the Minister of Colonies, after which the Dutch Parliament—without sufficient contact with Surinam—usually made drastic cutbacks in the colony's plans.

To Surinam's great annoyance, these economies were usually imposed on budgetary items considered crucial in the colony itself, while costly Dutch Government plans which roused little popular enthusiasm in Surinam, such as the Lawa railway project, and the Dutch Government's immigration policy only added to Surinam's financial predicament. The colony's chronic financial problems during this period and the dissatisfaction with the government in the mother country occasionally resulted in an atmosphere of tension and social unrest.

In the early years of this century, therefore, a plan was formulated whereby Surinam would become a republic, led by a president. Instead of the Koloniale Staten, two national representative assemblies were to be created. The colonial government and a number of top officials were to be sent back to The Netherlands. To cover damages ensuing from the loss of its colony, The Netherlands was to receive the sum of DM 25m. The new republic would take out a loan of DM 100m. on the international capital market to pay for this claim. Most of the remaining capital would be invested in productive sectors. A portion, however, would be reserved for improving the country's welfare level, particularly general health care for the people and the availability of such public utilities as running water and light. The exorbitantly expensive Lawa railway project would be abandoned. The incompetent army would be disbanded and the police force expanded. Corruption would be fought.

This plan was conceived and developed by a group led by the Hungarian-born police inspector Frans Pavel Vaclac Killinger, who had once served in the German Army and later came to Surinam as a soldier in the Dutch Colonial Army. The rank-and-file consisted largely of policemen and tradesmen. The group never carried out its planned coup before being arrested in May 1910. The Killinger Group trials did, however, lead to the setting-up of the Surinaamsche Volksbond (Surinamese People's Federation) in April 1911; this group drew its support from among the lower classes, and championed such causes as the liberalization of suffrage laws and the right to be elected to public office (Hira, 1982, p. 258).

Social unrest again swept the country in 1931, and the resulting demonstrations were violently dispersed by police. A Committee of Action was set up by a group of the unemployed, primarily those laid off owing to the crisis in the balata industry, and Surinamese workers back from Curaçao, where the oil industry had been hit hard by the international economic crisis. This committee demanded that the government create jobs, provide material support for the unemployed and distribute free food for undernourished children.

In 1932, a trade union organization, the Surinaamsche Arbeiders en Werknemers Organisatie (SAWO, Surinamese Workers' and Employees' Organization), was set up by a group that had been involved in the unemployed movement of 1931. This group maintained close contacts with Anton de Kom, a Surinamese schoolteacher who lived in The Netherlands and was part of the radical-leftist milieu in that country. De Kom felt his country's socio-economic problems could be solved by setting up large-scale industrial collectives, organized according to a modern model and belonging to the Surinamese people themselves. He returned to Surinam in January 1933, with the intention of generating solidarity among the masses and setting up a large-scale workers' organization. But de Kom was arrested on charges of subversion only one month later. The subsequent mass demonstrations for his release were brutally suppressed by the police. In May of that year, De Kom was discharged and he was put on the boat back to Holland the same day.

Owing in part to growing social unrest and to the Koloniale Staten's increasing bitterness about the lack of importance attached to its decisions by the Dutch government and parliament, the Government Order was once again amended in 1936. The colonial governor was granted more power to implement his decisions without the Koloniale Staten's endorsement. In critical situations he was empowered, by means of administrative decree or national ordinance, to impose statutory regulations regarding the necessary steps to be taken. He was also empowered to alter or suspend laws, royal decrees and national ordinances.

Furthermore, the Order of 1936 dictated the return to a Koloniale Staten composed of both elected and appointed members, with the understanding that five of the fifteen members were now to be appointed by the colonial governor. By way of justification, it was argued that this would result in better representation of the interests of the large group of East Indian and Indonesian immigrants. To this end, the voting population was also enlarged. All residents of Surinam paying taxes on an income of at least SG 1,000 per year (reduced from SG 1,400 in 1901), as well as those who met the requirements of intellectual development laid down in the electoral regulations, could participate in the Staten elections. Obviously, in view of their marginal incomes and the limited number who could comply with the intellectual requirements, few of the immigrants could entertain any hope of voting in the elections. It is interesting to note in this context that, even after the introduction of the Government Order of 1936, only 2 per cent of the population were eligible to vote in the Koloniale Staten elections.

Although the process of decolonization came into full swing throughout the world during the Second World War, it was not until 1955 that Surinam was granted autonomy in its domestic affairs, and it was 1975 before the country gained full political independence.

Modern Political History

Introduction of Universal Suffrage

Political developments in Surinam received great impetus from Queen Wilhelmina of The Netherlands' radio speech, broadcast from London, on 7 December 1942. The Queen presented the prospect of a new, post-war configuration of the Kingdom of The Netherlands, in which the colonies— The Netherlands East Indies, The Netherlands Antilles and Surinam—would be allowed to independently handle their own internal affairs. This announcement was primarily intended to appease the Indonesian nationalists, led by Sukarno, who had chosen the side of the Japanese occupying forces in the course of their struggle for independence. The announcement was favourably received in Surinam, coming as it did at a time of widespread discontent with the autocratic behaviour of the Dutch governor of the day. The slogan 'boss in your own home' was on virtually everyone's lips.

The Unie Suriname association, set up by the light-skinned Creole elite, was the most emphatic advocate of this creed. A major aim of this movement was to attain a better platform within the kingdom for the allocation of reinvestment funding for the ailing plantation economy.

As mentioned earlier, suffrage in Surinam was based on the census and capacity rule, and the voting population was no larger than some 2 per cent of the total population. Surinam's parliament, De Staten, as a mere advisory college to the Dutch colonial governor, had very limited powers. Mitrasing (1959, p. 77) therefore speaks of an 'anti-stimulus for extra-parliamentary political activity and the formation of political parties'. In their election campaigns, candidates for De Staten were supported by *ad hoc* electoral associations, which were disbanded immediately after the elections. Owing to the limitations on suffrage, the members of De Staten were largely representatives of the light-skinned, middle and upper class, and belonged to the Unie Suriname.

Political mobilization began immediately after the Second World War, in anticipation of the promised internal autonomy. The issue of universal suffrage served as a catalyst to this mobilization. The light-skinned Creole elite declared its opposition to universal suffrage. Limited suffrage would virtually entail the political exclusion of the East Indian and Javanese populations, as well as the black Creoles. It was therefore no less than logical that resistance to the elitist political attitude arose from these quarters. In order to expand their own constituencies, the opponents of limited suffrage tried to mobilize those excluded from the political process. This group was not so much attracted by the prospect of formal political power, but frequently rallied to back favourite members of the elite in their mutual conflicts.

The suffrage issue led to the setting-up of many political parties. The Creole opponents of universal suffrage set up the NPS (Nationale Partij Suriname). In its declaration of principles, the NPS presented itself as a national party offering refuge to all, regardless of race or religion. Yet this party drew only Creoles and, on the basis of its stance on suffrage alone, was unable to obtain the support of the Asiatic groups. The establishment of the NPS was actually a reaction to the setting-up of the PSV (Surinam Progressive People's Party). This group, with its Catholic origins, organized the common Creoles and fervently advocated universal suffrage. In the beginning, the East Indians and the Javanese were grouped within one political party, yet these ethnic groups were later to split. In this way, the VHP (United Hindu Party) was formed in 1949. An elite group of representatives of the higher castes, belonging to the orthodox Sanatan Dharm, were more attracted by the NPS standpoint on universal suffrage and did not join the VHP. The KTPI (Indonesian Joint Peasants' Party) became the major Indonesian party. The struggle for independence in Indonesia in particular had served to generate greater political awareness among the Indonesians in Surinam. The NPS, VHP and KTPI constituted the major political parties that would determine Surinam's political scene for decades to come.

The political mobilization followed ethnic lines. Surinam has frequently been depicted as an example of a 'plural society'. Furnivall, who introduced this notion, defined a plural society as one 'comprising two or more elements of social orders which live side by side, yet without mingling in one political unit'. Later writers, such as Rabushka and Shepsle, were to primarily emphasize the cultural differences between groups with generally incompatible sets of values. According to Rabushka & Shepsle, 'The hallmark of the plural society, and the feature that distinguishes it from its pluralistic counterpart, is the practice of politics almost exclusively along ethnic lines' and therefore one can speak of a plural society 'if it's culturally diverse and if its cultural sections are organised into cohesive political sections' (1972, p. 20).

Natural ethnic diversity existed among the various groups within the population of Surinam: racial characteristics, language, religion, etc. This ethnic diversity was reinforced by several other factors. The East Indian and Javanese groups continued, as they always had done, to work in the agricultural sector, while the Creoles had become far more urbanized. The accompanying geographical separation reinforced the communal feelings of identity, as well as the social isolation. West (1972, p. 488) has made the following general comment in this regard:

The outcome of colonial rule was often a society in which ethnic alignments tended to be reinforced by occupational, educational and even regional alignments. The essential feature of this sort of 'plural' new states is not simply the existence of important ethnic cleavages but their reinforcement by other social divisions.

For Surinam, an added factor was the enormous economic push which the Second World War had given the country as a large-scale bauxite producer. Economic opportunities therefore became greater for other groups in addition to the Creoles, and 'crowding' arose among these groups. As Dew (1978, p. 199) has put it: 'The economic consequences of the Second World War vastly broadened the opportunities of Hindostanis for education and social mobility, and the prospect of self-government and universal suffrage has awakened new possibilities, both positive and threatening.' Within this context, Dew (1978, p. 188) quotes Crawford Young, who said: 'Although intensity and identity of individuals with cultural segments varies widely in moments of threat, the group pressures escalate and strongly constrain individuals to align their overt behavior with the interests of the cultural collectivity'. For the East Indians and Indonesians, the formation of their own party was certainly not only a protective measure against the threat of possible Creole dominance, but also a powerful instrument for the emancipation of their own ethnic groups. Mitrasing notes that the Chinese and Jewish population groups had already been assimilated to a great extent, and therefore had no interest in emancipation or in their own political party (1959, p. 91).

Owing to the factors mentioned above, ethnic awareness had become strongly developed among these groups within Surinam's population. Furthermore, as Geertz correctly emphasizes, ethnic feelings have a special emotional intensity—a phenomenon he has termed 'primordial feelings' (1963, pp. 112-13). Accordingly, advantage had to be taken of the factors mentioned in order to mobilize voters. Within this context, Rabushka & Shepsle (1972, pp. 59-60) use the term 'political entrepreneur'. They state:

The natural cleavages that divide men in the community provide the obvious and perhaps strongest nuclei around which coalitions are built. The astute politician latches on to an issue precisely because of the groups he believes it will activate. This 'political entrepreneur' seeks political profit, electoral victory. Profit accrues to those who choose the issues, define the issues in ways that activate winning electoral coalitions. The successful entrepreneur, then, is the person who manipulates natural social cleavages, who makes certain of those cleavages politically salient, who exploits, uses and suppresses conflict.

The political parties in Surinam were, in fact, founded on the initiative of the upper layers of society, who needed to legitimize themselves in the political sense, both on the domestic front and with regard to The Netherlands. On the issue of universal suffrage, the NPS assumed a lone position in opposition to the other groups. However, this party did ultimately accept universal suffrage when it was posed by The Netherlands as an unconditional demand and when the other parties refused to accept internal autonomy before universal suffrage had been instituted. Yet, to allow itself nevertheless to consolidate its position of power, the NPS wished to implement a district electoral system. The Netherlands had left the establishment of the electoral system in the hands of De Staten. The light-skinned Creole elite, who dominated this body, belonged to the NPS. De Staten was therefore able effortlessly to introduce a nine electoral district system, on the principle of 'winner takes all'. In view of such operational procedures, Surinam's Parliament received the *nomen* 'egocentric oligarchy' (Mitrasing, 1959, p. 159). The electoral districts were arranged in such a way that the East Indians and Indonesians, who formed a slim majority of the population just after the Second World War, were unable to obtain an electoral majority. The NPS had mobilized nine, largely Creole, trade unions to ensure themselves of the necessary support. In the meantime, the party had developed sufficient self-confidence after having been proved able to mobilize considerable support among the lower-class Protestant Creoles, particularly among the country's well-represented Moravian Hernhutters. As Dew (1978, p. 70) commented in this context: 'The unavoidably Catholic character of the PSV (like it or not, its leader was a priest) tended to rally Protestants to the NPS, even though the latter's program was avowedly secular.' East Indians and the Indonesians offered no further resistance, and appeared to be content just to have a say at the highest political level. Aspiring political leaders now had the prospect of high-level positions. As Dew states: 'No group was very dissatisfied with the new order. An expanded legislature, elected on district lines, offered hope for many aspiring politicians' (1978, p. 73).

With the introduction of universal suffrage, the voting population had swelled from just under 3,000 to 96,000, yet the number of parliamentary seats awarded to each electoral district was entirely disproportionate to the total number of inhabitants and voters. In the district of Paramaribo, with its vast Creole majority, 34,230 voters were sufficient to fill ten of the twenty-one parliamentary seats in De Staten. In the East Indian-dominated Surinam district, 29,880 voters were able to elect no more than three representatives. Furthermore, this district was divided into three electoral 'circles', each one good for one parliamentary seat. Owing to the composition of the district's population, however, at least one of these seats would always go to the NPS. In the almost exclusively East Indian Nickerie district (western Surinam) 8,380 voters were able to elect only two representatives. The 1,680 voters in the largely black Creole district of Coronie, however, were also sufficient to elect one representative. Mitrasing (1959, p. 153) therefore refers to a 'discrimination of suffrage among the voters'.

The results of the first general election in 1949 no longer came as a surprise. The NPS won all ten seats in Paramaribo, plus the three remaining seats in the Creole districts, and therefore obtained an absolute majority in De Staten. The VHP received six parliamentary seats, while the KTPI won two in the district of Commewijne. The voting proportions according to district coincided almost perfectly with the ethnic populational proportions shown in the 1950 general census. Van Lier (1950, p. 28) therefore made the following comment: 'The election illustrated the total triumph of "segmentarism"'. The VHP was the clearest in its use of the ethnic foundation for the mobilization of voters. 'Hindu, Moslem, Sikh and Christian; all are brothers; India is the mother of all', was one of their campaign slogans (Mitrasing, 1959, p. 161). The electoral system reinforced the ethnic factor in the country's politics. As unprofitable as it would have been for the NPS to mobilize voters in the Nickerie district, it would have been just as futile for the VHP to have carried its campaign to Paramaribo; the electoral system ensured that the votes obtained by minority parties would ultimately be thrown away.

Ideological differences could barely be discerned between the parties. Mitrasing (1959, p. 93) says in this regard:

A comparison of the objectives and programmes of the political parties shows a great degree of similarity. They all favoured autonomy within the framework of the Kingdom, decentralisation, social and economic welfare, state intervention in economic life only in cases of emergency, the equality of religious education, etc. No contradiction was to be seen either in the parties' recommendations for the path to be followed or the means to be applied. These points would rather indicate a certain parallelism or convergency.

The election had introduced a number of new faces to De Staten. Two of these representatives were to play a major role in Surinam's politics. The first was Jaggernath Lachmon, Surinam's first East Indian lawyer, who saw his leadership of the VHP formalized. The second was Johan Adolf 'Jopie' Pengel, who would first play a subordinate role in the NPS before rather quickly making his mark. Lachmon had figured from as early as 1946 in the struggle for universal suffrage. He led a movement which originally included both East Indians and Indonesians. But the latter group quickly split off to form its own party. Internal conflicts later led to a split-off by the Islamitic East Indians. Yet this Moslem group, from which some voters transferred to the NPS, was small and the VHP therefore suffered almost no electoral consequences.

Of greater importance were the problems within the NPS. The NPS parliamentarians largely belonged to the light-skinned Creole elite. A number of them had already been members of De Staten during the time of restricted suffrage. Conflicts with the black Creoles, who joined the party during the 1949 elections, did not fail to arise. Mitrasing (1959, p. 198) says of this:

Although the NPS was shown to have the largest number of supporters, this party bore within itself the latent germ of dissension, in that the party top was largely comprised of coloured persons, a fact which has produced a degree of reaction, as well as in the fact that these leaders were no strangers to personal controversies.

Pengel clearly showed himself to be the leader of the black Creoles. He seized the opportunity of a ministerial conflict to attempt to force the resignation of his own NPS government. His motion was not passed, but it did lead to eight light-skinned NPS MPs being drummed out of the party. The split within the party had already led to a shift in the party administration in favour of the black Creoles. The hegemony of the coloured faction of the NPS would gradually come to an end. Aversion to the nascent cooperation between Pengel and Lachmon also played a role in the dismissal of the light-skinned NPS parliamentarians. Lachmon would say later that he and Pengel had been regarded by the elite as 'second-class' members of De Staten. In saying this, he was referring not only to the light-skinned Creoles in the NPS, but also to the upper-caste representatives and the supporters of the orthodox Sanatan Dharm within his own party. Pengel and Lachmon had also agreed to mobilize their respective rank-and-files—the Creole workers and the East Indian farmers—in order to gain control over De Staten.

The NPS parliamentarians who had left the party bundled their efforts for the 1955 elections within the EF (Unity Front). This elite group was annoyed with Pengel's tactics, and had no interest in cooperating with the VHP. Several East Indians closed ranks with the EF, as did the PSV. The formation of the EF prompted Pengel and Lachmon to further tighten their partnership. The electoral battle which followed was one of the most turbulent in Surinam's history, despite the lack of reported violence. Pengel's major opponent in the EF, David Findlay, did not hesitate to bring the racial element to bear. 'Do you wish to be governed by the VHP, do you desire mass immigration from a certain Eastern country?', he wrote before the elections in the *De West* daily, of which he was editor-in-chief (Mitrasing, 1959, p. 271). The electoral system had now turned on the NPS. With 50 per cent of the votes, the NPS and VHP obtained only eight of the twenty-one seats in De Staten, while the EF and the KTPI won thirteen seats, and therefore the parliamentary majority, with only 47 per cent of the votes. The EF won all ten of the parliamentary seats in the Paramaribo district that had formerly been occupied by the NPS. Mitrasing (1959, p. 278) had the following to say about the defeat of the NPS/VHP coalition:

It would seem quite probable that, normally speaking, every right-hearted and right-thinking citizen of Suriname would not only sincerely welcome an inter-racial coalition in such a multi-racial society as that in Suriname, but would also attempt to promote such cooperation. Yet it was on precisely this point that the coalition of the Creole NPS and the East Indian VHP, as the election results showed, was not able to convince the majority, because this majority understood that this coalition constituted no brotherly cooperation on the basis of idealistic principles, but rather was purely based on the mutual personal feelings of the coalition's leading figures [1959, p. 278.]

Although Mitrasing's conclusions may be seen as excessively cut-and-dried, personal relationships certainly did play a role. This was particularly applicable to Lachmon. He remained an admirer of his Creole mentor, the lawyer (and former prime minister) Julius Caesar Miranda. Furthermore, Lachmon was married to a Creole woman. In 1955, Lachmon even went so far as to offer a VHP parliamentary seat to Pengel, who himself had been unable to win a seat (in Paramaribo district). Lachmon's move served to preserve the turbulence within the Creole parties. The NPS leader accepted the offer from Lachmon, who first had to overcome considerable resistance within his own party. During his campaign, Pengel had even appeared in a dhoti (East Indian loincloth).

The cooperation between the VHP and the NPS did not wither under the election defeat, but actually received a renewed stimulus. It is worth noting that this reinforcement of ties took place at precisely the same time that, in neighbouring Guyana, the cooperative arrangement between East Indian leader Cheddi Jagan and the Creole leader Forbes Burnham within the PPP (People's Progressive Party) had undergone tumultuous disintegration. There can be no doubt that the NPS was sailing before the winds of social development, a fact related to the forceful social rise of the black Creoles after the Second World War. This process was clearly reflected in the country's politics. The NPS became the representative of this new black middle class. Pengel was very much aware of this trend. In 1952, he had provided himself with a strong electoral base among the working class by organizing the 'Moederbond' trade union organization. VHP leader Lachmon, who politically harnessed the East Indians' urge towards emancipation, was Pengel's legal adviser during the setting-up of the 'Moederbond'. Time was on the side of both politicians. An electoral victory by their coalition could not be long in coming. Mitrasing (1959, p. 278) sketched the social process which favoured the new NPS, and which resulted in the expulsion of the party's coloured leaders, as:

A process of erosion—which need not in itself be abnormal in such a pluriform and multi-racial society as that in Suriname, which was still in search of its political form as a nation—but which in this case partly reflects the rise of the 'new middle class'.

Elite-Cartel Democracy

The 1958 elections did indeed produce the anticipated political break-through for the NPS–VHP coalition. The fact that the PSV provided the NPS with political support in exchange for several eligible positions on the list of candidates was decisive. The PSV, principally supported by the Catholic portion of the Creole working class, had begun to feel somewhat out of place within the ranks of the Eenheidsfront, generally regarded as elitist.

The coalition government, which was to remain in office until 1967, entered the country's history as the implementor of the great political reconciliation. This period was also regarded as that of the greatest political stability and general welfare since Surinam had become self-governing. For the first time, the VHP had (two) ministers in the cabinet, which did not, however, include Lachmon. He and Pengel guided the cabinet from their parliamentary positions.

During this period, Surinam exhibited many of the characteristics of what Arend Lijphart has termed a 'consociational democracy'. Lijphart (1969, p. 216) defines this phenomenon as follows: 'Consociational democracy means government by elite cartel designed to turn a democracy with a fragmented political culture into a stable democracy.' The alliance between Pengel and Lachmon can reasonably be regarded as a cartel of elites. This has to do with the manner in which the NPS and VHP (as well as the other Surinamese political parties) tended to operate. Hoppe (1975, p. 151) has accurately spoken in this regard of 'top-level or caucus parties'. This means that the parties are actually run by a small group of active members, financiers (usually from within trade and industry) and members of parliament.

The power wielded at these top levels was only augmented by the fact that the local party branches were only active during the elections. Voters were at that time mobilized via an extensive propaganda apparatus. Following the elections, it was the top level alone that ran the party. Mitrasing (1959, p. 85), for example, made the following observation with regard to the VHP: 'The party executive, composing itself as it were, acts authoritatively and in actual fact comprises the party between election campaigns'.

Things were hardly different with the NPS, although this party did adhere to somewhat more democratic procedures for the selection of candidates. Van Lier (1977, p. 296) has noted that (after Pengel came on the scene) a gap once again arose between the new Creole upper class and the middle class which had only recently emerged from the working class (1977, p. 299). The party memo 'NPS 20 jaar' (Ormskirk, 1966, pp. 28–9) noted: 'Most of the members of the party executive belonged to our country's upper and middle classes'. A survey carried out by Kruijer (1973, p. 147) showed that the party members felt their influence on decision-making was limited.

The parties comprised a cross-section of various classes and could therefore be termed 'corporate groups' (see Smooha, 1975, pp. 71 ff.). Class conflicts did not pass through party ranks. As noted earlier, the party leadership mobilized the rank and file along ethnic–religious lines. Van Lier (1977, p. 296) states that: 'The parties exhibit much more the character of organized special interest groups, clustered within the existing ethnic or religious channels around various political personalities who appeal to the popular imagination'.

Patronage played an increasingly important role in mobilizing voters, as is shown by the steady growth of the civil service apparatus. Kruijer (1973, p. 103) defines patronage as follows: 'A powerful person provides favours for a less powerful person and so involves the less powerful person in an obligation which ultimately provides greater advantage for the most powerful of the two. The term embraces what is often referred to as a "patron–client" relationship.' According to Kruijer (1973, p. 103) this is 'a relationship between an individual with access to one or more resources (the patron) and an individual with more limited access to those resources he desires'. Kruijer notes that, in one of the districts a huge number of affidavits were distributed during the elections stating that the holder was insolvent, or almost so, and so eligible for free medical care. The campaign propagandists, who can be regarded as the political 'brokers', were promised new or better posts. Van Lier (1977, p. 296) therefore states that the political parties were supported by networks within the working class in particular, with the propagandists serving as linkmen. An empirical study by Derveld (1981, p. 92) into the role of patronage in the largely Indonesian district of Commewijne shows how deeply rooted and important the patronage system was in Surinam. One of the Indonesians interviewed told Derveld:

Two years ago, I was still working for the Marienburg sugar concern. Cutting cane in the sun. It was hard work. I didn't earn enough and by the afternoon I was too tired to plant anything . . . I asked Kromo whether he knew of a job for me, because I was on his side (KTPI). Kromo went out looking for a job for me. After a while I had a job at the Ministry of Agriculture.

The political broker Kromo admitted that he was 'given jobs' by Minister of Agriculture and KTPI leader Willy Soemita: 'Otherwise I couldn't work for him'.

Kruijer (1973, p. 106) notes that the patronage relationships serve to veil social inequalities: 'The bond of patronage allows the poor client to identify with his patron to a certain degree . . . Patronage has a conservative effect, it maintains the status quo. Patronage is a force which undermines tendencies towards structural change in society. As such, it is also used by those groups with vested interests in maintaining the existing order.'

Under certain circumstances, ethno-political parties with the above-mentioned characteristics can maintain a somewhat stable political system in accordance with the model of 'consociational democracy'. Surinam's political system largely exhibited the characteristics of the so-called 'equivalent incorporation of consociation', a version of S. G. Smith's 'mode of incorporation' whereby persons are divided into different corporate groups through which they participate in the public domain (See Smooha, 1975, p. 73).

It is helpful at this point to provide a brief summary of the conditions formulated by Lijphart (1969, pp. 207–25) and analysed for Surinam by Dew (1972, pp. 35–57). To a major extent, these conditions deal with the behaviour of the ethnic elites. Firstly, elites must have the ability to accommodate the divergent interests and demands of the sub-cultures. Secondly, this requires that they have the ability to transcend cleavages and to join in a common effort with the elites of rival sub-cultures. Thirdly, this in turn depends on their commitments to the maintenance of the system and to the improvement of its cohesion and stability. Finally, the elites understand the perils of political fragmentation.

Most of these conditions were met throughout the period 1958–67, with the NPS–VHP coalition. As Dew (1972, p. 44) supposes, the first condition also involves the 'allocation of goods and services by the elites for their own ethnic rank and file'. In other words, patronage plays an important role in the maintenance of political equilibrium. Surinam consistently failed to meet the second condition. The VHP's much-used slogan 'Unity in diversity' applied perfectly to this party; assimilation was therefore not a real proposition. The third and fourth conditions were certainly met, as Dew (1972, pp. 41–2) has stated. With regard to understanding the perils of political fragmentation, Dew notes the bloody race riots in neighbouring Guyana in 1962, which were used in Surinam as an example of how things could go wrong. Furthermore, the VHP also used Guyana's 'Black Friday' to mobilize its own voters.

The continuation of the cooperative ties between the NPS and the VHP even after the electoral defeat of 1955 underscores the conclusion that both Lachmon and Pengel felt duty-bound to the coalition. This was made even more clear by Lachmon's offer of a parliamentary seat to Pengel. In this context, Dew (1972, p. 43) has emphasized that, because of Creole domination of the electoral process, cross-cultural coalitions did not become mathematically necessary until 1969. 'That they have been adopted since 1955 partly reflects the intense rivalry among Creole leaders. But it also attests to the viability that they ascribe to consociational government.'

In addition to the behavioural prerequisites for the ethnic elite, Lijphart (1969, pp. 216 ff.) also mentions an additional and extensive list of 'system-conditions' which are favourable to the establishment and persistence of consociational democracy. These are:

(a) the length of time consociational democracy has been in operation;
(b) a multiple balance of power among the subcultures, instead of either a dual balance of power or a clear hegemony by one subculture;
(c) a relatively low total load on the decision-making apparatus. The more issues to be solved, the greater the risk of conflicts;
(d) distinct lines of cleavage or, as Lijphart (1971, p. 12) puts it, 'good social fences';
(e) internal political cohesion of the sub-cultures;
(f) adequate articulation of the interests of the sub-cultures;
(g) widespread approval of the principal of government by elite cartel;
(h) outside threat.

Further consideration can be given to several of these factors in the case of Surinam. With regard to the second factor, Surinam could be said to have a multi-polar system rather than a bi-polar one. The country's Indonesian population can assume a balancing position. A coalition including an Indonesian party would, in any event, have been able to provide greater legitimacy for the various elite cartels. However, the limited size of the Indonesian population in Surinam prevented the equally successful expression of the country's multi-polarity.

Surinam also did not comply with the fourth factor. The 'over-crowding' in the middle class in particular provided potential material for conflict. With regard to the fifth factor, Dew (1972, p. 49) notes that the absence of cohesion among Creoles can be a source of instability. Agreements with another ethnic group can then be rejected by groups from within the ethnic population. Dew (1972, p. 50) is positive about the articulation of interests. Furthermore, he believes that the Creole parties, as a primary instrument of articulation, are supplemented by Creole mining and industrial and civil service unions. Within this context, it must be noted that the unions, particularly in later years, became much more emphatically multi-racial organizations. This contributed to the improvement of relations between ethnic groups.

Hindustani articulation appears, as Dew (1972, p. 50) states, to be serviced by the variety of regional, religious, occupational and other group affiliations represented within the VHP leadership itself. 'Ideologically neutral compared to its Guyanese counterpart, the People's Progressive Party, the VHP is more like the Indian Congress Party as a monitor of articulation and instrument of broad-based aggregation.' On the basis of all these factors, Dew was optimistic concerning the stability of Surinam's consociational democracy. The party elites in particular are very committed to consociationalism, they have the ability to accommodate sub-cultural interests. With regard to the other 'system-factors', the same positive indications are obtained for multi-polarity, group cohesion and the public's feelings of legitimacy about the system. Furthermore, the Dutch colonial presence certainly contributed to the willingness to cooperate politically. The idea that only concerted efforts could compel the Dutch to provide the financial means for Surinam's upkeep served as a unifying force.

The 1963 elections confirmed the image of the stable elite-cartel democracy. The new cabinet was a coalition of NPS and VHP, with the KTPI soon entering the cabinet after replacing the PSV. The country's major ethnic groups were therefore now represented in the government. The electoral system was slightly altered by the addition of ten new parliamentary seats, in accordance with the system of proportional representation. Yet this led to no substantial changes in the political balance of power. Pengel himself now became prime minister.

With twice as many ministerial posts as the VHP, the NPS had a strikingly dominant position in the cabinet. By means of political patronage, both parties provided their supporters with civil service jobs, which in a certain sense promoted the emancipation of the rank and file. The Creoles were most strongly represented in the civil service apparatus. According to the 1964 census, 63 per cent of the government posts were occupied by Creoles, with the Hindustanis occupying barely 20 per cent.

Nationalism in Party Politics

The NPS/VHP coalition's easy victory did not mean a total absence of political challengers. From within the Hindustani population, a group of intellectuals was active which felt that Creoles occupied far too many top positions. But even this Actiegroep was forced to cooperate with a Creole party during the elections in order to win several parliamentary seats. The so-called 'out-bidding' by groups of ethnic extremists (see Rabushka & Shepsle, 1972, pp. 82 ff.), which can have such a deleterious effect on a multi-ethnic coalition, remained very much the exception in Surinam. Another interesting challenge for the country's established political machinery, albeit one originally quite limited in scope, was the formation in 1961 of the ideologically orientated Nationalist Republican Party (PNR). Nationalism had always remained vague in Surinam, a fact not at all surprising in such an ethnically diverse society. Surinam's internal autonomy had been formalized in the Statute of 1954, but the PNR wished to take things a step further and so adopted the demand for total independence. This party favoured such nationalistic movements as those led by Kwame Nkrumah and Patrice Lumumba in the African colonial regions. Although the PNR was left-of-centre and, in fact, the first more ideologically orientated Surinamese party since the introduction of universal suffrage, its tenets were largely nationalistic. The party leader, lawyer Eddy Bruma, said the PNR's aim was 'to bring together all progressive men and women, as well as Surinamese youth, into a well-organized political party, in order to give the Surinamese people a guiding body for the achievement of the nationalist revolution' (speech of 2 September 1961). The party was not a Marxist-Leninist one, despite the impression that some NPS followers wished to create. Years afterwards, the PNR was even to govern in a coalition with the NPS.

The PNR was born of the 'Wi egi sani' (Our Own Thing) cultural movement of the 1950s, of which Bruma was a major proponent. This movement presented itself as, among other things, an advocate of the 'Sranan tongo', the Creole language that was barely taken seriously at that time. Appreciation of the unique cultural identity, separate from the colonial culture, played a prominent role within the movement. Cultural emancipation was therefore one of its major objectives (see pp. 163–5).

In 1959, a number of the 'Wi egi sani' movement's members, led by the poet Robin Ravales ('Dobru'), set up the NBS (Surinam Nationalist Movement). In doing so, they gave political form to the cultural expresion of 'Wi egi sani'. The NBS immediately launched the idea of total independence. Pengel now also stressed that the Statute of 1954 was 'no eternal agreement', thereby leaving ajar the door to independence. His idea of independence, however, went no further than a rather vague concept of a commonwealth arrangement. By way of a symbolic gesture, Surinam created its own flag and drafted its own national anthem, with one couplet in 'Sranan tongo'. Furthermore, 1 July, the day on which slavery was abolished, became a national holiday. By way of compromise towards the VHP, which saw 1 July as a Creole affair, the day was referred to as the 'day of freedom and human rights'.

The ideas of 'Wi egi san' exercised a certain attraction on the Creole intellectuals within the government of that day. Pengel had the difficult task of recruiting to the NPS those badly needed intellectuals returning after graduation in The Netherlands, and keeping them from the clutches of radical Creole organizations. This he accomplished partly via the promise of independence.

To broaden its support, the NBS, predecessor of the PNR, also tried to spread its activities to the working classes. Accordingly, Bruma declared himself defender of Creole farmers in the Para district, who were faced with eviction in connection with the building of the Brokopondo hydroelectric station. Despite the NBS's attempts to present itself as a national party, it still remained a largely Creole affair. Sranan tongo, advocated by the NBS, had indeed developed into a lingua franca, but nevertheless remained the cultural property of the Creoles.

Yet the issue of independence became the centre of discussion. The VHP showed itself willing to make several concessions, so as to avoid a cabinet collapse and take the wind out of the radical's sails. Lachmon allowed it to filter through that he might agree to the status of 'dominion' for Surinam. Pengel then called for a new Round Table meeting between Surinam and The Netherlands, a summons to which The Netherlands was quick to reply in the affirmative. It now became clear, however, that the goal of independence did not enjoy broad support within Surinamese society. The orthodox Hindustanis in particular made their protests known. The Actiegroep mentioned above warned that independence would entail the election of a 'negro president' and 'Creole rule'. The Round Table conference remained without results, as the Surinamese delegation withdrew its proposals.

The conference's failure provided the stimulus for the setting-up of the PNR, which hoped to achieve independence on 1 July 1963—exactly a hundred years after the abolition of slavery in Surinam. Partly owing to the ethnic violence in neighbouring British Guyana, however, independence was no longer a burning political question in Surinam. The PNR received just over 3,000 votes in the elections, insufficient for a parliamentary seat. It is possible that voters were scared away by the NPS's accusation that the PNR was a communist party. The PNR party remained no significant political factor, and the relative political peace enjoyed by the NPS/VHP coalition remained virtually undisturbed. Patronage, which fulfilled a stabilizing function, certainly played a part in this. Had the NPS in particular been unable to reward its followers with civil service jobs, the PNR would almost certainly have done better in the elections.

A rift arose in the NPS/VHP coalition following the 1967 elections. On the basis of the increased number of parliamentary seats, made possible in part by an expansion of the system of proportional representation, the VHP demanded an additional ministerial post. Pengel refused to honour this demand. Both he and Lachmon were under pressure from the Dutch government, which was increasingly less willing to finance further expansions in Surinam's civil service. Pengel was therefore not prepared to give up yet another ministry and so diminish his party's opportunities for patronage. Lachmon was being pressured by the orthodox Hindustani Actiegroep. Pengel ultimately chose to cooperate with this small party. This constituted a setback for the functioning of the elite-cartel democracy in Surinam. On the basis of the election results, Pengel could just as well have opted for an entire Creole coalition. Yet he realized, as did Lachmon, that such a choice might unleash a 'Guyanese situation'. Pengel indicated on a number of occasions that he did not favour racial polarization. A further striking fact was the orthodox Actiegroep's cooperation with a Creole party. However, this coalition ultimately proved relatively brittle. The Actiegroep was quickly plagued with internal dissension regarding the cooperative venture.

Yet the coalition's fall still came as a surprise. The cabinet crisis was prompted by strikes in the educational sector, with The Netherlands playing an indirect role. As mentioned earlier, Holland had refused to further supplement Surinam's government budget. For a number of years, therefore, wage increases for teachers and others within this sector could not be paid. The strikes which came served to strengthen the position of the PNR. Just as Pengel had once provided himself with an electoral base via the Moederbond trade union organization, Bruma was now aware that he could strengthen his party's position via the trade unions. The activities of various unions finally led to the setting-up of the C-47 trade union organization, chaired by Bruma himself. It came as no surprise when these activities yielded results in the 1969 elections, in the form of a parliamentary position for Bruma. The NPS was also weakened by an exodus of its intellectuals, who set up the Progressieve Nationale Partij (PNP). In fact, the formation of this party was a challenge to Pengel's leadership. Pengel was quite autocratic by nature, and had extreme difficulty in granting a major role in the party to those who had returned from schooling in The Netherlands. The integration of the returning intellectuals into the political system would continue to present a problem, a fact which, as we shall see later, also played a role in the setting-up of several left-wing parties during the 1970s.

The PNP achieved electoral success with a campaign against alleged corruption and Pengel's authoritarian stance. However, the VHP was ultimately the major winner. Once again a multi-ethnic coalition was formed, this time consisting of the VHP and the PNP. The VHP was the largest party by far, but Lachmon conscientiously distributed the ministerial posts among all the ethnic groups and left the post of prime minister to the PNP. The coalition's term of office was hardly a calm one for the VHP and the PNP. The coalition was faced with strikes from the very beginning, in which all trade union organizations played a role. Owing to their position of strength within the trade union movement, the NPS and the PNR acted as the driving forces behind these industrial actions. The strikes, which lasted almost continuously for two years, resulted in a more heavily polarized racial atmosphere. The 1973 elections confirmed this fact.

Pengel had died in 1970, and the leadership passed into the hands of Henck Arron. Arron made successful overtures towards the PSV, the KTPI and even the formerly abhorred PNR. This Nationale Partij Kombinatie (NPK) won the elections with twenty-two parliamentary seats. The remaining seventeen seats went to the VHP, which had made an unsuccessful attempt to shed its racial image by changing its name to Vooruitstrevende Hervormings Partij (Progressive Reformational Party).

For the first time, Hindustanis were not represented in the government. The consociational model therefore suffered heavy damage. Ethnic polarization further increased when Prime Minister Arron, in his government's 1974 policy programme, announced that Surinam would become independent at the end of 1975. It was the Hindustanis in particular who had always resisted the rapid arrival of independence, out of fear for Creole domination.

However, powerful forces in favour of independence were at work in both

Surinam and The Netherlands. Via the joint NPK electoral list, the PNR had won four seats in parliament, markedly increasing its influence. Furthermore, some of the younger party leaders within the NPS greatly favoured independence. A certain 'now or never' feeling was noted among the Creole majority in parliament. In The Netherlands, the ruling Socialist party had explicitly included Surinam's independence in its policy programme. This progressive party felt the time for maintaining colonies, regardless of any degree of autonomy, had passed. Furthermore, the Dutch socialists wished to rule out the recurrence of any situation such as that which had arisen on Curaçao (The Netherlands Antilles) in 1969. At that time The Netherlands, in accordance with the statutes of its realm, was forced to send in marines to put an end to large-scale plundering and arson by workers on the island.

The approach of independence created extreme tension. The uncertainty had already prompted a veritable stream of Hindustanis to emigrate to The Netherlands. Yet an explosion of racial violence never occurred. The presence of several dissidents within each of the parties was one of the factors that moved them to caution. But it was also clear that the country's two most important political leaders, Arron and Lachmon, had no intention of allowing an actual confrontation to take place. Lachmon in particular finally gave in, saying he would be willing under certain conditions to discuss independence in 1975. He especially desired human rights guarantees in the new constitution. An ethnic balance in Surinam's armed forces was also an important point for the Hindustanis. Furthermore, Lachmon wanted proportional representation, to put an end to the electoral imbalance in favour of the Creoles. The VHP also demanded elections within six months of independence.

The talks began only shortly before the 25 November target date for independence. Several compromises were ultimately reached, with Lachmon making the biggest sacrifices. With regard to electoral system reform, Arron was willing to go no further than the appointment of a commission to study the proposal. He did, however, promise that elections would be held within eight months. The new constitution, drafted by a pluriform constitutional commission, received unanimous endorsement at the very last minute. And so, on 25 November, Arron and Lachmon were none the less able to join in a symbolic embrace.

Yet Lachmon and his party could not be truly satisfied with this development. The mass emigration of Hindustanis in the months immediately preceding independence was sufficient to show how VHP supporters were 'voting with their feet'. In view of all the objections, it was certainly surprising that Lachmon had acceded to independence on 25 November. In a

November 1985 interview with one of the authors, he gave the following explanation: 'I didn't want to disturb the country's peace. A racial conflict was looming. I could either allow it to escalate or accept the new constitution. As a responsible politician who wanted to do something for his country, I had no choice'.

In the matter of Surinamese independence, the Hindustanis in fact once again received the short end of the stick, as they had when the electoral system was established in 1948. Their subordinate role—in relation to the composition of the population—was also expressed in the distribution of ministerial and civil service posts in the years that followed. Choenni, in a comparative study, concluded that the Hindustanis, like their counterparts in the former British colonies Guyana and Trinidad, had been unable to wrest away political power at government level; this, despite the fact that the Hindustanis formed either the largest or the second largest ethnic group in these countries. Choenni (1982, p. 13) developed the following thesis in this regard: 'Their ethnic exclusivity, combined with the social and cultural exclusivity of the Hindustani population, caused the rest of society—and the Creoles in particular—not to view them as a legitimate, potentially governing power in these countries'. He further states that, according to the dominant Creole population, this exclusivity on the part of the East Indians meant that, once in power, they would work for sub-national rather than for national goals—in other words the goals of their own ethnic group. It appeared that even the Hindustani leaders realized their ethnic group would do better to play a somewhat more modest role in the political arena. The Hindustanis were well aware that their dominant role in the economy already formed a source of irritation for the Creoles. Lachmon's granting of the post of prime minister to the PNP in 1969, as well as his stance regarding Surinamese independence, pointed in this direction. In this context, Choenni (1982, p. 61) refers to a comparable situation in Trinidad, and notes the promise by Hindustani political leader B. Maraj, made before that country's 1956 elections: 'East Indians will never gain power in Trinidad, nor do they have that ambition'.

All the ethnic groups identified to only a limited extent with a Surinamese nation, although this lack of identification applied particularly to the Asian groups. In this, Surinam appears to differ little from the other Caribbean countries. Naipaul (1981, p. 275) describes the lack of internal cohesion which characterizes some Caribbean nations as follows:

These caribbean territories are not like those in Africa or Asia, with their own internal reverences, that have been returned to themselves after a period of colonial rule. They are manufactured societies, labour camps, creations of empires; and for long they were dependent on empires for law, language, institutions, culture, even officials. Nothing was generated locally; dependence became a habit.

Although the PNR's powerful nationalistic movement certainly exercised a formative influence on the thinking of the Creole population in particular, nationalism in Surinam still primarily remained a matter for the intellectual upper crust, a fact which resulted in a certain inherent instability in Surinam's political system following independence.

Emergence of Marxist Groups

Several left-wing parties arose during the 1970s with a strong nationalist and anti-colonialist platform. Various explanations exist for the rise of these parties. As mentioned earlier, the consociational model had suffered a number of broadsides, a fact which led to a certain degree of social instability. The strikes of 1969 and 1973 illustrated this. These industrial actions, which resulted in cabinet crises, had already provided the impetus for Surinam's left. In addition, a major role was played by the return of intellectuals who had studied in The Netherlands. In the late 1960s, these students had become familiar with the leftist currents so influential in the Europe (and particularly in the European academic world) of that day. These influences could often be directly traced in the manifestos and programmes drafted in Holland and brought to Surinam. The return of the intellectuals was accompanied by the problem of their integration in Surinam's political system. Owing to the fairly undemocratic internal procedures, adaptation was a demand with which many in the 'old' parties had no desire to comply. This problem appears to be a somewhat universal one in formerly colonial areas, and was in fact no new phenomenon in Surinam, as has already been discussed with regard to the setting-up of the PNP by Creole intellectuals leaving the Pengel-dominated NPS. Bovenkerk (1981, pp. 158 ff.) points out that integration is a common problem for re-migrants. In Surinam, he says, the rest of the population regard these re-migrants as something of a new 'ethnic minority', because of their arrogance and their pedantry.

The three left-wing parties set up in the 1970s were the PALU (Progressive Union of Workers and Peasants), the DVF (Democratic People's Front) and the VP (People's Party). The Surinamese Socialist Union (SSU), set up in 1970, presented itself as a movement. After a few years, the SSU formed an electoral alliance with the VHP and so ceased playing a political role. The party platforms of the PALU, DVF and VP exhibited many similarities. All three party platforms broke a lance against obvious social injustices and structural defects. As the PNR in the 1960s had primarily addressed itself to cultural and political nationalism, so the PALU, VP and DVF now placed additional emphasis on economic nationalism. Foreign domination in the country's economy was bitterly attacked.

In their 1977 campaign platforms, all three parties stressed the need for the development of a broader economic base, to be created largely by means of agricultural modernization and national industry. The DVF went furthest in its lone call for the gradual nationalization of the all-important bauxite companies. The PALU wanted the government to assume a majority share in the banking and insurance sectors; yet none of the left-wing parties called for complete nationalization of all Surinam's productive resources; instead, they strongly favoured the development of a well-founded national entrepreneurial class.

The parties also wanted to effect changes in the political-administrative system. Elected administrative bodies were to be set up on a district basis. This was put to an end to that centralized administration which had made grass-roots democratization so difficult to achieve. The PALU and VP also favoured lowering the voting age to 18—the ultimate implementation of which would have served these parties to no small extent.

The PALU executive consisted largely of those who had received agricultural university training in The Netherlands. The leaders could be roughly characterized as middle-class technocrats. The party's strategy was primarily aimed at taking over important positions within the government apparatus. At first, the PALU was the driving force behind a number of trade union activities, but this role was never of any great significance. During its initial stages in particular, the party's platform presented the PALU as a Marxist-influenced movement. The party manifesto of March 1977 was based on a dialectical social analysis. Yet the PALU maintained no contacts with foreign Marxist organizations.

The programme of the DVF, a political descendent of the Kommunistische Partij Suriname (KPS), was based on the Marxist–Leninist analysis of the Surinam situation ('Towards A Combative Socialism'), published in 1971 by its leader Humphrey Keerveld. In actual practice the party leaned towards Maoism. Members of the DVF executive were sporadically active in trade union activities, yet their participation was never very great. In the 1977 elections, this party participated in a joint platform with several other groups, the most important of which was the FAL Peasants Federation. It must be emphasized that, for the most part, parties were hardly more than small groups of devotees propagandizing their cause and vying for electoral support.

The Volkspartij, officially set up in 1975, was by far the most active of the three at the grass-roots level. The party set up 'people's committees' in various Paramaribo neighbourhoods. These committees provided social advice and information, as well as medical services. They also organized cultural and recreational activities. These people's committees in fact functioned as special-interest groups. The Volkspartij was the only one of the three left-wing parties with contacts among foreign Marxist groups. The party's Youth and Women's organizations were affiliated with the World Federation of Democratic Youth and the World Federation of Democratic Women respectively.

All three left-wing parties were multi-ethnic in character and composition, which was one reason why they enjoyed the sympathy of young people in particular. Great hopes were held out for the 1977 elections, and it was generally expected that at least the Volkspartij, owing to its vastly popular work at the grass-roots level, would succeed in obtaining a parliamentary seat. Disappointment was therefore even greater when none of the left-wing parties won a seat in parliament. With just over 4,500 votes (2.5 per cent), the VP received barely one-half of the parliamentary electoral quota. The PALU and DVF received nothing more than around 1,000 votes. Even the PNR, which—owing to the NPS refusal to meet their demand concerning the number of parliamentary seats—was now running independently, received only about 6,000 votes: too few for a single seat in parliament.

Dissension within Surinam's left was one of the reasons for its electoral defeat. Had all the votes cast for the left and the PNR been combined, the joint parties would have won two parliamentary seats (one in the national electoral district and one in the Paramaribo city electoral district). Furthermore, NPS leader Arron's hard-hitting election campaign, in which he accused the Volkspartij (seen by the NPS as something of a threat) of communist inclinations, did not fail to find its mark. For many Surinamese, such allegations were enough to prompt them to vote for the traditional parties. The small left-wing parties also lacked the funds from trade and industry enjoyed by the NPS and VHP. Another major factor was the left-wing parties' total inability to crack the patronage system. Even if the Volkpartij was able to draw thousands to its rallies, in the voting booth the individual's own position within the civil service apparatus was often more decisive than any sympathy for a progressive political movement.

There was yet another factor, and perhaps the most important one, working against the left. A hefty electoral victory was predicted for the VHP, which had formed a coalition with several smaller parties. This prompted many Creole voters to abstain from voting for the left and to none the less provide support for the NPS which, in the form of the NPK (Nationale Partij Kombinatie), had established a joint platform with the PSV, KTPI and one extremely small Hindustani party. The ethnic factor once again proved decisive. Under the influence of the district electoral system, the NPK achieved an almost unbelievable landslide victory, with twenty-two parliamentary seats. The remaining seventeen seats went to the VHP coalition. In terms of the number of votes received, these rival parties virtually tied.

Disappointment within the left was so bitter that many lost faith in the ballot box as a tool for exercising independent political influence. The DVF even established cooperative ties with the NPS. The Volkspartij continued its independent course. A rift occurred within the PNR. Part of this party's executive, namely those had been active in setting up the PNR—such as the poet Robin Ravales—remained true to their 'mentor' Eddy Bruma. These Brumists later formed a coalition with the VHP, a party which they had once heavily criticized. A second faction, consisting largely of trade unionists led by union leader Fred Derby, split off and began working with the PALU. Yet the left-wing parties proved to be only a marginal factor in a political system still dominated by ethnic allegiance.

The neck by neck race between the VHP and the NPS reflected the country's demographic development. The Hindustani population had grown very quickly, a fact which generated fears of a takeover among the Creoles. The inevitable result was ethnic polarization. This polarization became even more pronounced after the elections, when clear indications were found of electoral fraud on the part of the NPK. According to Surinam's General Statistical Office, 30,000 voters too many had been registered within a total voting population of just over 180,000. It appeared that the Hindustani population was to perennially be denied political power.

A general atmosphere of *malaise* was noted during this period, largely prompted by the Arron government's ineffectual economic policy, which did nothing to reduce unemployment or improve the social position of most of the population. In addition, the incoming flow of Dutch development aid had caused corruption to mount even further. This effect was produced by the relatively large sums allocated and the limited number of profitable projects. The Netherlands therefore tended to approve development projects much too easily while monitoring of these projects remained lax.

This *malaise* was rapidly expressed in the form of a new flood of emigrants to The Netherlands. Unlike that before independence, this new group of emigrants was multi-ethnic. Thousands of Creoles were now leaving the country as well. Bovenkerk (1983, pp. 158 ff.) has shown that Surinamese emigration in the 1970s can sooner be explained by 'push-factors' in Surinam than by 'pull-factors' in The Netherlands. Even after independence, emigration remained possible via a special agreement with The Netherlands. Just before this arrangement expired in 1980, the flow of emigrants reached a new peak. This emigration served as a safety valve for the incumbent NPK government. Social discontent could in this way be diffused—yet another reason for the left's poor election results. The Arron government therefore had absolutely no reason to halt the flow of emigrants.

For many, the socio-economic and political situation in Surinam at the end of the 1970s had become hopeless. The short-lived expectations raised at the time of independence had been driven into the ground. Ethnic polarization had even come close to causing a constitutional crisis in 1979. After the death of a parliamentarian from the NPK—which had recently been weakened by several resignations—the VHP refused to provide the parliamentary quorum needed to swear in a successor. Only the president's threat to resign, and so render the country literally ungovernable, finally resulted in a compromise and the announcement of early elections in 1980. Owing to unforeseen developments, however, these elections were never to be held.

Historical Analysis of the Regime Since its Formation

The Sergeants' Coup

On 25 February 1980, a group of sixteen poorly-armed sergeants, led by Desi Bouterse, seized power in Surinam. The surprise coup was welcomed by the majority of the population. Dissatisfaction with the country's 'old' organized politics was so widespread that any change was seen as a chance for improvement. Yet it would not be correct to say that a revolutionary situation existed in Surinam at the time. There had been no long-lasting struggle for liberation in which a front of workers and/or farmers had finally triumphed against a repressive power. Political behaviour was determined more by tradition than by any existing and well-focused dissatisfaction. As noted earlier, most of Surinam was still entangled in the ethnic politics of patronage and nepotism, scarcely based in any ideology. The vast majority of the people were mostly insensitive to revolutionary rhetoric. If feelings of dissatisfaction were to be expressed, this took place through the trade unions, as was the case in 1969 and 1973.

But the people's general dissatisfaction and their desire for a change was nevertheless a factor in the turbulence leading to the coup. Yet it was matters concerning the military itself which directly prompted the mutiny. The situation within the military and its position in society had fanned the fires of frustration among the young corps of officers. Following independence in 1975, Surinam had begun with the transformation of the existing foreign Army detachment into its owned armed forces, with the aid of an extensive Dutch military mission. A portion of the officers' corps consisted of Surinamese commissioned and non-commissioned officers who had received their training, served in The Netherlands and returned to Surinam when the country gained independence. Herein lies a significant explanation for the frustrations of the NCOs and their alienation from their superiors and the civilian government. The non-commissioned officers were primarily dissatisfied with the military's policy of promotion, the inferior equipment and the pay-scale. Those soldiers who had served in The Netherlands received supplementary pay, which naturally generated a certain friction within the ranks. The young corps also clashed with the authoritarian and archaic policies of their supreme military leader. The NCOs had received different treatment in The Netherlands. Another background issue was the fact that Surinam's Army had not been transformed into a so-called 'development Army', with duties related to the economic development of the country. Such a situation could have put an end to the ennui and enforced idleness in the ranks. In contradiction to his intention expressed at the time that independence was granted, Prime Minister Arron refused to implement this idea. Involvement of the army in civilian tasks would have placed an unacceptable limitation on the prime minister's opportunities to serve his political clientele. Those in favour of a development army, such as PNR Minister of Military and Police Eddy Hoost, were therefore promoted to positions safely out of the way.

Following the Dutch example, the non-commissioned officers set up a military union (Bomika) in 1979 to protect their own interests. The government refused to recognize the union and had several of Bomika's board members arrested in early 1980. Among those arrested was Badrissein Sital, who was later to play a major role in the post-coup period. These arrests led to the coup of 25 February. Several hours before the court was to have delivered its verdict, Arron's government was overthrown. Some said that 'the military wanted a union and got a country'. Yet the conflict surrounding the military union was nothing more than a goad to action. As Bouterse himself was to comment later, 'The matter of the union was of indirect influence'.

Various plans for a coup had existed for more than a year. Preparations were being made not only by the group around Desi Bouterse, but also by commissioned officers led by Surendre Ramobocus and by such sergeants as

Badrissein Sital and Chas Mijnals. The latter two had ties with the VP (People's Party), and were the only conspirators with a clear political orientation. Shortly after the coup, Bouterse said he had begun conspiring with the sergeants Badrissein Sital, Chas Mijnals, Laurens Neede and Roy Horb under cover of the military union (Slagveer, 1980, pp 25 ff.).

Another factor in the coup's success was the (financial) support Bouterse was already receiving from the 'national bourgeoisie'. These national entrepreneurs, on the whole from trading companies but also from manufacturing and construction companies, opposed the perennial political domination of the 'compradore bourgeoisie' with its strong dependence on foreign support. It was this vision that prompted the Surinam term '*foetoebois*' (errand boys or lackeys). Successive governments had provided virtually no support for the nation's industry. The soldiers were aware of the trade union organizations' support for their coup attempt, with only the Moederbond adopting a reluctant position. Another significant factor was the position of the chief of the Dutch military mission. His support for the NCOs in their grievances against the inefficient military apparatus gave the sergeants the impression that The Netherlands would, in any event, not reject a *coup d'état* out of hand. It is not unlikely that the mission chief (Col. Hans Valk), either unwittingly or out of sheer partisanship, had stimulated the coup. An official Dutch investigative study, however, simply arrived at the conclusion that the diplomat had maintained insufficient distance from the matter and that his actions had provided the non-combatants with moral support.

Militarily speaking, Bouterse's coup was well-prepared. But, as would quickly be seen, all political preparation was lacking. There was no political ideology, and conflicts in this regard would flare up quickly enough. On the heels of the coup, power was placed in the hands of the nine-member National Military Council (NMR). The NMR was chaired by Badrissein Sital, whose leftist-radical ideals received support from only a minority within the council. Sital owed his position primarily to his former activities in the military union. The NMR adopted a very cautious position. A proposal for the name 'Revolutionary Military Council' was rejected as being too daring. In the council's first communiqué, dated 25 February 1980, all citizens of Surinam, 'regardless of race, religion, political conviction and profession' were called on to submit to the process of 'socio-economic, social and moral re-orientation' and to the development of Surinam. As early as their second communiqué, the soldiers clearly declared their intention to establish a 'civilian council', to be charged with administrative duties. One thing was clear: the military victors of the coup were neither willing nor able to go it alone. Their first press conferences were primarily characterized by a lack of confidence. To underscore their moderate intentions, their communiqué emphasized that foreign investors would not be interfered with. The coup was quickly rechristened the 'intervention'.

The soldiers called on the lawyer Eddy Bruma to form a civilian council. It was no coincidence that they chose the founder of the PNR. Bruma had served as a counsellor to the three board members of the military union after their arrest. The two most important military men of the coup, Desi Bouterse and Roy Horb, therefore felt that Bruma was the obvious choice, although they also felt that he—as a representative of the 'old' political machinery—was too controversial to assume a position in the civilian council itself. More radical factions, including Sital and Mijnals, were not at all pleased with Bruma's role.

The reference to the coup as an intervention appeared entirely justified. The sergeants had not suspended the constitution, and it was the constitutional president, Johan Ferrier, who inaugurated the civilian council. Ferrier also spoke stubbornly of an 'interim cabinet' and not of a civilian council which, according to the NMR, was to play only an advisory role. The president did not recognize the unconstitutional formation of a civilian council and also refused to accept the NMR as supreme national power. Even Surinam's parliament remained intact, albeit devoid of actual powers. Parliament could no longer dismiss the government. 'Surinam is currently in an exceptional situation', Bruma noted at the time, with more than a hint of understatement. Surinam had, in fact, come up with an extremely remarkable and, at the same time, extremely unclear constitutional configuration. Later, parliament was even to approve a bill of amnesty to absolve the military leaders of any charges resulting from several killings which took place during the coup. Very much against the will of the NMR, this same bill termed the coup a punishable offence, but dismissed the participants from prosecution. Via an enabling act in April of that year, parliament handed the reins of power over to the government.

Within this context, it is striking that the VHP was less reluctant than the NPS. VHP leader Lachmon called on parliament to help in the transference of political power 'to allow the government room to make a clear sweep in the country'. It was obvious that the VHP had less to lose from the coup than did the NPS.

If the coup itself was already unique owing to its execution by sergeants, it was made even more so by the fact that all this took place within the constitutional framework. The military leaders appeared thoroughly swept off their feet by their own lack of political experience. During the first weeks, an NMR spokesman even went so far as to issue a request for several handbooks on *coups d'état*. By remaining within the constitutional boundaries, the new strongmen also hoped to win confidence from abroad. As early as the beginning of March 1980, American officials announced that they were 'no longer worried by the possibility that the coup would produce a leftist government'. On behalf of the Andes Pact countries, Venezuela thanked President Ferrier for his efforts to preserve the democracy.

The civilian government inaugurated on 15 March was led by Henk Chin a Sen from the moderate wing of the PNR (the Brumists), a physician of impeccable behaviour but totally lacking in political experience. This lack of experience applied to most other cabinet members as well. The new prime minister's Chinese descent rendered him ethnically neutral, and thus acceptable to both the Creole and East Indian groups in the population. The government, which included two representatives of the military, was largely technocratic in nature, but it was the PNR that was none the less able to exert the most formative influence on it. Both the radical and moderate wings of the party were represented. The inauguration was attended by a pandit, a *molvi* and a pastor, to symbolize the national character of the government. No political programme existed as yet. In those first weeks, however, there was little that could abate the euphoria resulting from the toppling of the Arron government. The NMR members visited factories and schools in order to gain personal experience of the problems there. In one of the districts, soldiers brought the children to school when the school bus broke down. The NMR members also visited street markets to personally ensure that merchants adhered to the price regulations. Pension benefits were now paid out punctually, and refuse collection services were operational once more. Civil servants were now to be at their posts throughout official working hours—in order to weed out those who were merely on the payroll. A suggestion box, in which civilians could deposit their written comments and ideas, was also placed at the entrance to the military camp. And within the framework of the crime prevention programme, criminals were given public beatings, a development which caused some to shudder but which generated a feeling of safety among the majority of the people. With these measures, inspired more by populism than by ideology, the military were able to maintain their popularity for the time being as 'our boys'.

On 1 May, almost two months after its inauguration, the Chin a Sen government presented its declaration of policy, which included a socio-economic and political section. In this declaration, the events of 25 February were termed a 'severance'. 'On that day a system saturated with injustice, corruption, social injustices, bureaucracy and nepotism ignominiously fell'. And, in an anticipatory mood: 'For the people of Suriname, February 25, 1980 means a day of liberation, of new hope, a re-birth. The old order has passed away, a new age has dawned for our country and our people'. Chin a Sen dutifully vowed that the hope that which had been kindled would never again be extinguished.

The new government's programme could be termed pragmatic, yet it did not avoid decision-making. The premises set out in the declaration were based on four renewals:

— renewal of the political/administrative order;
— renewal of the social order;
— renewal of the educational order, and
— renewal of the socio-economic order.

The declaration formulated a number of major points concerning the political/administrative order. A constitutional commission was to study the possible need for constitutional amendments. The drafting of a bill on political parties was announced, which was to redress the errors of the old system and, among other things, guarantee internal democracy under the party system. The voting age was to be lowered from 21 to 18. The formation of district councils to promote regional democracy was announced, a major improvement in a country that had always been administered from Paramaribo. According to the government's programme, functional (social) groups were also to be involved in policy-making. A special court of law was to be set up to investigate and prosecute cases of corruption from the pre-coup period. The civil service was to be purged of corrupt officials. The Army was not to be definitely transformed into a development Army. The government was even ready with a date for a general election: 'Barring unforeseen circumstances, new elections can be expected around October 1982'. The programme inspired confidence, both within Surinam and abroad.

However, this confidence could not conceal the escalating battle of competence between the civilian and military sectors. President Ferrier, now more than ever exceeding the bounds of his ceremonial function, 'formateur' Bruma and Prime Minister Chin a Sen had, from the very start, done their best to defuse the NMR as the centre of power. The NMR's view of the relationship was made clear directly after the installation of the Chin a Sen cabinet. NMR chairman Badrissein Sital said then that the National Military Council had delegated administrative tasks to a civilian council, and that the regional and sectoral policies were to be implemented on the basis of 'directives' from the NMR. In his policy declaration of 1 May, Chin a Sen was already attempting to provide clarity.

With the swearing-in of the government by the president of the Republic of Suriname on March 15, 1980, the power of government has once again been placed in civilian hands. In addition to this, the National Military Council has remained in force. It is that government which was sworn in on March 15 which governs this country. In doing so, the government receives powerful support from the NMR, which takes part in the government via its two cabinet representatives. The government does not wish to deny the fact that it has not come into power by means of those procedures provided for in the constitution, in other words, by means of elections, or that the power to govern has been handed over to the government by the NMR, the true seat of power in the republic until March 15. These circumstances, supplemented by the fact that the maintenance of public order and national security continue to demand a high degree of vigilance, prescribe, in the government's view, that this country be governed in close consultation with the military power.

The battle of competence between the civilian and military sectors was not laid aside with this peace speech, but would continue to run as a thin red line through Surinam's recent history. Perhaps of even greater significance was the debilitating dissension within the civilian sector itself. One faction, the left-wing groups that had not succeeded in winning parliamentary seats during earlier elections, had hoped that more room would be allowed after the coup to tinker with the existing constitution and structures. The chairman of the left-wing nationalist PALU party, Iwan Krolis, subscribed to the opinion that a mistake had been made in remaining within the boundaries of the constitution after the coup. 'The constitutional aspect was the weakest facet of the coup', he told an interviewer at the time. 'They should have realised that foreign intervention only takes place when international interests are threatened, which was not the case.' The PALU and the nationalists within the radical wing of the PNR unconditionally chose the side of the military. A controversy arose within the People's Party about the desirability of supporting the military, and about whether the party apparatus might be made available to the military leadership. A group of leftist-radical intellectuals, with Cuba as their political model, split from the VP and formed the Revolutionary People's Party (RVP). The main arguments used by the left to rationalize its participation have been noted by Gowricharn (1983, p. 211):

— the political dominance of the 'compradores' must never be restored;
— the coup provided the unique opportunity to implement, with the help of the government apparatus, major changes in Suriname's society;
— as it was the military which had removed the old, corrupt and right-wing politicians from power, it could be assumed that these military leaders were themselves incorruptible and anti-right wing, or even leftists. The military lacked

only a political vision and experience in political administration, qualities which could be supplied by the left.

Iwan Krolis and future foreign affairs minister Harvey Naarendorp sat on the NMR's advisory council, as did trade union leader Fred Derby from the radical wing of the PNR and Henk Herrenberg, who was later to be appointed Surinam's ambassador to The Netherlands and minister of foreign affairs. For the country's left, the shots fired on 25 February appeared to herald the approach of a true revolution. At the time, coup leader Desi Bouterse emphasized his own moderate position by stating that: 'This advisory group is sure to be supplemented with what is often referred to as "the forces of the right", so that a certain equilibrium can be achieved within the advisory council'.

It appeared that the NMR would be able to further its influence with the support of the advisory council. The primary concern of the radical members of the advisory council was to drive an even greater wedge between the government and the NMR. The NMR operated as a virtually independent force in the investigations into corruption and the establishment of people's or civilian committees. During the first months, the military arrested various politicians and civil servants, including the deposed prime minister Henck Arron (who would none the less never be convicted). The NMR had adopted the idea of the people's committees from the People's Party.

It was largely the left-radical soldiers Sital and Mijnals, chairman and vice-chairman of the NMR respectively, who wished to strengthen the position of the military council. They were quick to make clear that the NMR was to form the 'vanguard of the revolution'. Yet the NMR was suffering all too heavily from a lack of unity. The left-radical wing of the NMR, supported by the advisory commission, attempted in July of that year to carry out a mobilization during a visit to Surinam by the Dutch minister of development cooperation. Several thousand people, including many schoolchildren, demonstrated for price-indexation of Dutch development aid. The coup had unquestionably resulted in heightened national consciousness, and the demonstration was an expression of this. Yet Prime Minister Chin a Sen also appeared to have rapidly learned a bit about political strategy. Having earlier adopted the demand for indexation, he could turn the tenor of the demonstration on Paramaribo's Independence Square into one of devotion to himself.

Politically speaking, the left-wing movement within the NMR was very weak. This faction lacked a political programme and detailed ideas about how society was to be reformed. When asked shortly after the coup how he thought the lives of the people could be improved, Mijnals replied that he 'didn't know yet'. Furthermore, the Chin a Sen government already had a programme for improving the lives of the poorest section of the population, a fact which served in advance to take the wind out of the sails of the left.

Meanwhile, the NMR was being undermined even further. In late June of 1980, Bouterse and Horb were commander-in-chief and garrison commander of the council respectively. Only two weeks later, both men had left the NMR. In this way, they intentionally destabilized the NMR to further their own positions. This, of course, meshed extremely well with the strategy of Prime Minister Chin a Sen. The prime minister's adviser at the time, André Haakmat, spoke in his political memoirs (1987, p. 50) of a strategy aimed at 'driving a wedge' within the NMR as the only means to gradually restore an adapted form of parliamentary democracy. But Bouterse and Horb went on to form a new seat of power, over which they themselves had control: the military leadership. This was to lay the foundation for an ongoing battle of competence between the civilian government and the military leadership.

A Break with the Old Republic

The amorphous constitutional arrangement created after 25 February appeared barely serviceable. In any event, it confirmed the fact that the coup was unique and could not be compared with the more familiar powerplay by a Latin American caudillo. The ceremonial president had maintained his position and the constitution remained in force, yet this also provided the old order with the opportunity to resume its overtures to power. On 13 August, therefore, a break was made with the 'old' republic.

The immediate cause was constitutional President Ferrier's stubborn demand that the central budget be presented to a parliament which had in fact already been effectively neutralized. This demand was unacceptable to both Prime Minister Chin a Sen and the military leadership, for it was seen as an attempt to restore the old order. Ferrier was forced to step down, and Chin a Sen was presented with the presidency in addition to his prime ministership. The constitution was simultaneously suspended and a state of emergency was declared. In fact, the 25 February coup was only now complete for the first time, after almost six months. The dissatisfaction with the legal procedures in the corruption trials had also provided fertile ground for a settling of accounts with the former republic. Prominent parliamentarians, civil servants and government officials arrested on charges of corruption were acquitted by the court on what were often merely procedural grounds. Commander-in-Chief Bouterse said of this: 'the bureaucracy has frustrated attempts to see justice done'. Shortly after 13 August, several VIPs were arrested and a Special Court was established to deal with cases of corruption; yet virtually no heavy sentences were passed.

Along with the nipping in the bud of restorative tendencies, 13 August also witnessed the dropping of the curtain on the extreme left. Leftist military men, including Badrissein Sital and Chas Mijnals, and several civilians from Revolutionary People's Party circles were arrested on charges of conspiring against the regime. Bouterse spoke of a counter-coup 'with the armed aid of a foreign power which will remain anonymous'; it was clear to all that he was referring to Cuba. During the trial several months later, however, this accusation could not be substantiated. It could not be denied that those arrested were dissatisfied with the course of events in their country, nor that there had also been regular contacts between the RVP members and Cuban visitors to Surinam, but the existence of plans for a coup was never proved. The arrests were sooner prompted by Bouterse's fear of competition in the struggle for power. He watched mistrustfully as the NMR became increasingly interested in ideological matters. This had to do with the NMR's commissioned involvement with the civilian mobilization. The NMR had therefore developed good contacts with the RVP, which viewed civilian mobilization as the major means to achieve its revolutionary goals. With his 'administrative coup' of 13 August, Bouterse had killed two birds with one stone.

The cabinet was revised but remained technocratic in nature. An important newcomer was André Haakmat, mentioned above, a close acquaintance of Chin a Sen. As deputy prime minister and minister of foreign affairs, justice, army and police, Haakmat assumed an influential position. In an interview at the time, he analysed the intervention of 13 August as follows:

These measures were needed to prevent Suriname from taking a politically extreme course. We desire no adventures, from either left or right. The second republic will ply an independent, neutral course. We desire a socially just government without isolation by the left, although we do assume a position to the left of centre. We are striving for a social democracy. There were those who wished to swing to the extreme left or right, and they have been removed from their posts. [Haakmat also commented on President Ferrier's demand for the restoration of the powers of parliament:] We could not accept that, because we must first purify the government of those who misbehaved during the Arron period. That can only be done if the democracy is restored gradually. Had we buckled under to the president's demands, we would have run the very real danger of returning to the situation as it was before the revolution.

Prime Minister Chin a Sen, now President as well, said shortly after August 13 that a 'radical intervention' had been needed because of 'conflicts regarding competence, opposition and stagnation'. According to Chin a Sen, certain groups had possessed blueprints for imported revolutions. 'But we do not wish to import any revolution; not a Chinese revolution, not a Russian revolution and not a Cuban one.' Chin a Sen described the situation in Surinam as a 'revolution based on national aspirations'. The term 'Surinamism' was used in this context to underscore the new national consciousness.

Although the civilian leaders praised the intervention of 13 August, this 'administrative coup' at the same time weakened their position. With the declaration of the state of emergency and the suspension of the constitution, the Chin a Sen government had sacrificed much ground, despite the fact that the prime minister had received the presidency as well. Prior to 13 August, legislative power was in the hands of the government. After that date, legislative decrees were also signed by the military leadership, which had assumed the role of co-legislator. The ground won by the government in the undermining of the NMR had now been lost again. The Chin a Sen government underestimated the consequences. The increased power of the military leadership was formalized several months later in the form of a decree which provided the military commander, in given circumstances, with the power of acting presidency. This marked the decisive defeat of those who had accorded the military a mere 'watchdog function' after the 25 February coup. The political position of the military leadership was further formalized by the setting-up of the Policy Centre, a policy-making body consisting of the military chief, the Chairman of the NMR and the President.

Relations with those foreign powers most important to Surinam—namely The Netherlands and the United States—had not suffered from the political changes. On the contrary; these countries appeared pleased with the fact that Surinam's left had been pushed out of the picture. The Netherlands had at an earlier point already expressed its confidence in the moderate pragmatist Chin a Sen, and had made 500 m. guilders available for the carrying out of a 'crash programme' (see Chapter 4). Selected soldiers from Surinam's Army were now trained not only in The Netherlands, but in the United States as well.

Yet the country's internal relations were under great strain. The arrest of the three left-wing military leaders provided a catalyst for dissatisfaction. Demonstrations in protest against the curfew, the ban on public gatherings and the limitations on press freedom grew in size and intensity, as did the number of random arrests made by the military police. The sentences of one or two years passed on the three soldiers were considered in Surinam to be more of a successful attempt by Bouterse to justify and complete his 'coup' of August 13 than any fair punishment for offences committed.

The affair surrounding the leftist military men took a sudden and quite remarkable turn in March of 1981. Under orders from the military leadership, the left-wing leaders were released. A spectacular reconciliation with Bouterse followed, before the watching press, yet without any notice having been given to Surinam's government. This was the first time the military leadership was to demonstrate its leverage over the civilian government. Bouterse now suddenly heralded a 'revolutionary process in the direction of a socialist society'. Sital confidently announced that work was to begin on a people's democracy. If a plan had been lacking since 25 February, the day had now apparently dawned for a declaration of the course to be taken.

The political shifts in favour of those left-wing radical factions close to the seat of military power resulted in the publication on 1 May 1981 of the 'Manifesto of the Revolution'. This was the first time since the coup that Surinam's left had presented political ideas to the country. The plan had been drafted by PALU leader Iwan Krolis, at times quoting from his own party manifesto published some years earlier, and was not endorsed by the Chin a Sen government. The major portion of the document dealt, however, with the situation as it had been prior to 1980. The coup was once again re-christened, this time as the 'revolution'. The manifesto stated that 25 February 1980 had been 'a decisive turning-point, for it was the first time that the struggling masses succeeded in wresting themselves free of the political power of our country's colonial and neo-colonial rulers'. The manifesto referred to the military perpetrators of the coup as 'the brave sons of our people', and equated their struggle with that of the Maroons. The revolution's most important mandate was the development of a new society 'built on the ruins of the neo-colonial society'.

The lack of a revolutionary movement, however, had created a vacuum that would allow various individuals and groups to try to ease themselves into the seat of power and influence the military leadership. Because of their inexperience and lack of real expertise, the soldiers had shown their vulnerability in this regard. After all, they had demonstrated their helplessness immediately after the coup by calling on the civilians for their assistance.

With the release of Sital and the others, a course of polarization was established which was to continue for some time to come. The Manifesto of the Revolution was a first signal. However, the revolutionary rhetoric struck a singularly unresponsive chord. Sital himself admitted that the mobilization of the people had met with little success. In a July 1981 interview he stated: 'The NMR is active at the grass-roots level through such means as the people's committees, yet the results are of little substance.' Sital also did not shrink from admitting that the soldiers' authority had, in fact, disappeared. 'The fact that the military actually holds sway over the country is experienced as a limitation to freedom. A clear connection must be established between the people and the military apparatus. The military is lacking in popularity.' The military were also able to exhibit but few successes from which the people could directly benefit. A fairer distribution of land and income, for example, had not yet been effected on any large scale.

The efforts of the military leaders would from this point on be largely aimed at the formation of a front. The strong impression was created that the military leadership and the radical left-wing intellectuals hoped in this way to limit the actual powers of the president even further. Several days after the publication of the revolutionary manifesto, the prominent Palu member Iwan Krolis, Harvey Naarendorp and Garrison Commander Roy Horb were added to the Policy Centre. In this, Surinam's highest policy-making body, the President was now confronted with three soldiers and two radical left-wing civilians. Krolis's party had already succeeded in late 1980 in obtaining a cabinet ministry with Errol Alibux. Naarendorp had been Minister of Foreign Affairs and Minister of Justice as from early 1981, after the resignation of André Haakmat. Three months later, Badrissein Sital would enter the cabinet as Minister of Public Health. In June of that year, relations with Cuba were upgraded. Shortly afterwards, the Cubans opened an office in Paramaribo for their chargé d'affaires—the direct result of Naarendorp's own initiative in his role as Minister of Foreign Affairs. The RVP in particular maintained regular contacts with the Cuban diplomatic mission, with the Cubans providing advice on the development of a revolutionary organization. At an earlier stage, Naarendorp had abolished the visa requirement for Cubans, allowing them to enter and leave Surinam as they pleased. In this way, tiny Surinam threatened to become a bone of contention between East and West.

The formation of the Revolutionary Front was proclaimed in late August; its chairman was military leader Desi Bouterse, who had in the meantime risen to the rank of lieutenant-colonel. The Front's composition was broad, with associated bodies including some of the trade union organizations (C-47, CLO and PWO) and the FAL Federation of Peasants. Among the political parties, the PALU, RVP and the PNR had also joined the Front. According to Bouterse, the Front was to establish the much-needed connection between the Army and the government on the one hand and the population on the other. Chin a Sen was not opposed to the formation of a front *per se*, yet he believed this body ought to 'democratize' the revolution and not become a tool for the military leadership. The idea for the formation of a front was the special brainchild of the radical left-wing military men Sital and Mijnals. Meanwhile, Bouterse became increasingly emphatic in his assertions that the Army was nowhere near returning to the barracks. This paved the way for a conflict with Chin a Sen. The President-cum-Prime Minister wished to keep to the policy programme announced on 1 May 1980 and so hold elections in late October of 1982, based on a law on political parties that would rule out any system functioning on an ethnic basis. The struggle of ideologies and for political power became increasingly overt. Chin a Sen deliberately contributed to this development with the publication in September of that year of a draft constitution, drawn up by a special commission. In this way he hoped to precipitate a public discussion, much against the will of the military, and so place the military leadership and the left wing under pressure, in order to obtain leeway to implement his policy programme. The draft constitution included an administrative model that allowed room for political parties and functional groups, as well as for popular democratic bodies. The draft was intended, as one member of the constitutional commission said, to prevent Surinam from taking an administrative backslide into the situation it had been in before 1980. It provided the military with nothing more than an advisory status, within the framework of a 'Revolutionary Council'. This no longer fitted in with Bouterse's view of things. Inspired by his advisers, he had begun to cherish political ambitions. The publication of the draft constitution added new fuel to the fires of conflict. Bouterse stated publicly that the position of the military in the central government would have to be arranged more satisfactorily. Furthermore, the military leaders were less than enthusiastic about the re-emergence of political parties. They preferred a system within which only functional groups and popular political structures could function, as such a system allowed them to exert greater control.

The late Eddy Hoost (at one point a member of the constitutional commission) said: 'The soldiers will accept no system which moves them out of the picture' (off-the-record discussion with one of the authors, October 1981). The definitive parting of the ways between the Chin a Sen government and the military authorities followed on 17 December 1981. A rally had been organized in Paramaribo for Army Commander Bouterse's proclamation of the Revolutionary Front. The presence of representatives from Nicaragua's Sandinista front, Guyana's Marxist PPP (People's Progressive Party), the Salvadorean insurgents and the Cuban diplomatic mission provided the festivities with a certain international allure. Yet the rally received little response from Surinam's people. At the same moment, in the district of Coronie, President Chin a Sen was railing publicly against the 'evil forces threatening to take over our society'. Although he did not explicitly name the forces in question, the President was clearly referring to Cuba.

Leftist-Revolutionary Groups at the Centre of Political Power

The government's resignation on 5 February 1982 could no longer come as a surprise. It was, in fact, the logical conclusion to a process that had begun shortly after the coup. The direct cause was Chin a Sen's refusal to read a speech drafted by Iwan Krolis which explicitly failed to mention the promised elections. Chin a Sen resigned after a conflict with two PALU ministers which ended in a call for the President to step down. Even though a demonstrative birthday celebration in the presidential palace, organized by national trade and industry, had drawn thousands of guests only one month earlier, Chin a Sen's resignation was marked by an almost complete absence of statements of support. Chin a Sen could expect little from the 'old' parties, who saw him more as the one who—along with the military—had put an end to their regime than as an ally in the struggle against a rising dictatorship.

Two years after the coup, therefore, the radical left (PALU and RVP) had succeeded in strengthening its position at the centre of power. In doing so, this faction had taken able advantage of the trend towards power politics which played an increasingly clearer role in the thinking of the military leadership. With its largely university-trained leadership, the PALU had succeeded in winning a series of strategic positions in the government apparatus. This success was indeed so great that critics spoke of a 'monopolization' of the revolution. The RVP, on the other hand, played a prominent role in the apparatus of the civilian mobilization, with this party seen as the driving force behind the revolution.

Yet mistrust and aversion towards those in power were growing among the population. The continuation of restrictive measures and the continual postponement of democratization led to even more intense criticism. On the whole, the Revolutionary Front enjoyed little popularity among the people. It was hardly realistic to expect moderate trade union organizations to function within one front together with such parties as the PALU and the RVP. An attempted coup on 11 March 1982 by a group of soldiers led by Surendre Rambocus—who, as we have noted earlier, had plans for a coup even before 1980—shook the Bouterse regime to its foundations.

The attempted coup made several things clear. Firstly, it showed that dissension existed within the Army concerning the course to be followed. A major faction wanted the restoration of democratic institutions in Surinam in the short term. The coup attempt also demonstrated once more that the regime could count on only limited and rather shaky support from the population. When Rambocus, during the short period in which it appeared that he had seized power, announced the return of the Army to its barracks, various people's committees promptly began removing the nameplates of their organizations. One could barely speak of any popular attachment to the regime. Racial sentiments also appeared to play a role. Many regarded the attempted coup as a 'Hindustani' affair. Bouterse himself reinforced this idea with the comment that the organizers of the attempted coup had hoped 'to strike the racial key'.

Crushing the coup attempt had certainly not added to the popularity of the military regime. The summary execution of one of the conspirators, Wilfred Hawker, who had two years earlier been one of the sixteen sergeants participating with Bouterse in the successful coup, even generated popular dismay. The regime was becoming increasingly autocratic. The policy programme from the new largely unaffiliated government spoke only vaguely of a return to democracy. And not one word was dedicated to the re-institution of political parties. The political structures announced in the new policy programme were populistic and corporative in nature. The drawing-up of yet another draft constitution was announced, and the setting-up of a National Assembly would be 'aspired to'.

Yet, of much greater importance were the changes in administrative structure effected after the resignation of the Chin a Sen government. The military leadership assumed full power, and a junta model was proclaimed by decree. The executive presidential system was disbanded. In addition to the prime minister, there was now to be a ceremonial president. The highest administrative power was placed in the hands of the Policy Centre, which began functioning as a junta. The Commander-in-Chief (Desi Bouterse) and the Deputy Commander-in-Chief (Roy Horb) were Chairman and Vice-Chairman of the Policy Centre respectively, and the prime minister was by definition a member of the supreme authoritative body. Under the decree, the composition of the Policy Centre was placed entirely in the hands of the military authorities. It was the Policy Centre that was to determine 'the direction of the revolutionary process' and government policy. The military's administrative supremacy was in this way formally established for the first time since the coup of 25 February 1980. The exertion of political influence by the civilian sector could now only take place through informal channels. It was precisely the radical left-wing groups that found access to these channels, as they unconditionally accepted the power of the military.

For those now in power, the Ministry of Civilian Mobilization began playing an increasingly important role. The approach became more professional, and of a more ideological hue. Civilian mobilization became more emphatically a brains trust for revolutionary and ideological thought, within which models were developed for a populistic political structure. A 1982 memorandum from this ministry reflects the increased Cuban influence. The tasks for people's committees outlined in the memorandum display striking resemblances to the Revolutionary Defence Committees (CDRs) in Cuba (see pp. 81-9).

It was against this background that criticisms of the trade union movement became more intense. On 1 March 1982 Cyrill Daal, leader of the Moederbond, gave a belligerent speech for bauxite workers. In this speech he emphasized that the trade union movement could only function in a democracy. And he added to this the threatening comment that 'trade unions have in the past caused Surinam governments to take to their heels.' But the mounting resistance came not only from the Moederbond, which could still be accused of having ties with the 'old' NPS party. Gradually, more criticism was aired by other trade unions as well. The protest actions by small-scale rice farmers in August in the Nickerie district of western Surinam had a catalysing effect. They demanded that the government establish higher minimum prices. The authorities refused and so, in effect, chose the side of the large rice dealers. Lieut.-Col. Bouterse dispatched a military unit to Nickerie, led by Hørb, when the farmers blockaded the airport and roads. For the first time since the coup, Surinam soldiers confronted the country's citizens. Ten board members of the FAL Peasants' Federation, an organization that had actually shown consistent support for the 25 February coup, were arrested.

Strikes in the health care and educational sectors served to worsen the climate. The military leaders also brought the wrath of many down on their heads when they arrested two soldiers suspected of conspiracy who had just been acquitted by the courts. Unrest came to the university when the authorities announced plans to install a 'revolutionary' academic board. Medical students responded with the demand that members of the people's militia should leave the campus.

The setting-up of the people's militia in August had already cast a considerable pall over the political climate. The militia was the instrument (the 'eyes and ears') of the Army and the revolutionary left, and was considered to be a threat by many. An institution such as the people's militia was also entirely foreign to Surinam society, which as an elite-cartel democracy had always been relatively peaceful. Yet now a strongly polarized atmosphere had been created. Critics of the regime were labelled 'enemies of the revolution', and the term 'counter-revolutionary worms' (after the Cuban '*gusanos*') was also commonly applied. It was principally the RVP supporters who had introduced the image of the enemy within. They had largely taken over the state media and they now used it as an instrument for propaganda.

The last three months of 1982 witnessed a confrontation such as Surinam had never seen, culminating in the killing of fifteen prominent opponents of the regime. Here too the revolution was to devour its own children. Moederbond leader Cyrill Daal emerged as the first to drive a wedge into the military leadership's position of power. The incident began with Daal's arrest on the grounds that he had used insulting language in reference to Bouterse and to Grenada's Prime Minister, Maurice Bishop, who was visiting Surinam at the time. The atmosphere was already tense, owing to a strike by air-traffic controllers associated with the Moederbond. Only after being threatened by armed soldiers did the strikers consent to cooperate in landing Bishop's plane. Daal and his union saw Bishop as a symbol of the 'imported revolution' which they so fervently hated. Surinam's revolutionary leadership, however, identified with Grenada and with Bishop. Something had been achieved in Grenada which appealed to the imagination, and something similar should therefore also be possible in Surinam. Bouterse himself certainly identified strongly with his 'personal friend' Bishop. During Bishop's visit, both men's faces appeared on posters with the caption 'Up to the Final Bastion'. Daal must have known that there was no better way to strike out at Bouterse than to call out strikes during Bishop's visit. Daal's arrest was a spark in the powder keg. Other strikes followed, such as those by the telephone service, insurance companies and the port services. Owing to a strike at the electrical company, Bouterse suffered the humiliation of having to receive his friend Bishop by candlelight, precisely at the time he had hoped to show his counterpart the achievements of Surinam's revolution. After a demonstration before the military headquarters, Daal was released. But events had already gained in momentum. During the strike the following day, which had been announced as to last only two hours, in protest against the treatment of the air-traffic controllers, Daal suddenly announced that the industrial action would continue until the demand for general elections had been met. The strike would be rounded off with a mass meeting on Sunday, 30 October, precisely at the moment when Bouterse and Bishop were to hold a joint rally at another location in Paramaribo. On that day, 15,000 demonstrators rallied to Daal's side, while no more than 1,500 people attended Bouterse and Bishop's rally. One could scarcely imagine a more forceful challenge for Bouterse. Maurice Bishop was clearly alarmed by what he saw as a counter-revolutionary movement, and in his speech he stated: 'The Surinamese revolution is too friendly, reactionary forces too strong. You have to eliminate them, otherwise they eliminate you.' Although Bishop's comment was obviously not meant to be taken literally, he none the less contributed to an escalation of the conflict.

Daal's industrial action ultimately failed, owing to a lack of support from the three other trade union organizations. Traditional conflicts within Surinam's trade union movement played a role in this. The C-47, led by Fred Derby, saw Daal's efforts partly as an attempt to restore the situation as it had been before 1980. This view was based on the ties between the Moederbond and the NPS, as well as on the firm support Daal had received from a section of trade and industry. Furthermore, Derby feared Daal would overplay his hand by demanding the immediate return of the military to the barracks. According to Derby, the conflict of interests had become too intense to reasonably expect an immediate step-down by the military. In addition, Daal's campaign had been provided with an extra dimension by accusations that he was receiving orders from the American embassy. There can be no doubt that the American embassy was following the strikes very closely. Just before Daal's mass demonstration, the American chargé d'affaires telephoned the offices of C-47 to ask 'what the position of Derby will be'. Against this background, Derby found it difficult to join the ranks.

The lack of support considerably weakened Daal's position. The Moederbond's industrial action therefore came to a rapid halt following Garrison Commander Roy Horb's talks, on behalf of the Policy Centre, with Daal. The Moederbond leader came away from these talks with nothing more than the promise that the authorities would work on effecting 'new and tangible democratric structures', a formula that merely echoed the government's policy programme. The accord with Daal also heralded the beginning of the split between Bouterse and Horb. The latter felt he had been deceived when the Policy Centre, contrary to an assurance it had made, did not work on a joint communiqué after the talks with the trade union leader. Daal's industrial action could have been dismissed as an attempt by a trade union, in alliance with the 'old' political parties, to implement a return to the pre-coup situation, were it not that barely one week later a much broader drive for democratization came into full swing on a national scale. The other trade union organizations and the FAL Peasant's Federation, led by C-47, presented their own plan for a return to democratic institutions. The Moederbond also joined in, which meant that a plan had now been put forward by Surinam's entire trade union movement. The plan was much more cautious in its approach than the Moederbond's original package of demands. Because of its step-by-step approach, it was commonly referred to as the 'phases plan'. The plan's major elements were:

— the formation of a national assembly before 1 January 1983, consisting of democratically elected representatives from (functional) social groups such as trade unions and employers;
— endorsement by the assembly in February 1983 of a law providing for political parties;
— the drafting and ratification by the assembly of a constitution in March 1983;
— the drafting of a plan for economic reconstruction.

Shortly after the plan's publication, talks with the Policy Centre were initiated at the trade union organizations' request. After the tensions surrounding Daal's campaign, a certain degree of optimism was present. After all, a plan had been presented which could count on broad support from Surinam's people. Yet the talks made clear that no common vision was held by the authorities themselves. Prime Minister Henry Neijhorst, also a member of the Policy Centre, said the phases plan contained no elements to which the cabinet was opposed (interview with one of the authors, November 1982). Foreign Affairs Minister Harvey Naarendorp, however, emphasized that objections certainly did exist to the plan (interview with one of the authors, November 1982). Naarendorp in this way gave voice to the vision of the radicals, who had continued to win more and more positions at the centre of power. In addition to Harvey Naarendorp, Iwan Krolis of the PALU, who belonged to Bouterse's circle of advisers, also played a major role in squashing the phase plan. None of their interests were served by such a democratization plan, for any form of representative democratic system would only entail the loss of their position and opportunities for revolutionary change. Yet an ideological schism was also becoming increasingly obvious within the military leadership itself. While his deputy Roy Horb felt that concessions should be made to the trade union movement, Bouterse had swung in the direction of his radical advisers.

While the negotiations on the phase plan were still underway, Bouterse, in a television speech (15 November 1982), suddenly announced his rejection of the plan. He stated that

Democracy without leadership leads to anarchy, and anarchy leads to demise. And of course no one in this world wants that, especially not in our country. . . . For this reason we, as leaders, will provide the further drafting and formulation of the general outlines of the new democratic structures, based on the wealth of experience and the multitude of insights we have gained in recent years in dialogue with you. And we will present you with the outlines which we have drafted and formulated no later than the end of March 1983, and we will announce the manner in which the discussions with you are to take place.

Bouterse's statement can be seen as a turning-point in the tempestuous developments of the autumn of 1982. It had become clear that the military leaders were in no way willing to be dictated to concerning the desired form of democratic structures.

The trade union organizations reacted furiously. In a joint declaration the unions retorted:

The announcement of November 15 is a clear demonstration that those in power and their 'confidential' advisers have not understood one iota of the common convictions of Suriname's people. The military authorities and their advisers have once again confirmed the fact that they live in an ivory tower, high above the heads of the people, and that despite their progressive rhetoric they lack any actual bonds with the people. ... He [Bouterse] has clearly indicated that the military acts as though it were willing to allow the people to have a say in fundamental matters, but regards the people's true rule as only to obey and not to take part in decision-making ... It is clear that the current situation does not lend itself to such a speech. Had the chairman of the Policy Centre given this same speech two years ago, it would have been an unqualified success. But the current situation calls loudly for actions regarding democratisation and not for words and lengthy procedures which strongly resemble delays and postponements. [The statement ended with a summons:] The trade union organisations and the FAL will continue undaunted in their efforts to implement the phase plan. We hereby call on all workers, farmers, young people, women and other workers to remain poised to continue the struggle for true social and political renewal until victory has been achieved.

Bouterse was now opposed by the entire trade union movement.

In its demands and criticisms, the trade union movement was supported by about ten major groups, united in the 'Association for Democracy'. These groups included all of Surinam's religious organizations and the country's employers, including the national employers—united in the Association of Surinam Manufacturers (ASFA)—and the employers of the Association of Surinam Trade and Industry (VSB), who were largely involved in foreign trade. On 23 November, these groups sent a letter to Commander-in-Chief Bouterse. The fundamental character of this document is reflected in the following excerpts:

Although you speak of democratic structures and consultation, participation, monitoring and the acceptance of responsibility, the people must accept the government leadership, as represented by you among others, as an unalterable fact. Apparently, you do not consider the people to be as yet capable of the insight needed to choose their own representatives. We understand this view to be one in which the socio-educational and political-administrative approach which you have advocated has failed in sufficiently conditioning the people to enable them to choose for that which you yourself favour. Yet this is certainly not a democratic, but much sooner a totalitarian concept of government. Characteristic of such a view is that the leadership's vision is definitive, and only those who on the whole loyally support that vision are allowed to participate in its further development and implementation . . . Adult and free citizens consider it their inalienable right to choose, within a governmental context, their own leaders; this is, after all, the essence of that bundle of rights which is referred to as 'political rights and freedoms'. To attempt in the 20th century to convince a people such as ours that this is not the case appears to us, in view of their level of intellect, their cultural and historical background, their political tradition and their interest in political developments, to be an act of utter futility. You cannot dismiss the fact that our people have passed through a centuries-long development, from colony to independent nation.

According to the Associations' view the military's concept of democracy would 'lead to acts of repression such as have never been seen in Surinam'. This repression would in turn result in the polarization and disintegration of Surinamese society.

By late November, the military regime found itself opposed by the majority of Surinam's people. The regime was faced with a choice: either accept a moderate and reformative solution or attempt to enforce its own model while running the risk of a head-on conflict. For Bouterse, the time for compromises appeared to have passed. In early December a demonstration by several thousand students was brutally dispersed. The trade union movement declared its solidarity with the demonstrators, and the Association for Democracy wrote in another letter to Bouterse: 'It was unfortunately again shown on this occasion that a stubborn attempt to impose the will of a small minority on a large majority ultimately ends in the use of senseless violence'.

The confrontation came earlier than anyone had expected, and in a way in which no one in Surinam would have believed possible. On the night of 8 December, the offices of the Moederbond trade union organization, two radio stations and the offices of a daily newspaper burst into flames. At the same moment, fifteen prominent opposition leaders were arrested and brought to the military headquarters, where they were tortured and then executed. The victims included union leader Cyrill Daal, Surendre Rambocus (the imprisoned leader of the failed March 1982 coup) and Rambocus's lawyer and former cabinet minister Eddy Hoost, as well as several signatories of the Association for Democracy's declaration. C-47 leader Fred Derby was originally among those arrested. He was released after twenty-four hours and so became the sole survivor.

Shortly after the arrests, Bouterse announced that 'the revolutionary leadership had succeeded in frustrating an attempted coup which was designed to restore the situation whereby a small economic elite would come to power and trample underfoot the interests of the workers, peasants and masses of our people.' This explanation was all the more striking since it followed on the heels of the joint trade union protest. And, in view of the divergent political standpoint of the victims, the announcement hardly carried credibility. The conflict situation of late 1982 exhibited parallels with that of autumn 1981 concerning a draft constitution. Conflicts now arose when the demand was made for the provision of concrete plans for democratic institutions. The military leaders apparently preferred to continue operating in a constitutional vacuum, since this presented the fewest obstructions to their power.

The official statement read that the fifteen detainees had all 'been shot while trying to escape' from the military headquarters. The United Nations' special rapporteur on summary and arbitrary executions, the Kenyan Amos Wako, carried out an investigation for the UN Commission on Human Rights (UNCHR). In his report of 12 February 1985 (UN Economic and Social Council), Wako concluded: 'On the basis of information in his possession, the Special Rapporteur finds that summary executions took place on the night of 8–9 December in "Fort Zeelandia"'. Wako drew no conclusions with regard to direct personal involvement. He did, however, quote five anonymous eyewitnesses who had made incriminating statements. Wako states that, according to these five eyewitnesses, among those present at the fort at the time were Lieut.-Col. Bouterse, Major Horb and, for part of the time, the prominent PALU member Errol Alibux, and Harvey Naarendorp. During his 1984 visit to Surinam, Wako also asked Wim Udenhout, Prime Minister at the time, why a legal investigation had never been carried out into the affair. Udenhout's reply was: 'It's a problem of having to ask the question. What will be served by ascertaining the facts and bringing to justice all those responsible, directly or indirectly? What would be served by this kind of justice? It might lead to violence again.'

Within the Army there were groups who no longer wished to be identified with the military leaders after this event. As early as January 1983, Bouterse placed some ten of these officers on non-active duty. Some of them fled the country. But Bouterse saw the greatest danger in the person of his deputy, Roy Horb. The rift between Bouterse and Horb had become increasingly obvious during the final months of 1982. The moderate and right-wing forces saw in the simple-minded yet straightforward Horb the only figure possibly able to topple Bouterse by means of an internal coup. These groups were in fact striving for the return of former president Chin a Sen, who had left for a medical refresher course in the United States after he had been removed from office. Horb, whose relationship with Chin a Sen was good, had paid a visit to the former president in October, with the knowledge and approval of Bouterse. The visit led to speculations that the two men were considering implementing a political reversal with the support of the United States.

Shortly after the December executions, Horb had tendered his resignation, a fact which made him quite popular among the population and within the Army. Bouterse increasingly feared that Horb, reinforced by the support he enjoyed, would attempt to seize power. In late January of 1983, Horb, his bodyguards and several civilians were arrested on conspiracy charges. Three days later, the former garrison commander was found dead in his cell. The official statement spoke of suicide. The regime had accused Horb of conspiring with the American CIA. No evidence of such a conspiracy was produced. Some months later, in May of 1983, the American ABC broadcasting corporation revealed that American President Ronald Reagan had approved a CIA plan to topple the Surinamese regime, because of Cuban influence in that country. According to ABC, the plan was shelved for lack of support from the United States Congress which objected to the plan.

It appeared that, for Bouterse, the revolution was only now beginning. In an interview with the French daily *Le Monde* (7 January 1983), he said:

Having crippled the counter-revolution, the time has now come to accelerate the revolutionary process. Until 8 December we had a quiet revolution, without violence. Yet we lacked a centre which would provide direction for our political activities. Because we allowed them too much freedom, our opponents were able to profit from this and regain the territory they had lost. That's why the army is now more on the alert, and wants to promote the civilian mobilisation. Space will now be created for all those who wish to take part in the revolution. But the privileged must abstain in the people's interest.

The revolutionary course was also more clearly expressed in the composition of the new government. Following a government which had been consistently technocratic in nature, a radical cabinet had now been formed in which the two most loyal revolutionary allies, the PALU and the RVP, held the major ministerial posts. The cabinet was led by Errol Alibux. Bouterse had chosen him as one who had proved loyal even in the darkest hours, and who totally accepted the leadership of the military strongman. 'Bouterse is the shining example. We wanted him and we will always want him', Alibux said shortly after accepting his post. Badrissein Sital received the post of Civilian Mobilization, a position which gave him major influence in the development of populistic structures. Bouterse hardly had any choice but to ask the PALU and RVP to take part in the government. There were, in fact, no other groups still willing to do so.

Bouterse's settling of accounts with the opposition had given him a certain amount of room to manœuvre. The shock to Surinam ensured that the opposition forces fell silent for the time being. Yet Surinam, now more than ever, drew the attention of foreign powers, a fact which was not without influence on the country's domestic policy and the position of the regime. The suspension of Netherlands' development aid was a severe economic blow (see Chapter 4). And the increasingly radical course taken also prompted historically unprecedented alertness on the part of Brazil and the United States. The Brazilians became openly involved in developments in Surinam. Mounting Cuban influence was the factor which prompted Brazilian concern. The United States had also emphatically urged Brazil to become more actively involved in Surinam's affairs. According to one of Bouterse's former advisers, ex-trade union leader and journalist Rudi Kross, the United States even went so far as to put the Brazilians under heavy pressure by referring meaningfully to the South American country's foreign debt. Brazil carried its involvement quite far. In an unprecedented step, Brazilian President Figuereido in April 1983 sent his top security official and adviser, General Denilo Venturini, on a lightning mission to Paramaribo.

The general's visit was so unexpected that his 'diplomatic invasion' literally violated Surinam's airspace. Venturini told Bouterse point-blank that Brazil would not tolerate a position of strong Cuban influence on its borders. One year later Bouterse's former adviser Kross related how the Brazilians, during an official visit to their country, had informed him of their position regarding Surinam. While assisting the Surinamese Minister of Economic Affairs in talks on trade and technical assistance, he reported that the Brazilian military side-stepped both its own civilian government and the Surinamese delegation in handling the affair. Kross related that he was bluntly informed by top officials that Brazil was not at all interested in Surinam, but that it was prepared to react drastically if pressured to do so now that it appeared Brazil was sharing a border with Cuba via Surinam. This message was confirmed in both private talks and a press campaign depicting the special deployment of Brazilian expeditionary troops close to the border with Surinam and the troops' armaments. Venturini's visit, with its veiled threat of an intervention, was not without the desired effect. Bouterse promised to honour the Brazilian demand concerning foreign influence in Surinam, in return for which Brazil offered Surinam the opportunity to improve trade relations and even to purchase military equipment.

At the same time, the programme of the newly inaugurated Alibux government was divested of radical rhetoric. Yet the rapprochement between Surinam and Brazil led to dissension within the Army and government. The PALU was not displeased with the Brazilian move. A reduction of Cuban influence could serve to pull the rug out from under the rival RVP. This did ultimately take place when, in June 1983, Badrissein Sital was forced to leave the cabinet and enter voluntary exile in Cuba. Sital viewed Brazil's offer of help as a 'dictate' which should not be complied with. An official statement concerning Sital's dismissal spoke of 'serious differences' between the revolutionary leadership and the minister. In private conversations, top officials said Sital's views on civilian mobilization were too closely allied with the Cuban model. After the pressure exerted by Brazil, Bouterse wanted to adopt a somewhat more careful course, at least in terms of the image presented to the outside world. Another factor here was that Sital had been actively developing his own position of power within the Directorate for Civilian Mobilization.

In this effort, he was able to use the people's militia as an instrument. Sital's temporary exile, urgently advised by the RVP, the PALU and Bouterse, was intended to quiet things down for Surinam. This ploy was hardly successful, for the country was aware that the eyes of the world had been turned even more intensely on it since the events of 8 December 1982. Related pressure remained on the country's internal policy, a matter to which Bouterse was not entirely insensitive. It must have been a shock for him when Maurice Bishop, referred to by some as Bouterse's 'revolutionary godfather', was killed by fellow revolutionaries and his country invaded in the course of an American intervention. What had happened in Grenada could also take place in Surinam. Immediately after these events, Bouterse expelled Cuba's crack ambassador, Osvaldo Junquera Cardenas. During the United Nations General Assembly in New York, the Americans had informally made clear to Surinam that its reaction to the Brazilian move had been insufficient. Both immediately before and after the expulsion of Ambassador Cardenas, Bouterse had held lengthy talks with the American ambassador in Paramaribo.

Cuban influence had grown to such a point that information from the Policy Centre often landed the same day on Cardenas's desk. Bouterse also saw in this situation a possible threat to his own position, considering the way in which Bishop had been removed from power by members of his own party. Upon announcing the expulsion of Cardenas, Bouterse undiplomatically referred to the ambassador's 'somewhat peculiar' working methods. Bouterse's adviser Kross was a little clearer. According to Kross, then employed at the Ministry of Economic Affairs, Cardenas had issued a letter in which he told his subordinates that all Surinamese civil servants, under orders from the Policy Centre, were to provide the Cubans with any information they might require.

The most serious defect of Surinam's revolution continued to be the lack of a mass movement which was needed to further the process. After the failed experiment with the Revolutionary Front, which was quickly disbanded owing to internal dissension, the attempt was once again made to set up a revolutionary movement of unity. The '25 February Movement' was set up in November of 1983. Membership was now open, not to organizations, but to individuals. In this way it was hoped that the danger of dissolution could be minimized. The military authorities wanted their own base of power, without interference from different organizations (see pp. 81-9). The military leadership itself formed the leadership of the 25 February Movement. The Chairman was Lieut.-Col. Desi Bouterse, with Capt. Etienne Boereveen and Lieut. Paul Bhagwandas as members of the board. Bouterse felt the Army should still be seen as the 'vanguard and mainstay' of the revolution.

Bouterse's leadership was once again put to an extreme test in late 1983 by a massive strike which began in the all-important bauxite sector. At the end of December of that year, all the workers at Suralco (an ALCOA subsidiary) and Billiton (a Shell subsidiary) went on an all-out strike. The strikes were prompted by the Alibux government's plans for tax hikes (see Chapter 4). The scope of the industrial action grew quickly when political demands such as elections under the secret ballot system were added to the list of grievances. Work also stopped in banks, at the state electrical utility and in the private bus services. Students boycotted their classes. The strikes were of a different nature, owing to the lack of identifiable leaders. One year after the executions, no one dared assume that role. The trade union leaders refused to support the industrial action. C-47-leader Derby made the futile attempt to persuade his members to resume work, in order to avoid political difficulties. Yet Derby's authority had waned since his release on 8 December 1982, which raised the suspicion that he was under pressure from the regime.

In the beginning, the authorities refused to move an inch. Bouterse even despatched troops to the Suralco plant, 'to protect those willing to work'. But the military unit's commander returned home without accomplishing his task, noting that the strikers did not constitute a 'small group of terrorists'. Owing to possible political complications, it would in any event have hardly been conceivable that a military unit should force its way onto the production site of an American multinational. The strikers appeared to be well aware of this fact. Bouterse finally conceded by having the Alibux government resign for the 'mistakes' it had made (see also Chapter 4). The strikers were not satisfied, but continued to press for the resignation of those actually in power. Only after ALCOA had closed the bauxite plant for an indeterminate period of time did the striking workers allow themselves to be bought out with a few financial compensations. Had the civil servants joined the strike, the military regime might have been brought down. There are two reasons why this did not happen. The Suralco workers are the best-paid workers in Surinam, and so are seen as an elite group. In addition, government reprisals were feared. Bouterse only needed to sacrifice the Alibux government in order to save himself. This, however, meant the political demise of the PALU.

The Dissolution of the Surinamese Revolution

The dismissal of the PALU/RVP government in fact symbolized the failure of Surinam's revolution. Total political isolation and the escalating economic crisis compelled Bouterse to seek support, or at least cooperation, from organizations with a broader social base. Bouterse turned to organized trade and industry and the trade union organizations, the same group that had offered him such bitter resistance in the fall of 1982. This act can safely be described as nothing less than having come, politically, full circle. Bouterse not only initiated talks with the national entrepreneurs, united in the ASFA, but also with the VSB, which represented the large trading concerns and had once been labelled 'compradore bourgeoisie'.

A new government, comprised of the trade union movement, trade and industry and the military authorities, was—during an eleven-month transitional period (until December 1984)—to create 'lasting democratic structures' and to deal with the economic crisis as well. A special think-tank, including representatives from the military (the 25 February Movement), the trade unions and industry, was set up to draft a democratization plan. The trade union leadership had no easy time convincing their rank and file to participate in the new government. This was largely due to the rank and file's loss of confidence in their union leaders after their failure to stand behind the bauxite strikes of late 1983. Hard feelings towards the military authorities were also common within the VSB. The trade unions and trade and industry demanded, and were granted, a complete say in the appointment and dismissal of cabinet ministers. They hoped in this way to prevent the military from exercising arbitrary decisions in these matters. This move somewhat strengthened the position of the civilian partners.

The new government was led by Wim Udenhout, one of Bouterse's advisers. With the inauguration of the new government, the military quite successfully damped down social unrest for the time being. The interim period, implied by the promise of democratization, provided the regime with a certain amount of breathing-space.

Abhorrence for the 'old system' remained the major justification for the continuation of military rule. Even after the government's popular base had been broadened through participation by trade and industry and organized labour, Bouterse was still thinking in terms of a revolutionary movement of unity. In a speech at the time, he spoke of the 25 February Movement as the 'backbone of the revolution'.

It is certainly not surprising that opinions differed widely within the think-tank concerning the direction that democratization was to take. In fact, the discussions within this body strongly resembled those which had already been carried out in preceding years. In their report, the representatives of the 25 February Movement called for a 'participative democracy', in which a 'continuing dialogue' was to be maintained with the administration, as the prime means to achieve revolutionary goals. The question of just how such an administration could be set up was once again left unanswered.

The trade union movement wanted the government to be a mixture of representative democracy and a corporate system, in which both political parties and social groups would be granted a major role. Under such a system, the trade union organization would also be able to exercise direct influence. This vision actually differed little from the 'phases plan' presented by the trade union organizations in late 1982. According to organized labour, the military leadership should simply function as one of these social groups. Organized trade and industry called for a system of representative democracy, with parliament as a legislative body. The think-tank's final report, which could truly be nothing more than a compromise, resulted in the setting-up of the National Assembly. Within a transitional period of twenty-seven months, this assembly was to simultaneously draft a constitution and act as a legislative body. The assembly included representatives from the 25 February Movement (fourteen seats), organized labour (eleven seats) and trade and industry (six seats). A new government, comprised of these three partners, was once again placed under the leadership of Wim Udenhout. The VSB employers' organization refrained from participation out of dissatisfaction with the distribution of seats in the assembly.

The population had noticeably little confidence in the government. A significant factor in this was the rank and file's decreased respect for the trade union leaders. These leaders' rejection of the 1983 strikes and the conciliatory attitude towards the military particularly prompted hard feelings among many workers. The government's social base therefore remained narrow, despite participation by organized labour and trade and industry. The possibility that this government would find a solution to the country's political and economic problems therefore appeared scarcely feasible. Finding such a solution was made even more difficult by the suspension of Dutch development aid.

Another striking political twist took place in 1985, when Bouterse opened dialogues with a wide range of social and religious groups. The official explanation was that the ideal of unity was to be stimulated in this way. But the talks took on much more significance when a dialogue was also initiated with VHP leader Jaggernath Lachmon and the leader of the NPS and former (ousted) prime minister, Henck Arron. Both these political parties were, in fact, still banned. Talks had, however, already been held between Bouterse and the 'old' political leaders. At Bouterse's request, Lachmon had drawn up a democratization plan in May 1984, with Arron's co-signature. The draft plan called for direct elections and awarded only an indirect supervisory role to the military. But the plan was shelved, and the dialogue appeared to have reached a dead-end. Yet the talks were warily resumed. Bouterse tried to play down the scope of the talks by insisting that he was speaking with the 'old' political leaders only 'as individuals'. But it was clear to all that the dialogue had a much more far-reaching significance. Later came official recognition of the fact that this was a 'structural dialogue concerning fundamental matters'.

Bouterse had a number of reasons for involving the 'old' parties in the country's administration. Such participation could provide his regime with a more acceptable image, both at home and abroad. Without a doubt, the 'old' parties continued to enjoy widespread support. Furthermore, there were many who saw these parties as at least one means of bringing about political change, especially now that the trade union leadership was suffering a loss of credibility.

The negotiations, in which the NPS and VHP—as well as the Indonesian KTPI party—took part, proceeded laboriously. Time was on the side of the political parties, and they appeared to be keenly aware of this. As participation by the left-wing parties had already proved a failure, and as organized labour could provide no sufficient popular base, the 'old' parties remained the sole alternative. Lachmon and Arron demanded the right to discuss their mandate in the dialogue within the upper levels of their parties. Bouterse capitulated after several months. However, the negotiations concerning the new democratic structure were even more laborious. The VHP and NPS insisted on sticking to their own 1984 democratization plan. Bouterse wished to reach an accord before 25 November 1985, come what may, to allow for the public announcement of the results of the dialogue in the form of a manifesto on the tenth anniversary of Surinamese independence. And, indeed, an agreement was reached only a few days before the deadline.

The incumbent government would remain in office until April 1987, the end of the agreed transitional period. The agreement read that Surinam would before that time receive a constitution and a representative body, to be set up 'in accordance with the principles of a true democracy'. The VHP and the NPS had ultimately to be satisfied with this vague description. According to the agreement, Lachmon, Arron and KTPI leader Soemita were to take part in the 'Supreme Council' which had already begun operating as the country's highest administrative body (see Chapter 3). The three political leaders were furthermore only to involve themselves in political-administrative matters, to facilitate monitoring the implementation of the accord. Lachmon made no attempt to disguise the fact that this formula was a compromise. In a reaction after the signing of the agreement, he said: 'I can hardly claim that the entire document lives up to expectations, but give-and-take is necessary for agreement in any dialogue. When one is thinking in terms of national interest, it won't do to be too adamant about one's own standpoint.' The political leaders emphatically voiced their qualms by their limited participation in the administration.

The incumbent government had now become something of a lame duck in the political whole. It could interpret the agreement with the 'old' parties as a vote of no-confidence from the military leadership. Criticism of the government mounted within the National Assembly. The cabinet was heckled as being indecisive in matters including those measures needed for economic recovery. Several ministers resigned amid accusations of corruption. Similar accusations were levelled against the military leaders.

As noted earlier, organized labour's waning authority denied the trade union organizations the necessary popular support. The trade union movement was already deeply divided when, owing to an internal conflict, it stepped out of the Udenhout government in 1985. And the dissension mounted even further in early 1986, when the Supreme Council accused the C-47 trade union of 'terrorism' after it had supported a strike at Suralco. These rifts served only to strengthen the position of the 'old' parties.

The VHP, NPS and KTPI began participating more fully when they entered the new cabinet in July 1986. The post of prime minister went to the VHP-affiliated Pertab Radakishun. His appointment underscored the new political turn of events. Radakishun was a former chairman of the VSB employers' organization, a special-interest group that had always opposed the government and that had in turn been blackballed as being 'neo-colonialist'. Radakishun was also Surinam's first VHP prime minister. Yet it was not entirely illogical that the prime minister was to come from the VHP and not the NPS, for it was the former party that had maintained the initiative in the preliminary dialogue. The VHP was in a much easier position in this regard than the NPS, which had been dealt a much more direct blow by the 1980 coup.

According to its policy programme, the Radakishun government was to implement the accord of 25 November 1985. A noteworthy point in this accord was the outlining of a foreign policy of 'reinforcing historical ties with eligible countries'. This was an implicit reference to The Netherlands and the United States, and served to further underscore Surinam's new political course. A striking point in the programme was its reference to the need to combat corruption. This was in fact the most explicit recognition of the failure to achieve one of the major revolutionary goals of the first hour.

Although the major political parties were now taking part in the administration, the domestic situation remained extremely unstable and unpredictable. The accord between the military leadership and the political parties was rather vague, and both sides appeared to have different definitions of democratization. A conflict concerning the expulsion of the Dutch ambassador led in early 1987 to the resignation of VHP Prime Minister Pertab Radakishun (see Chapter 5). But the 'old' political parties continued to participate in the Supreme Council.

These parties expect definitive steps towards democracy to be taken with a new constitution and the preparation for free elections (see pp. 96–8). Several new developments now further complicated the political situation. In September 1986 a Miami court found the military's second-in-command, Lieut. Etienne Boereveen, guilty of attempting to set up a cocaine trade route via Surinam. Protection was to be granted to drug traffickers within Surinamese territory. The allegations and the court's verdict seriously discredited the Bouterse regime at the international level. Another development was the rise of a guerrilla movement led by former military man Ronnie Brunswijk in eastern Surinam, along the border with French Guyana (see pp. 90–8). The rise of this guerrilla movement and the recent increase in public unrest clearly undermined further Bouterse's position and prestige as leader.

2 Social Structure

Surinam's social structure is principally characterized by pluralism, heavy dependence on foreign partners and a one-sided production structure. The country's pluralistic social structure is mostly indicated by the findings of Van Lier (1977, p. 8 ff.). Van Lier states that the major feature of such a structure is the lack of racial, linguistic and economic unity and that these differences have not arisen within a single culture, but result from the multi-cultural origins of the population, with social classes running largely parallel to the division between these groups.

Surinam's great foreign dependence is primarily economic, while Dutch cultural domination has also been a factor. This dependence is caused not only by the foreign control of the country's major economic sectors, but also by the large proportion of the country's public spending traditionally financed by The Netherlands. This donor–recipient relationship allowed the Dutch government—even after Surinam had been granted political independence—to have a major say in its former colony's development policy.

Surinam's generally one-sided production structure is characterized by a strong orientation towards one sector, in which a dominant role is played by one industrial branch or product. Even during the years following the 1980 coup, with the military regime emphasizing that a revolutionary process was under way and would reach completion, few substantial changes have been seen in this situation. Clearly, however, the formation of social classes and the rise of class conflicts which cut through ethnic categories have become more pronounced. Furthermore, the preoccupation with one industrial branch (since the Second World War, the bauxite sector) has slackened since the early 1970s, owing to the weakened position of Surinamese bauxite on the international market. The influence of foreign trade and industry has also clearly decreased during the rule of the military regime. This is not the result, however, of a deliberate policy of diversification and self-reliance, but rather of the further decline in Surinam bauxite's international market position, a decrease in the already marginal interest on the part of foreign investors in Surinam—primarily caused by the political instability and relatively high labour costs resulting from the overvalued Surinam guilder—and the suspension of Dutch development aid. This chapter will present a brief historical overview of the development of Surinam's social structure.

Historical Overview

The earliest records of factors which have proved formative for Surinamese society date from the mid-seventeenth century, when the first British colonists introduced plantation agriculture for the production of staple crops for the European market. Investments in plantation production were financed with European capital. The planter was often also the plantation owner, but investments were also made with borrowed capital. Labour was provided through the import of African slaves.

During the early slavery period, society consisted largely of two classes; a small group of white European masters and a large group of black African slaves. Although these groups came from extremely different cultures, they had in common the fact that they had been uprooted from their original cultural environment. Both groups therefore no longer functioned within their own environments, but transferred to their new milieu those native elements that had been preserved, adapted or else had disappeared altogether (Van Lier, 1977, pp. 16–18).

After a time, therefore, the slaves began speaking 'Neger-Engels' (later named Sranan tongo), a linguistic composite of English, Dutch, Portuguese and a number of West African languages. According to Van Lier, this language—which has since gained official status—was fully formed by as early as 1700. Several other cultural elements involving religion, oral tradition, music and dance have been preserved to this day.

The original inhabitants of this sparsely populated country, the Indians, were quickly either massacred or driven into the jungle after attempts to use them as slaves on the plantations had failed. With the importation of African slaves, a new and growing group of runaway slaves was created which, like the Indians, took refuge in the jungles and formed more-or-less separate communities. Small groups of fugitive slaves (*schuilders*) also hid in the forests close to the plantations, where they lived by thievery and small-scale farming on plots known as *kostgrondjes*.

Plantations during this period were more or less autonomous communities, for the planter was empowered by law to punish his slaves. Only a small corps of colonial officials existed. The highest of these officials were usually chosen from among the white elite, and a few plantation owners even attained the rank of colonial governor.

A society of the kind formed during this period in Surinam is often referred to as a 'plantation colony' (see Keller *et al*. 1908), with only limited emigration from the mother country. The small group of colonists consisted almost entirely of men who did not work the land themselves, but forced slaves to do so for them. In such a society, the social unit is not the nuclear family but the individual. Van Lier (1977, p. 5 ff.) refers to plantation colonies such as that established in Surinam as 'borderline societies', having developed at the outer limits of the European cultural sphere. Both masters and slaves were uprooted from their respective cultures, and were forced to adapt to situations they found new and strange; they lived in a continual 'borderline situation'.

Surinamese society gradually became differentiated. This was due in large part to the rise of means of existence for professional groups other than planters, overseers and colonial administrators. These new colonists included civil servants, traders, craftsmen, clergy, and especially soldiers, who were used to defend the plantation and hunt for runaway slaves.

As mentioned above, the White British and (later) Dutch colonists were soon joined by Europeans of various nationalities and religions. The slaves also came from a variety of African regions and tribes, but of even greater significance was the variety of activities they were called upon to perform.

Van Lier (1977, p. 102) distinguishes between city and plantation slaves, and breaks these main groups down into the sub-classification of household slaves, craftsmen's slaves and field slaves. The field slaves living in the cities performed gardening chores or were lent to the plantations.

Differences in types of labour and severity of discipline also served to determine whether slaves worked on sugar plantations, coffee plantations, cotton plantations or in wood production. Work on the sugar plantations, for example, was more taxing than that in wood production. Yet, in view of the much greater opportunities for escape, slaves on the wood plantations were punished much more severely than their counterparts in other production sectors.

Although Spanish and Portuguese Jesuits were hard at work even in the plantation colony's early days converting Indians and the 'Marrons' (Maroons), missionaries were officially admitted to Surinam only at a relatively late date. Slave-owners long remained opposed to the preaching of the doctrine of equality to the slaves, which they were afraid could lead their human chattels to draw logical religious and social conclusions with regard to their masters (Van Lier, 1977, p. 52). Furthermore, the adoption of Christianity would also pose the risk of demands for free Sundays and Christian holidays.

The missionary activities of the Moravian Brethren among the Marrons began in 1735, and were later directed towards the Indians as well. Missionary work in Paramaribo began in 1765 and this denomination consistently attempted to remain self-supporting by carrying out economic activities in Surinam itself. A mission company, led by Christoph Kersten, was set up to this end in 1767. In 1787, Roman Catholic missionaries were also officially admitted to Surinam, largely for evangelical work among the slaves. The other Christian Churches, such as the Lutherans and the Dutch Reformed, were not active among the slaves and remained the Churches of the White masters and later of the upper classes. The Moravian Brethren and the Roman Catholic Churches remain to this day the only true Churches popular among the masses.

Following the ban on the slave trade in 1808, great emphasis was placed on both the physical and spiritual care of the slaves, in order to maintain the country's labour force. In addition to the introduction of medical care for Blacks, it was felt that the introduction of Christianity could serve to strengthen the slaves' marital ties and so boost their relatively low birth-rate. The Society for the promotion of religious education among the slaves and other Heathen peoples in the colony of Surinam was set up in 1828, and Christianity spread quickly through the Black population.

A school for mulatto children was set up as early as 1760, thus providing a starting-point for the social progress of the country's non-Whites. In that same year, permission was granted for the free practice of missionary activities and religious education. This permission also applied to the Roman Catholic mission when it came to Surinam in 1787. In view of the impossibility of carrying out missionary work on the plantations without permission from the planters themselves, it was 1844 before a start was made with the setting-up of schools to provide rudimentary education for slave children.

Van Lier (1977, pp. 53 ff.) states that, although the slaves' increasing interest in religion certainly influenced their morals, the example set by the Christian masters did not serve to clearly reinforce the Blacks' marital ties—in any event not before emancipation. Concubinage, which Van Lier says arises when legal, social or economic bondage exists, was a common phenomenon in Surinam at this time. This was reinforced by the fact that the colony contained many more White men than White women. Until 1817, the colonial administration tried (albeit unsuccessfully), by means of negative sanctions in the Plantation Orders, to prevent marriage or even sexual relations between Whites and non-Whites. This served, however, only to reinforce the practice of concubinage.

The racial group of mulattos or Coloureds arose early in the slave period owing to miscegenation, usually in the form of sexual relations between White masters and women slaves. The increasingly common release of these mulattos from slavery soon resulted in an intermediate class, between slaves and masters. Slaves were freed with greater frequency during the eighteenth century as well. With the approach of emancipation, the practice of manumission (release from slavery by means of the payment of a considerable sum of money and following approval by the Colonial Police Court) became increasingly common.

As noted earlier, until the early 1770s the planters were usually also the plantation owners. Most of them had settled in Surinam with their families, and had financed their investments with Western European capital. During the Dutch period, most of this capital came from within The Netherlands, with the Amsterdam trading houses playing an increasingly major role in the course of the eighteenth century. Following the Amsterdam bourse 'crash' of 1773, however, many Surinamese planters were forced to sell their plantations and the number of absentee owners grew. These new owners did not live in Surinam and left the actual running of the plantations to their plantation supervisors.

The slave trade was banned in the early 1800s, and the emancipation process was completed in the course of the same century. This process can primarily be credited to the rising demand for labour in Africa for the production of basic materials intended for export to the burgeoning Western European industrial centres. These activities primarily involved the production of palm kernels and palm-oil for the then-important production of candles and soap (McPhee, 1926, pp. 28 ff.). This development led to drastic changes in Surinam's social structure. In addition to the virtual standstill in the importation of slaves, the practice of manumission and the increasing number of runaway slaves caused the plantation owners to search frantically for a solution to the huge labour shortage—which they at first thought lay in the recruitment of contract labourers.

The development towards a plural society was greatly stimulated by the introduction of foreign contract labourers mentioned earlier. Although these labourers came from a variety of regions within their respective countries and from varying professional and social classes, the new situation in Surinam (particularly during the initial period) caused them to act as unified racial groups. This particularly applied to the East Indians, who not only came from various different Indian provinces but also from different castes. Furthermore, this group of immigrants was also religiously heterogeneous; 82 per cent were Hindu and the rest were Moslem (De Klerk, 1953, pp. 98 ff.). The first East Indian organization, the Surinaamsche Immigranten Vereniging (Surinamese Immigrants' Association), was founded in 1910. This general association had as its objective the protection of the interests of those contract labourers in general, and East Indians in particular, who had chosen to remain in Surinam after their labour contracts had expired (De Klerk, 1953, p. 168). After a time, organizations arose within this ethnic group that were related to specific social classes and religions.

As from the period of abolition and mass immigration, a policy of assimilation was implemented in Surinam that had as its central goal the adaptation to Dutch cultural values. Not only was Dutch the language of the schools, but the curricula were also almost identical to those used in The Netherlands. The intellectual emphasis was primarily on The Netherlands and Dutch culture. A visit to Europe and a Dutch education for one's children (by providing them with the opportunity to study in The Netherlands if possible) was seen as the highest good. In addition to the missions, various private organizations also contributed to the spread of Dutch culture in Surinam. Another major factor in this regard was the establishment of a regular shipping line with Holland in 1884 (see Chapter 5). Tolerance was usually exercised towards the Asian immigrants with regard to the practice of their religion, but only the Christian and Jewish communities were eligible for government subsidies.

This assimilation policy, however, changed drastically in 1934 with the ideas and plans of Dutch Minister of Colonies C. J. I. M. Welter and J. C. Kielstra, Colonial Governor at that time. Both men had served in the former Nederlands Indie (Indonesia), and both were concerned with the well-being of the Indonesians in Surinam.

Kielstra, a former professor at the Agricultural University of Wageningen in The Netherlands, rejected the Western-orientated model of development and advocated instead one based on agricultural production and strong rural communities, with populations homogeneous in terms of both race and religion. In addition to stimulating small-scale agriculture, his plan also called for the revival of export-orientated plantation production through the recruitment of one hundred thousand Indonesian contract labourers and an additional ten thousand Indonesian colonists. This latter group of colonists was to provide leadership for the rural communities. Although a start was made with the implementation of this plan in 1939, the outbreak of the Second World War prevented its completion.

Because of the waning importance of plantation agriculture, the government began stimulating small-scale agriculture even before emancipation. Small-scale farming to supply Paramaribo became crucial when the growing labour shortage caused the plantation operators to move their efforts to production for export. Paramaribo's plight in this regard became particularly clear after 1873, when the freed slaves were finally allowed to leave the plantations, and did so *en masse*.

The rise of small-scale farming began as early as 1845, with the immigration of Dutch farmers. Furthermore, land close to the city of Paramaribo was distributed among freed slaves. But agricultural production by African slaves and their descendants aimed at supplying Paramaribo never truly succeeded, for most of these Creoles only practised subsistence farming and preferred other professions. Once the plantations became unable to do so, the job of supplying provisions to the capital was taken over by the Dutch farmers. These farmers gradually encountered growing competition from East Indians who had begun as small-scale farmers after their labour contracts had expired.

During the period immediately following emancipation, small-scale farming was largely carried out by Creoles. But, as from 1890, this sector passed first into the hands of the East Indians and later to the Indonesian settlers. Both groups concentrated primarily on the production of their main staple, rice, which was first introduced to Surinam around this time. Since this time, rice has become the major staple of the Creole population as well, in addition to being the country's major agricultural export product.

The Creole group grew substantially after emancipation, owing to miscegenation, and the race- and colour-based class hierarchy became less dominant. Only a limited number of White colonists remained in the country. Van Lier (1977, pp. 191 ff.) states that the departure of the European Whites served greatly to increase the status of the Jewish population—which had until this point occupied one of the lowest positions among the White groups. The Jews were the largest group of remaining White colonists, and assumed leadership of Surinam's public life.

The senior officials posted from The Netherlands also formed part of the highest group within the class hierarchy, but usually returned to Holland after only a few years. This 'upper crust' remained closed to Blacks, East Indians and Indonesians, and until the Second World War the number of people of mixed race within its ranks remained minimal.

The upper middle class consisted largely of coloureds and Jews, as well as a few ambitious Blacks and East Indians. The lower middle class was largely reserved for Blacks, and was gradually supplemented by East Indians, while the lower class consisted almost entirely of Blacks, East Indians and Indonesians.

The various ethnic groups have usually adapted to the social milieu by following the path which led from the plantations to the rural homestead and then to the city. During this social journey, however, these groups have been largely successful in preserving their individual cultures.

As from the early 1940s, gradual but clear changes have taken place in the country's social structure. These changes can largely be attributed to:

— Surinam's re-incorporation into the world economy through the extraction of its available bauxite reserves: at first for the arms industry—and the aircraft industry in particular—and later for increasing industrial uses for aluminium;
— the great increase in development aid (mostly from The Netherlands) as from the late 1950s;
— major political changes, namely the introduction of universal suffrage and the country's political autonomy (first with regard to domestic affairs and later full political independence).

The massive post-war growth of bauxite production and the start of the local processing of bauxite into alumina and aluminium in the 1960s (as a result of direct investment by multinational aluminium concerns) created a group of privileged workers earning three to four times as much as their counterparts in the small local firms serving the domestic market.

Workers employed by those foreign firms active in forestry and wood-processing, agriculture and commercial fisheries also earn significantly more than their counterparts in the smaller local firms. It should be noted in this regard that it is primarily the higher-level personnel who are relatively well-paid, while the wages of the lowest qualified personnel (particularly in the agricultural sector) are usually not much higher than those of comparable workers in the local firms. Developments in the country's foreign-dominated banking and insurance sector have also led to relatively high wage levels. The high wages and salaries in the bauxite sector exercise an upward pressure on wage levels, and especially those for trained labourers in other sectors.

The number of trading houses has greatly increased, due in part to large government investments funded by development aid, and an important group of local importers and wholesalers has arisen. Activities in transport and other commercial services, such as engineering offices and contracting firms, accountantships and consultancies, have picked up subtantially. These firms and activities are largely owned or controlled by foreign concerns.

The steady growth of the public sector has been accompanied by a disproportionately large increase in the number of civil servants, rendering the government by far the country's largest employer. Civil servants' wages, however, traditionally lag far behind those in the private sector. The lowest-level civil servants in particular receive low wages, and attempt to supplement their incomes through unofficial activities.

Yet the poorest-paid remain the small farmers and unskilled farm workers, as well as (in view of the marginal social welfare facilities) the unemployed, who account for about 20 per cent of the labour force. It must also be noted in this regard that the pronounced segmentation in the labour market is reinforced by the traditional organization of labour on a firm-by-firm basis.

Proceeding on the basis of three social classes—namely the bourgeoisie, the *petit bourgeoisie* and the proletariat—Kruijer (1973, pp. 156 ff.) states that the Surinamese bourgeoisie is unique in both character and composition. Local Surinamese entrepreneurs are poorly represented in this class, for a national business community has never successfully taken root. In view of the dominance of foreign firms, says Kruijer, the local bourgeoisie plays the supporting role of assistant and consumer not typical of a true entrepreneurial bourgeoisie but of the type referred to in Surinam as the *foetoeboi* bourgeoisie (errand-boy bourgeoisie).

Kruijer says that the pinnacle of Surinam's bourgeoisie consists of the heads of large firms, the highest government officials, the trading elite, several major local businessmen and a number of professionals, and is thoroughly permeated by foreign elements. The country's *petit bourgeoisie* consists of employees, minor officials, retailers, medium-scale farmers, etc., who identify with the ruling class. Kruijer assigns most farmers to the proletariat. He also places industrial workers (with the exception of those in the bauxite firms) in this class, as well as the practitioners of those professions 'which don't bring in a penny', such as street merchants, market sellers, cleaners, household personnel and beggars. Poverty is the central feature of life in this group, whose members subsist by what Breman (1975, p. 214) has renamed the system of '*hosselen*' and '*pinaren*'.

Kruijer's analysis only takes into account social segmentation, but Smooha (1975, pp. 71 ff.) points out that a pluralistic society requires a multi-dimensional analysis. The 'new pluralists' take into account not only a social dimension, but a cultural one as well. An analysis of social relationships in Surinam, they feel, should take into account the major effect of the society's ethno-cultural divergence on the behaviour of its people. Surinam differs in this regard from other Latin American countries, where the religious uniformity (Catholicism) imposed by the Spanish has led to the virtual obliteration of native cultural values and institutions.

Until the 1950s, the highest government posts were largely occupied by Dutch nationals. A gradual change followed, however, and the 'Surinamization' of the government became complete during the early 1970s. The placement of Surinamers in leadership positions in foreign firms and in foreign-controlled industries only began in the early 1970s, and was completed at an accelerated pace during this decade.

Van Lier (1977, pp. 299 ff.) notes that the pattern of social stratification has changed markedly since 1940. Blacks and East Indians, formerly belonging to the lower middle and middle classes, have entered the upper and upper middle classes. Gradually, a few Indonesians, and even the occasional Bush Negro or Indian, have entered the higher social classes. These changes have been made possible both by the greatly improved educational facilities (with the scholarship system for studying in The Netherlands playing a major role) and by the introduction of universal suffrage and the creation of political parties. As noted earlier, the leadership of the political parties consisted, until the late 1950s, almost exclusively of light-skinned Creoles. Upward political mobility for people from the working class was largely the achievement of the NPS, under the leadership of J. A. Pengel, but was also promoted by the rise of East Indian parties (especially the VHP) and political parties representing the country's Indonesian and Bush Negro groups.

All of Surinam's major ethnic groups began in the lowest social class. All Blacks were first slaves, and all East Indians and Indonesians were first contract labourers. Although the class structure gradually assumed a course somewhat less parallel to ethnic segmentations, the departure was not complete.

Using the attained level of education as a criterion, Kruijer (1973, p. 192) has drawn up the following hierarchical ranking of Surinam's ethnic groups: Europeans, Chinese, Creoles, East Indians and Indonesians. The Bush Negro and Indian groups are at the end of this social queue. In his comments on the three largest ethnic groups, Kruijer states that both Creoles and East Indians are represented in all three social classes mentioned above, with a relatively large East Indian proletariat. This East Indian proletariat consists largely of small-scale farmers with a few possessions, but Kruijer says the East Indian upper class plays a much less important role in Surinamese society than does the Creole upper crust. More Indonesians than East Indians are found among the proletariat, and far more at the extreme bottom of the social scale. This group is, however, poorly represented in both the *petit* and *grand bourgeoisie*.

Modern Surinamese society still exhibits a remarkable diversity in ethnic groups. According to the most recent census, held in 1980 by Surinam's General Bureau of Statistics, the East Indians are the country's largest ethnic group—with 35 per cent of the total population. The East Indians were followed by the Creoles (32 per cent), the Indonesians (15 per cent) and the Bush Negroes (10.5 per cent). In addition, Surinam's relatively minor ethnic groups include the native Indian inhabitants, the Chinese, the descendants of Dutch immigrants and farmers, Jews, Lebanese, the descendants of Portuguese Madeirans, a few North Americans and Creoles from the West Indies.

Helman (1977, pp. 11 ff.) has described Surinamese culture as 'a sort of mosaic', in reference to the fact that a large number of ethnically and culturally hetereogeneous groups live side-by-side, either with or without interacting, in a relatively small area. Throughout Surinam's history, the White colonists attempted to impose their own cultural standards on the native inhabitants, and later on the successive (ethnic) groups of imported labourers. Helman notes that, after emancipation, the label 'acceptable' was given only to those slaves and those descendants of slaves who conformed as much as possible to the norms of Western civilization. This also applied to the East Indian and Indonesian immigrants. These latter groups, however, offered greater resistance and clung more emphatically to their own cultural values than had the Creoles. This discrepancy in willingness to adapt contributed to social stratification, allowing the Creoles greater access to the upper social classes. Despite the conscious idea of ethnic purity held by most groups, all were gradually forced to submit to the process of racial amalgamation (see pp. 163–5)

Christianity, imposed on the Surinamese population by the Western (and particularly the Dutch) colonizers and especially well received by the Creole group, has contributed to this process of amalgamation. But it has also complicated the situation by adding to the already considerable diversity. Christianity is a clear presence in Surinam and, as is the case everywhere, a house divided. Furthermore, Christianity in Surinam is an imported commodity. The country contains some nineteen denominations, with the Roman Catholic and the older Reformed Churches—of which the EBGS (Evangelical Brethren Community of Surinam, formerly the Moravian Brethren) is the most important—enjoying the highest membership (Van Raalte, 1977, pp. 292 ff.).

Other religious traditions and groups are also clearly present, however. The East Indians and the Indonesians are still predominantly Hindu or Moslem, while Confucianism is still adhered to by many of the Chinese. Judaism, already present in Surinam in the early sixteenth century, is still practised, while the African and native Indian tribal religions still exist. Van Raalte (1977, p. 298) notes that this plethora of religious groups must not only tolerate each others' presence, but that each group is also confronted with a Western model of behaviour and thought which takes into account only scientific, political, social, economic and technical factors (see pp. 166–70).

Western culture, however, has been imposed most emphatically in the field of education, which conforms almost entirely to the Dutch model. This entails a process of alienation from the natural environment which begins at the elementary-school level. The great emphasis placed on Holland and on Dutch culture means that the child is not taught to place itself within the context of its own surroundings (see pp. 158–63).

Recent Developments

The political independence gained in 1975, which was welcomed by only a part of the population, as well as the clear indications after the 1980 coup that the new military authorities lacked a clear socio-economic strategy and political policy, brought no marked change in Surinam's social structure. Although Surinam today cannot be seen simply as a strictly segmented society, its plural character has been largely preserved. Brandsma (1983, p. 13) states that the majority of the population has learned to think in such terms and act accordingly. The maintenance of one's own cultural identity continues to be an important tool in the ethno-cultural groups' struggle for emancipation. The Indian and Indonesian embassies in Surinam are especially active in reinforcing and expanding cultural ties with the native countries of their respective ethnic groups. The wave of nationalism in the 1970s is often seen as the most interesting development in this regard. Yet this nationalism has only been able to take solid root within the labour movement, and has not yet led to a major breakthrough in the compart-mentalized political system. This nationalism has primarily found acceptance among the dark-skinned Creoles, and has led to greater regard for the African elements in this group's own culture.

A start was made after independence on the development of an educa-tional system which would place greater emphasis on Surinam itself. In addition, attempts to eliminate Dutch influences in the educational system were intensified after the 1980 coup; but owing in part to insufficient funding, no major changes have yet taken place. Results have, however, been achieved with regard to the 'Surinamization' of the corps of teachers and professors and in the adaptation of teaching materials.

The major political parties are still organized along ethno-cultural lines. The system of patronage and populism, which aids in preserving segmenta-tion, still functions well. Many cultural organizations, particularly in the area of religion, are still organized along ethnic lines. Even since the coup, no obvious changes have been noted in this context. The old political parties, with their radical orientation, were banned after the coup. Attempts to mobilize the lower classes, however, have failed. The old political parties have been granted a degree of freedom since July 1986, and will most likely return to the centre of national politics in the foreseeable future. These developments illustrate that little has changed in the ethno-cultural structure of the Surinamese political system.

3 Political Systems

The 25 February Movement

It was not long after the coup of 25 February 1980 that the first attempts were made to set up popular structures which could potentially provide the basis for a revolutionary movement. The Bureau of Popular Mobilization played a prominent role in this. This bureau, initially responsible to the National Military Council (NMR), could therefore be regarded as a major revolutionary instrument. Within eighteen months of the coup, more than one hundred people's committees had been set up. The Bureau of Popular Mobilization provided the stimulus for such organizations, and often acted as initiator.

The Bureau of Popular Mobilization assumed the function of a revolutionary think-tank, particularly after the release in March 1982 of three soldiers, including Badrissein Sital and Chas Mijnals, accused of conspiracy. The Cuban-orientated RVP members were very active in this think-tank, as they were in the setting-up of the people's committees (PCs). The revolutionary thinkers were searching for an administrative system in which new mass organizations could play a major role. The Manifesto of the Revolution, published on 1 May 1981 and written by PALU leader Iwan Krolis, had already indicated several of the major lines of thought used in this search. It stated:

We will create a new administrative order in which true democracy will reign and real influence on political decision-making and action throughout all levels of the community will be guaranteed to all portions of the community. This means that we will thoroughly raze the false parliamentary democracy of neo-colonialism, in order to build a new and real democracy in which true influence by our people's specialised mass organisations will be guaranteed, and for which the decentralisation of the administration will serve as a true indicator. [And, concerning the dialectical philosophy upon which this real democracy was to be based:] Revolution never proceeds on the basis of the lowest common denominator of interests and opinions unearthed from among the rubble of neo-colonial society, but proceeds from and is led by well-chosen societal interests which are recognised as fundamental and essential facets of the larger national interest. In Suriname, these are the interests of those larger portions of our people who have been placed in positions of disadvantage by colonialism and neo-colonialism. These are the interests of the people as a whole, with the exception of the compradores, those opportunists who have assembled their empty existence from the crumbs which have fallen from the table of our exploiters and who wish to maintain that existence at any cost.

These compradores are now scattered throughout our community, agitating and spreading panic, betrayal and discord. They have pushed their way even on to the front ranks of the revolution, where, disguised as true revolutionaries, they are actively trying to frustrate and endanger the process of that revolution. Let us unmask them, these pseudo-revolutionaries who hope to reverse the process. Let us meet them head on, these pseudo-revolutionaries who now express their concern with community problems which they themselves have created, and who have not yet been able to undo the revolution.

The manifesto ended with a direct summons to 'all true revolutionaries among our people' to combine forces and form a 'revolutionary, united front to lead the revolution, to protect it and to bring it to a successful conclusion'. Compliance with this summons would serve to fill a major gap, as the one thing that the coup had lacked was a mass political movement, for the soldiers had conquered the country, but had not won over the people.

The Bureau of Popular Mobilization, as the political arm of the revolution, was absorbed in the attempt to prompt a revolutionary mass movement. In Popular Mobilization's view, people's committees would necessarily play a major role in this, somewhat after the model of Cuba's CDRs (Comités de Defensa de la Revolucion). A 1982 policy paper from the Department of Popular Mobilization reflected the increased Cuban influence.

The people's committees are charged with supporting, propagating and defending the revolution ... Defending the revolution includes the prompt identification of possible saboteurs, reporting to the leaders the movements and manoeuvres of enemies of the revolution and strict compliance with orders concerning the tactical dealings with these enemies ... The leaders of the people's committees are to be fervent supporters of the revolution of February 25. They are the political commandos among the masses ... The leadership can only stand open to those who show themselves to be devout, dedicated and hard-working supporters of the revolution ['Goal and structure of the people's committees', unpublished paper, 1982].

The paper went on to sketch a centralistic administrative structure. Only Committee leaders could be chosen to sit in higher bodies. The paper stated: 'This means the higher bodies are comprised of only the most aware, most dedicated and, in other words, the best revolutionaries'. The pinnacle of this administrative pyramid was to be occupied by a National Congress; the daily management of the revolution was to be put in the hands of a Politburo.

It was over four years after the coup that a revolutionary unity movement, the 25 February Movement (Vijfentwintig Februari Beweging), at first referred to as 'Stanvaste' (after a hardy local flower), was officially established on 12 May 1984, after the official proclamation had been made in November 1983. The lengthy period preceding the setting-up of such a movement was primarily due to the absence of any revolutionary struggle before the coup. The formation of a unity movement could therefore only take place after the fact. This revolutionary unity movement was imbued with the ideas developed earlier by the Bureau of Popular Mobilization. The VFB was presented not as a party, but as a movement.

This was the explicit choice of its founders. The VFB's two major ideologists, Harvey Naarendorp and Jules Wijdenbosch (later to become Home Affairs Minister and Prime Minister) wrote the following about the choice of a movement: 'A party would actually have been the best. But the conditions were lacking for making a revolution via an extremely experienced organization with a high degree of political and ideological homogeneity' ('Structuur van de VFB', instructional memorandum, 3 February 1984). But, within the government structure, the VFB in fact operated as a true party.

The major objective of the 25 February Movement was the forging of a link between the military leadership, as vanguard of the revolution, and the working masses (industrial workers and farmers). In an introduction to the VFB programme, Commander-in-Chief Bouterse spoke of 'the heart of unity, which beats where the military vanguard becomes profoundly involved with the bearers of our direct national production: our workers and farmers' (introduction to VFB programme, 12 May 1984). Naarendorp & Wijdenbosch have stated:

The vanguard within the National Army has, during this phase of history, assumed the task of implementing a revolution. This revolution is intended to change society, that is, to eliminate repression. To this end, the revolution must involve itself with the working class. Not only because this class has 'power' and because it must produce for us, but also because it is the lifeblood of the revolution [Struktuur van de VFB, p. 8].

According to this train of thought, it was only logical that the General Assembly, at the establishment of the VFB, appointed the members of the Military Authority as the movement's central leadership. Lieut.-Col. Desi Bouterse became Chairman, while the military second- and third-in-line, Etienne Boerenveen and Paul Bhagwandas, became Secretary and Treasurer respectively. The VFB explicitly opted for a centralized decision-making process. According to Naarendorp & Wijdenbosch, centralism is characteristic of and justifiable in the early phases of any popular revolution. They have said:

If you hold new elections right away, you get the same situation as before. During the initial phase, the vanguard rules, because they showed the most courage in intervening in a situation which had gone wrong, because they put their lives on the line and fulfilled the role of vanguard, and because they made the clear choice for fundamental change . . . Although the people are aware of their own interests, it is essential to arrive at a point of joint discussion, a bit of centralism, in order to determine from that vantage point what is best for everyone. Policy is not, after all, the simple adding up of the people's interests [Structuur van de VFB, pp. 11, 12].

Structure and Functions

The VFB posed for itself the task of reaching all Surinamese in all sections of society. The Movement's programme was therefore to be implemented at the central government, regional and economic levels. The programme advanced the following major policy lines:

(a) The establishment of organizations everywhere that Surinamese people live and work. These organizations are to be based on revolutionary principles: consultation of the people, control by the people, responsibility to the people and the implementation of decisions made by the majority, supported by information and training.

(b) The democratic organization of the defence of the revolution, so that every Surinamese person can participate in the defence of the homeland.

(c) The development of a social and economic order based on national-democratic principles.

(d) The actual implementation of the required international solidarity.

The VFB's organizational structure reflects the task that the unity movement took upon itself in its policy programme. The Central Leadership (with the three military leaders) is the highest body within the movement. In order to carry out activities among the masses, this body is assisted by the Political Advisory Group (Politieke Advies Groep, PAG) and the Organization Committee (Organisatie Comité, OC). The PAG works at the theoretical level and actually serves as the Movement's think-tank. The PAG has four sections: Propaganda and Political Instruction, Discipline, Economics and International Relations. The chairmen of the first two sections serve concurrently on the Daily Executive, which also includes one member of the Central Leadership.

The OC is charged with working directly with grass-roots supporters, and is divided into eight sections for this purpose. These sections operate via their respective core groups, which consist of ten to fifteen members. These core groups are organized to coincide with those places where members are socially and economically active: neighbourhoods, companies and mass organizations. Core groups from the Labour Section, for example, are involved in the Labour movement, while core groups from the Young People's Section work with youth. Naarendorp & Wijdenbosch have explained the general tasks of the core groups as follows: developing and translating the revolutionary programme into everyday practice, training, distributing the movement paper, applying day-to-day democracy by nurturing discussion of opinions and ideas and recruiting members. The chairmen of these sections are members of the OC. The link between the OC and the Daily Executive is maintained by the fact that one member of the executive attends OC meetings.

Through its core group, the National Security Section is active in the People's Militia and the 'anti-intervention committees'. This involvement is intended to give substance to the priority given in the movement's programme to the democratization of the armed forces. According to the VFB programme, gradual participation by the population in national defence should be possible. The People's Militia had been set up 'to defend the revolution' as early as 1982, following Surendre Rambocus's aborted coup (see pp. 170-4). The anti-intervention committees were set up in 1983, under the leadership of the Department of People's Mobilization, after reports were made of preparations for an invasion with the aid of mercenaries. These committees had representatives in government ministries, companies and in local neighbourhoods. The National Security Section was of such vital importance that, according to the memorandum from Naarendorp & Wijdenbosch, only the 'most aware' could be included among its ranks.

The People's Structure Section was also of major importance. Within the people's committees and the regional and district councils, this section was charged with carrying out those activities deemed worthwhile by the Department of People's Mobilization. Along with the Labour and Agriculture Sections, People's Structures was one of the three sections granted initial priority because of the scarcity of qualified leaders.

The Chairman of the People's Structure Section, Lieut. Laurens Neede (before the coup, one of the administrators of the banned Military Union) provided a clear explanation of the VFB's objectives for the OC sections:

The core groups are to be formed within the existing structures; within the People's Committees, regional and district councils and within other organisations throughout society. This also entails a change in the form of these existing structures, in the sense that the VFB people will participate so actively that they will obtain a majority within these organizations, in order to achieve the movement's goals with the power and support of the majority of society [cited in Surinamese daily *De Ware Tijd*, 26 June 1984].

In the VFB's view, regional structures were to play a central role in the development of the new political administration. Local and regional bodies were therefore the foundation of all democratization plans submitted by the movement in the course of the discussions concerning a new constitution (see Chapter 3).

It was only logical that the military should attempt to create a political base by means of a mass movement. In his *Military Institutions and Coercion in Developing Nations* (1977), the American sociologist Morris Janowitz provides a clear analysis of the behaviour of military authorities in new nations such as Surinam. In this comparative study, he explores the extent to which the military can effect change with a minimum of coercion. Janowitz (1977, p. 73) states: 'I still maintain that the most successful military regimes, if one can use this term, are or will be in the long run those that are able to share political power with or even transform themselves into more civilian-based political institutions.'

After seizing power, new military authorities are confronted with the task of supplying national political leadership and of developing mass support for their programmes. Janowitz (1977, p. 105) states: 'If the military is to succeed in this political goal, it must develop a political apparatus outside the military apparatus under its direct domination.'

The setting-up of the VFB was an attempt to achieve just such a political goal. But, for a number of reasons, it was clear that the chances of success in the Surinamese situation were negligible. Generally speaking, the group of military and civilians regarding themselves as the 'revolutionary vanguard' clashed with the social and political recalcitrance of the system of elite-cartel democracy as it had functioned since the Second World War. The patronage system had left its mark and the loyalties of the lower classes continued to be focused largely on individuals' own ethnic groups. The military had not succeeded in providing another direction for these loyalties.

The people's committees were to have provided the base of power, yet they proved ineffectual even in the years immediately following the coup. They often included supporters of the old political parties, who hoped to benefit, just as they had in the past, from good relations with the powers-that-be. For them, this was in fact a mere continuation of traditional clientelism and nepotism.

The people's committees often drew up impossibly long lists of material requirements and this practice prompted one trade union leader to label them the 'new gold-diggers'. In a 1981 interview, the leftist military man Badrissein Sital commented that there was 'nothing to' the people's committees. He was largely referring to the fact that the PCs played no revolutionary role. For this same reason, the Department of People's Mobilization had tried to ensure loyal administrators within the committees by means of open voting and the preliminary selection of loyalists. But this mobilization only generated mistrust at the grass-roots level.

In the same interview cited above, Sital made it quite clear that government and the military leaders were supported by the Army alone. 'That's the sole political base', he said. It was obvious that mass mobilization could not go hand-in-hand with force and with restrictions on fundamental freedoms; and it was precisely this necessary freedom that was lacking. In this context, it is perhaps illustrative to note how, in June 1981, the military squashed the labour movement's mobilization activities for International Labour Day (see pp. 104–12). The *dirigiste* approach, coupled with a curfew and other repressive measures, had a converse effect on the Surinamese people, who have always valued their freedom.

Membership

According to its official statutes, the VFB strives to combine the forces of 'all persons of a patriotic and democratic bent, including: workers, farmers, women, young people, civil servants, national businessmen, intellectuals and the unemployed' (VFB Programme and Statutes, May 1984). The VFB's nucleus consists of soldiers, left-wing (semi-)intellectuals and members of the People's Militia. The movement's official membership count is unknown. Meetings of the VFB executive usually attract no more than a few hundred observers. Assuming the official count of ten to fifteen members per core group, the entire membership can total no more than three thousand, and there are no more than a few hundred real activists.

The VFB has too much of a military character to recruit a mass of supporters. Commander-in-Chief Bouterse has made a number of futile attempts to provide the movement with a more sympathetic national image. He has made increasing reference in his speeches to such historical figures as Anton de Kom and Ramdjane and to Marron leaders such as Joli Coeur and Boni, all of whom once fought for the raising-up and liberation of the oppressed Asiatic contract-labourers or the Black slaves. Bouterse has not hesitated to equate his activities with those of these historic figures. He nevertheless has continued to bear the stigma of the military, which has been held directly responsible for the physical elimination of prominent opposition leaders—an act generally labelled 'un-Surinamese.'

The military authorities were brought into further discredit in 1985 with the arrest for drug trafficking of VFB Secretary (and second man in the military hierarchy) Lieut. Etienne Boereveen. Boereveen was arrested in Miami, Florida by officers of the American Drug Enforcement Agency (DEA) and later imprisoned for attempting to establish a route for cocaine traffic through Surinam. On top of this, rumours increased concerning the economic misuse of power by certain military and other leaders.

Within the Surinamese social structure, political leaders have traditionally emerged from religious and ethnic groups, and can therefore count on a natural group of supporters. But the VFB failed on the whole to establish ties with such leaders. Attempts were made in the districts to involve local leaders of traditional organizations in the mobilization. Moslem groups in particular were approached, because of their traditionally antagonistic stance towards the old VHP party, with its clearly Hindu character. These attempts met with only limited success. Trade union leaders who associated themselves with the VFB paid for this step with the dissolution of their group of supporters (see pp. 104–12).

The left-wing intellectuals on the other hand were too far removed from the people to mobilize any significant support. Yet another comment from Badrissein Sital is telling in this regard. He said:

The people did not understand this development. The masses lagged far behind the leadership. Until now, we have not succeeded in establishing a close bond between the leaders and the people ... The revolution's basic premise is the presence of a proletariat. Class distinctions in Suriname are no simple matter. The strongest group is currently the middle class, which accounts for more than 55 per cent of the population. This group is not willing, certainly not at this stage, to support the development of a revolution.

But the revolutionary ideologists clung to the idea that mass mobilization was both possible and necessary: Sital, 'On the other hand, we are convinced that a revolution can be carried out in Suriname, despite the presence of a middle-class majority' (interview, 7 January 1984).

Not only was the middle class totally unwilling to be mobilized towards radicalism, but the lower class also refused to move. This was the boomerang effect of the leftist-revolutionary thinkers' lopsided socio-political analysis of the complicated society that Surinam was and is. The VFB entertained the same idea as the small left-wing parties of the 1970s had done: the possibility of making policy on the basis of class analysis alone. What they overlooked was the basic problem of applying such an analysis to multi-ethnic states: imposing class ideology where ethnicity obscures such distinctions inevitably results in a degree of oppression.

Movement/State Relations

However modest popular support for the 25 February Movement may be, the movement's direct ties with the military have granted it a position within the government apparatus far beyond its representative power. The centralist vision embraced by the VFB ideologists regarding their own movement must also, they felt, be applicable to the government structure.

This view, which goes well with the Marxist-Leninist model, has been expressed by Harvey Naarendorp and Jules Wijdenbosch in their above-mentioned memorandum. They state:

During the initial phase, the vanguard will rule. Why? Because they showed the greatest courage by intervening in a situation which had gone wrong. Because they risked their lives and took the vanguard. Because they have made a clear choice for fundamental change ... The comment is often heard: if the people are so sure of their interests, why not let them choose themselves? When those who make such comments think of democracy, they think only of a label, of a structure, and take no account of the content of democracy ... Although the people are aware of their interests, it is crucial to arrive at a point of common discussion, a bit of centralism from which we can determine what is best for all. Policy, after all, is not merely the sum of the people's interests ['Structuur van de VFB', pp. 11–12].

Through its leader, Commander-in-Chief Desi Bouterse, the VFB holds supreme political power. The special powers granted Bouterse, as Leader of the Government, under Decree A-19, are of particular importance. These involve assuring the 'proper observance and implementation of the objectives of the revolution' and the defence of 'the sovereignty and internal safety of the state of Suriname' (article 2, parts 1 and 3; see pp. 84–7).

The VFB also occupies a number of cabinet posts, of which the Ministry of Internal Affairs, Local Government and People's Mobilization is of strategic importance. Through this ministry, the VFB is able to exert a disproportionately great influence on the implementation of new democratic structures. Those funds allocated to People's Mobilization are in effect of the greatest benefit to the VFB, which is able in this way to finance part of its activities from the public coffers. The movement also occupies a number of important positions within the civil service and (semi-)public institutions. But one of the VFB's major defects is its lack of that professional quality and manpower needed to run the government apparatus.

As Janowitz (1977, p. 118) notes: 'Only in very large military establishments do officers get the kind of staff experience that prepares them for the highest administrative posts in government'. In Surinam, the military machinery was small and the leaders had received no more than the training of sergeant. The civil service continued to lean on the experienced personnel from the old political parties; and the VFB, owing in part to the continually deteriorating economic situation, were unable to buy their loyalty or their alliance. The centralist vision could therefore not be applied to the government model. The VFB needed coalition partners (see Chapter 5), not only for political reasons, but also to provide the logistical vision it lacked.

Constitutional Arrangements

Even before the coup of 25 February 1980, Surinamese constitutional law experts were examining possible new forms of constitution. They entertained considerable doubts about the functioning of the political system as set out in the constitution drafted at the time of independence. That constitution embraced a monarchist model, adopted almost word-for-word from that of The Netherlands, with a ceremonial president substituted for the role of monarch.

From the time of independence, Surinam had operated under a parliamentary system with ministers directly responsible to parliament. The constitutional law expert, C. D. Ooft (as Home Affairs Minister, he was one of the signatories of the 1975 constitution), delivered sharp criticism only a few years later. Ooft (1979, p. 11) wrote: 'Suriname would do well to maintain the system of parliamentary democracy, but then to provide this system with its own characteristics in accordance with an independent model benefiting Suriname's own constitutional and political needs.' He rejected the parliamentary system within which the government or ministers must maintain the confidence of a parliamentary majority. According to Ooft, parliament should be maintained, but then within a presidential system whereby the ministers are responsible to a directly elected president. He indicates why the parliamentary system with the 'confidence norm' cannot function in Surinam. His arguments reflect a certain criticism of the nepotism and ethnic factionalism present in Surinamese politics. Ooft (1980, p. 34) says:

(a) The procedure of expressing confidence or no confidence thoroughly lacks a sense of political reality in our Surinamese community. Annoyance with a minister, because he happens not to provide a position for the brother of a powerful politician or an executive member of his own party, can provide the cause to express a lack of confidence in him. This is unrealistic.

(b) The process of dissidence or floor-crossing, sometimes referred to as the betrayal process. Causes for crossing the floor (by government supporters to the opposition or vice versa) are legion. These causes are neatly nestled between true national interest and the crude material advantage which is the consistent result of such floor-crossing.

(c) The small scale and lack of stability in Surinamese political activities serve to obstruct the proper functioning of the parliamentary system. Small-scale in the establishment of both party platforms and government programmes, which consistently involve neither principles nor ideologies, but rather the implementation of government proposals and executive plans drafted and presented for execution regardless of any economic or political planning [Ooft, 1980, p. 34].

Following the 1980 coup, the constitutional issue automatically presented itself; and Ooft's ideas were certainly influential. The first post-coup government's policy programme had already heralded a new executive political order. The setting-up of a constitutional commission was announced. This commission was to draft a constitution 'which will better meet the (socio-economic) possibilities and aspirations of Surinamese society as a whole' (government policy programme, 1980, p. 9). The 1975 constitution and the parliament, however, were preserved for some time after the coup. This was largely due to the desire of those newly in power to win a certain degree of domestic and international confidence in this way. But it was no surprise that the traditional structures soon came to be regarded as excessively restrictive. In an enabling act of 20 May 1980, parliament therefore turned over its legislative powers to the government. The policy programme of 1 May 1980 had already stated that the government needed this expansion of powers 'in order to effect the turnabout needed to confirm the new order'.

The constitution itself was increasingly seen as a hindrance, particularly when ceremonial president Johan Ferrier began profiling himself as a political figure by demanding that parliament have the right to discuss and endorse the state budget. The suspension of the constitution on 13 August 1980 nevertheless came rather unexpectedly, with the military itself providing the direct cause. The discovery of an alleged conspiracy served to accelerate developments and provided the direct stimulus for the state of emergency proclaimed on the above date. General Decree A, dealing with the state of emergency, stated that 'tensions potentially injurious to the state have arisen within the National Military Council (NMR) and within the ranks of the military'. The confrontation with President Ferrier concerning the powers of parliament was stated as grounds and described in the decree as 'a critical constitutional conflict'. The judicial apparatus, accused by the cabinet and the military leaders of being too lax in prosecuting officials and politicians accused of corruption and of actually having provided these people with the chance of leaving the country, was included in the grounds for criticism in the decree. Prime Minister Chin a Sen at that time spoke generally of 'conflict and stagnation which necessitated radical intervention' (press conference, 20 August 1980).*

August 13 in fact marked the settling of accounts with the political system of the 'old' order. The proclamation of a state of emergency effectively neutralized the parliament and the Advisory Council (a legislative advisory body). At the same time, Prime Minister Chin a Sen was appointed to presidential office, thereby introducing the system of executive presidency. In view of the preceding constitutional discussion, this was not entirely unexpected. Yet, at the same time, the military authorities, now referred to for the first time, without further explanation, as the 'Military Leadership', became an institutional political factor. According to Article 2 of Decree A, governing power was to be wielded by the President, the Council of Ministers and the Military Leadership. Law took the form of decrees, which were to be signed not only by the President but also by the Military Leadership, which thereby became co-legislator. The political power of the military authority was established even more emphatically in Decree A-2 (20 November 1980). According to Article 9 of this decree, the Military Leadership, in consultation with the Council of Ministers, was to serve as acting president when and if the President was no longer able to exercise his powers, had resigned his position, or was absent.

The arrangement for an executive presidency in fact anticipated the proposed constitutional changes. Shortly after being set up, a government-appointed constitutional commission, consisting of legal experts (including C. D. Ooft), stated in a working paper that 'a shift in emphasis from parliament to the executive (president) is considered necessary. Within the system applied until now, parliament's dominant position has not allowed the state

---

* Furthermore, Decree B-4 stated that—despite the state of emergency—all laws, government bodies and rulings were to remain in effect unless otherwise altered or suspended by decree.

sufficiently effective powers and means to steer social developments towards society's objectives'.

Controversy Surrounding the New Constitution

The suspension of the 1975 constitution brought with it discussions concerning a new constitution. This issue has continued to play a major part in the national political debate. On behalf of the government, the constitutional commission mentioned above presented a draft document in the fall of 1981. As anticipated, the draft proceeded on the assumption of a presidential system with a directly-elected executive president. In addition, the draft document stated that there was to be a two-chamber system, consisting of a Political and a Social Chamber. Representatives of the political parties could be elected to the former, while the Social Chamber would consist of representatives of social groups and regional councils. The Social Chamber was primarily intended to do justice to regional standpoints and to prevent a return of the traditional situation in which the country was ruled only from Paramaribo.

The political parties were to be bound by law to strict conditions regarding internal party democracy. One member of the constitutional commission said at the time that the draft constitution was aimed at preventing a return to the old political system. As we have seen, the draft constitution led to a conflict between civilian President Chin a Sen and Commander Bouterse. Bouterse openly commented that the military's position within the political system needed to be more firmly outlined. According to the draft constitution, the military was to take part in a Revolutionary Council which would merely be awarded an advisory role. Furthermore, the military preferred a political system with a Social Chamber only. They believed it would be possible in this way to steer the composition of such a chamber in their favour through the Bureau of Popular Mobilization. The conflict surrounding the draft constitution led to the fall of the Chin a Sen government on 5 February 1982, when the majority of the cabinet adopted a stance in opposition to the military leadership, which was supported by the small, left-wing PALU and RVP parties (see Chapter 1).

One constitutional development of note took place on 18 March 1982. In the absence of a new cabinet, the Military Leadership was at that moment in complete power. Commander Bouterse announced that the Military Leadership had already (as early as 11 March 1982) proclaimed martial law in connection with the aborted coup led by former officer Surendre Rambocus (see Chapter 1). The most important stipulation regarding the state of martial law involved the court martial of those who had actually endangered national security during this period. Such people would generally be tried by the National Army leadership, referred to in the decree as the 'drumhead court martial'. According to the decree, this court was empowered to sentence people to death without providing the possibility of appeal. The fact that Bouterse announced the decree a full six days after the coup attempt caused the proclamation of this decree to be seen by many as a retroactive justification of the summary execution of one of the conspirators; this execution had stirred up widespread concern regarding the human rights situation in the country. Following strong protests by Surinam's major social groups, the state of martial law was lifted within one week of its public proclamation. And, in an apparent attempt to quieten public unrest concerning human rights, the military leadership published a decree on 25 March 1982, entitled 'Statute of Fundamental Rights and Obligations of the Surinamese People'. For the first time since the suspension of the constitution on 13 August 1980, the fundamental rights of the Surinamese were once again explicitly laid down.

The statute contained twenty-one articles, of which ten were included in the chapter 'Civil Rights and Responsibilities'. This chapter outlined the most common civil rights. Accordingly, article 2 reads:

All Surinamese are equal before the law and have the right to equal protection. No one may suffer discrimination on the basis of his birth, sex, language, religion, descent, education, economic position, social circumstances or any other status. It is the government's duty to promote those conditions needed for the real equality of all citizens.

And article 3 reads: 'All persons have the right to physical, mental and moral integrity. No one may be submitted to torture, humiliation or inhuman treatment or punishment'. Articles 7 to 10 emphatically state further fundamental freedoms. Article 7: 'All persons have the right to freedom of religion and belief.' Article 8: 'All persons have the right to freely express their opinions. Press freedom is recognized.' Article 9: 'All persons have the right to peaceful assembly.' Article 10: 'All persons have the right to petition'.

The statute also included chapters on social and cultural rights and responsibilities and on educational freedom. It stated that these rights could legally be subjected to limitations in the event of a state of siege, a state of emergency, or for reasons of national interest, national security, the public order or public morals. A number of freedoms therefore remained rather limited. The old political parties, for example, were forbidden to meet (see p. 112).

The publication of the statute on fundamental rights and duties, described by the authorities as a 'transitional constitution', did not put an end to the controversy. The temporary and retroactive proclamation of martial law had made it clear to many that the military leadership was able to alter statutory regulations virtually at will. The Neyhorst and Alibux governments both announced plans to draw up a draft constitution, but little came of either project. This was not due simply to the premature dissolution of both cabinets (see Chapter 1). The failures resulted to a much greater extent from the lack of urgency or even willingness on the part of the Military Leadership and the small left-wing parties to establish a constitutional structure. The Military Leadership and the parties apparently wished to maintain a certain amount of room for manœuvre. Immediately after the resignation of the Chin a Sen government, Bouterse said:

Why can't we draft a constitution? We are now in a revolutionary period. Institutions now exist which will soon no longer be there. If you lay down such things in the form of a constitution, that's pure idiocy ... A constitution cannot be written before the people's committees have determined which such a constitution will contain [speech in Saramacca].

More than a year later, after the broad-based movement for democraticization of November 1982 and the dramatic events of December of that year, the opinion of the 'revolutionary leadership' had not changed. Harvey Naarendorp, at the time Bouterse's most important adviser, explained:

Those who want a constitution in the short term are displaying no realism, because power cannot be bound by rules. I can formulate thousands of things. Drawing up a constitution isn't so difficult. The real problem, however, isn't to draft rules, but to establish a bond between the military and the people [interview with one of the authors, December 1983].

For the revolutionary leadership, a constitution in fact constituted a limitation on the possibilities for revolutionary change. It was much easier to operate within a constitutional vacuum.

A broad spectrum of groups, including trade unions and ecclesiastical organizations, voiced their fundamental dissatisfaction with this constitutional limbo. In a sharply critical statement, one of these groups, the authoritative Committee of Christian Churches (CCK) said:

After three years without a constitution, a major reason why a constitution must be quickly re-introduced is that, without such, the people are unaware of their rights— and particularly their duties—which ought to be established by law, and are ignorant of the cohesion between these laws. The people have no certainty. Furthermore, the tasks and the proper powers of the various institutions, particularly the new institutions, are extremely vague and unclear in the absence of a constitution, which can needlessly complicate the life of the individual citizen. All this creates confusion, fear and insecurity among the population (. . .) The major justification for a constitution is that its absence hinders full legal security. Without a constitution, even the best of programmes have an extremely unpredictable value [from official CCK statement on the 25 February Movement's draft programme, 15 November 1983].

Organized labour and trade and industry also felt that a speedy end should be put to the uncertainty. Even the (ceremonial) president, Fred Ramdat Misier, in a speech celebrating the eighth anniversary of Surinamese independence, stated that 'the disappearance of fear and worry is indispensable to the establishment of a healthy legal system (speech, 25 November 1983). But the chasm between the various groups regarding a new constitution appeared to be scarcely capable of being bridged. Harvey Naarendorp felt that those calling for a new constitution actually wanted to restore the old political order:

An extremely small group wants to return to the old political structure. A second, relatively large group, wants more or less the same as the first group, but then in a neatly polished form. These are those who want a constitution and elections right away, but then accompanied by a law allowing for political parties [interview, December 1983].

It was only after the 1983 strikes, which resulted in the collapse of the Alibux government, that the slightest change was noted in this uncompromising standpoint on the part of the Military Authority.

The new government, led by Wim Udenhout—the first in which organized labour and (a portion of) trade and industry were to take part—was charged with establishing 'lasting democratic structures'. A think-tank, comprised of representatives of the three government partners (Military Leadership, organized labour and trade and industry), presented an advisory report in December 1984. Its most important recommendation was that for the formation of a National Assembly, comprised of representatives of the three partners and empowered to draw up a draft constitution. The National Assembly was installed in January 1985, and was to hold office for a period of twenty-seven months, after which the 'lasting democratic structures' were to be put into effect. Meanwhile, Commander-in-Chief Bouterse had also invited the old parties to take part in the political discussion (see Chapter 1).

The dispute over a new constitution exposed the same discrepancies that had surfaced in earlier years. Were there to be direct elections, with political parties, and what was to be the position of the Military Leadership under a new system of government? These continued to be the major, unanswered questions. The various groups in the National Assembly submitted their proposals during November 1986, and the 'old' parties jointly published a draft constitution. The proposals showed clear differences of opinion between the 25 February Movement (VFB) and the old parties, organized labour and trade and industry. These latter groups all advocated direct elections by secret ballot, and a role for political parties. They favoured a directly elected president with executive powers. Organized labour's constitutional model contained corporate elements in its inclusion of organized social groups in the proposed legislative body. The VFB went no further than recommending indirect elections, whereby district councils were to be elected from among neighbourhood representative bodies. The National Assembly was to be elected in turn from the members of these district councils. The establishment of local and regional representative bodies is the primary task of the Ministry of Home Affairs' Directorate of Popular Mobilization (see pp. 101–4),and it is precisely this ministry that is controlled by the VFB. The suspicion held by political opponents that the VFB, within its proposed government structure, hopes to exert an influence far beyond the actual support this movement enjoys among the population is anything but far-fetched. Although the VFB favours a direct political role for the Military Leadership, the other groups foresee only an indirect supervisory function for the military. Out of what they term 'political realism', the old parties lay aside a majority position for the military in a State Council, which is to ensure the maintenance of democracy. This council would, however, be empowered to do little more than call a referendum.

The controversy surrounding a new constitution intensified as the established schedule elapsed and the old parties held tenaciously to their prime demand for immediate and free elections by secret ballot. A 'true' democracy was heralded in the 25 November 1985 agreement between the Military Leadership and groups including these political parties (see Chapter 1).

It was in late 1986 that Commander-in-Chief Bouterse first spoke of free elections to be held in spring 1988, to follow a 1987 referendum on a new constitution. This was generally regarded as a victory for the old parties and an effective suppression of the VFB's proposal for indirect elections. Although the new plans will entail the first-ever district elections, these will be independent of the national elections.

The most recent draft constitution, agreed by the military leaders and the old political parties in late March 1987, clearly awards the military a continuing, albeit less dominant, role in government. It limits the military's political participation to the above-mentioned State Council, with its watchdog function. This council, chaired by the country's president, is to include members of the military as well as organized social groups and political parties. Supreme legislative power will be granted to a directly-elected parliament (National Assembly), consisting exclusively of representatives of the political parties. The National Assembly in turn is to elect an executive president by no less than a two-thirds majority vote. This draft constitution, however, was to be presented for public endorsement by means of a referendum in September 1987. General elections were to follow within six months. But it remains to be seen to just what extent the military will be willing to play a subordinate role in national politics. One certainty remains: relations between Surinam's civilian and military sectors will remain problematic for some time to come.

The Government Structure

Turbulent political developments have kept Surinam's government system in a state of continual flux. As we have already seen, one of the turning-points was the break with the 'old' republic on 13 August 1980 and the suspension of the constitution. An executive president was introduced, to serve simultaneously as prime minister and chairman of the council of ministers. Even more important was that, along with the break with the old republic, the political power of the Military Leadership and thus of Commander-in-Chief Bouterse, became institutionalized. Laws were now no longer to be signed by the President and the Prime Minister alone, but were also to be co-signed by the Military Leadership. The military in this way became co-legislator.

Decree A of 13 August 1980, which dealt with the proclamation of a state of emergency, established the Military Leadership's formal participation in the government. This power was to be exercised in cooperation with the executive president and the council of ministers. Decree A2 of November 1980 further reinforced the military's position. Article 9 of this decree stated: 'The Military Authority, after consultation with the council of ministers, is to serve the function of acting president' when the president is unable to govern effectively.

The conflict between Bouterse and President Chin a Sen in February 1982 concerning a draft constitution led to the President's resignation and to new changes in the government structure. After Chin a Sen's resignation on 4 February of that year, the Military Leadership once again assumed full power pending the formation of a new cabinet. Not surprisingly, the Military Leadership were anxious to dispose of the system of executive presidency.

Maintaining such a prominent figure in the government system posed a threat of new constitutional conflicts.

On 25 March 1982, with the installation of a new cabinet, the government structure was once again laid down, in General Decree A-9. According to this decree, issued by the Military Leadership, the highest administrative power was placed in the hands of a 'Policy Centre'. Article 6 of the decree stated that the members of the Policy Centre were to be selected by the Military Authority. Decree A-9 was the first formal delineation of the military leadership's position of absolute power. According to article 5, the Policy Centre was to determine 'the direction and policy of the revolutionary process'. The centre was also to make government policy, as well as to nominate ministers for appointment by the (ceremonial) president. The ministers themselves were to be directly answerable to this same Policy Centre. According to the decree, ruling power was in the hands of the Policy Centre and the Council of Ministers. The prime minister, as chairman of the Council of Ministers, was, by definition, to be a member of the Policy Centre.

Another decree (C-64), issued on 25 March 1982 and dealing with the government's rules of order, stated that the Commander-in-Chief and Deputy Commander of the National Army were to serve as the Policy Centre's chairman and vice-chairman respectively.

A new structural change came on 21 August 1985. The major aspect was the even clearer emphasis placed on Commander-in-Chief Bouterse's position in the government system. As Chairman of the 25 February Movement, Bouterse had already received the title 'Leader of the Revolution'. Decree A-19 referred to the military commander as 'Leader of the Surinamese Government', to be replaced in his absence by another member of the Military Leadership. Article 2 of this decree awarded the government leader a number of special powers:

— to see the proper observance and implementation of the objectives of the revolution;
— to see the proper observance and implementation of the programmes of the government of Surinam;
— to protect the sovereignty and internal safety of the state of Surinam;
— to safeguard the general interests of the state of Surinam.

This decree placed Bouterse in a unique position of power. By appealing to the first and third of the above-mentioned powers in particular, the military commander-cum-government-leader could implement measures at will. The third power in fact entailed the introduction of the doctrine of internal security, in accordance with the Latin American model.

Article 3 of this decree also had the following to say of the powers of the government leader: 'The leader of the Government of Suriname shall convene meetings of the Government as often as he thinks desirable. The leader of the Government shall act as Chairman of such meetings consisting of members of the Military Authority and the Members of the Council of Ministers.'

Participation in the political process by the old political parties also entailed several changes in the government structure. After the November 25, 1985 accord between the Military Leadership and the VHP, NPS and KTPI, these parties had a seat on the 'Topberaad' (Supreme Council). This newly-established body had been operating informally since 1984, when the trade unions and trade and industry had entered the cabinet. After the accord with the old parties, however, the Supreme Council's position was more securely formalized. At first the political parties' participation in the Supreme Council was limited to matters relating to the restructuring of the national administrative system. As from 25 May 1986, the parties participated fully in these discussions. Two months later, on 16 July 1986, that participation was rewarded with the formation of a new cabinet, which included people who could justifiably be considered representatives of the old parties.

The government structure in effect since that time was described in a joint memorandum by Pertab Radakishun (VHP prime minister at the time) and then-deputy prime minister and minister of internal affairs, Jules Wijden-bosch. The memorandum, excerpts from which follow, was entitled 'The structure of the Government of Suriname'.

The head of state is the President of the Republic of Suriname. The Supreme Council is the highest political institution of the state. It comprises the following members:
(a) the 25 February Movement;
(b) organized labour;
(c) organized employers, and
(d) the major political parties (NPS, VHP and KTPI).

It is worth noting at this point that the most important trade union federation, C-47, does not participate in the Supreme Council (see pp. 104–12). The council is presided over by the Chairman of the 25 February Movement, Commander Desi Delano Bouterse. By definition, the prime minister and deputy-prime minister attend the meetings of the Supreme Council, but have no vote. Government ministers are nominated by the Supreme Council, and the council establishes the government's policy programme and checks government policy for compliance with the programme. If necessary, the

Supreme Council can amend the government's policy programme and it is the public body empowered to decide on 'matters of policy nature in the last resort'.

The council consists of a maximum of eighteen members, two members from each of the nine participating groups: the 25 February Movement, the NPS, VHP and KTPI political parties, the CLO, PWO and Moederbond trade union federations and the VSB and ASFA employers' organizations. The council's rules of order state that a decision need not be unanimous in order to be passed. If three or four of the partners are in opposition, the motion is suspended for no longer than thirty days. If four partners remain in opposition after this time, however, the motion is defeated. If no more than three are opposed, the motion is adopted. According to the rules of order, the 25 February Movement could theoretically be overruled in the Supreme Council, but the voting ratio in the council is relatively insignificant in view of the extensive powers of the Leader of the Government outlined in the above mentioned Decree A-19.

The Government consists of: the Military Leadership, including the Government Leader, the Council of Ministers. Legislative authority is jointly held by the Government and the National Assembly.

The Military Leadership consists of the following posts: the Commander of the National Army, the Chief of Staff, the Battalion Commander, the Chief of Materials and Logistics and the Chief of Operations and Training.

The Council of Ministers is appointed by the President of the Republic, after nomination by the Supreme Council. It is chaired by the Prime Minister, and is the principal executive policy instrument for the implementation of the Supreme Council's guidelines.

Local Governments

Political decision-making in Surinam has always been centred exclusively in the capital city of Paramaribo. No administrative decentralization has ever taken place. This was certainly one of the political system's major flaws, contributing to local people's sense of exclusion from the country's political administration. Surinam has been divided into administrative districts from as early as 1863. These districts, however, have always remained administrative subsections of the central government in Paramaribo. In other words, the delegation of administrative responsibility is entirely lacking. The legal channels needed for the decentralization of administrative power have existed since 1865, yet virtually no use has been made of them.

The Rural Communities Decree was proclaimed in 1937, but had little to do with administrative decentralization. This decree was primarily intended to allow community members to receive a parcel of agricultural ground from the government under perpetual lease. The colonial governor of the day, J. C. Kielstra, had, as a former colonial official in the Dutch East Indies, a certain affinity with the Asiatic groups. Kielstra intended this decree to protect the Indonesians against economically more powerful groups. At the same time, the decree served as a tool whereby the colonial government could assure itself of sufficient labour by binding peasants to villages close to their plantations. Only twenty-two of these rural communities were established during the period 1937 to 1945, but even these played no significant role in the administrative process. One could say that district administration was primarily an executorial tool of colonial politics, intended to guarantee an adequate supply of labour in the agricultural areas. The administrative structure established at that time has remained virtually unchanged.

The possibility of administrative decentralization was laid down in the so-called Polity of 1955, and again in the 1975 constitution, with implementation left to the legislative body; and, as early as 1951, the Home Affairs Ministry had its own, separate department for administrative decentralization. The issue was also dealt with in a number of party electoral platforms. Yet, until the 1980 coup, no serious attempts were made to reduce the capital's administrative dominance.

Vollers (1974, p. 175) points out that in Surinam, more than elsewhere, factors associated with party politics appear to have played the most important role in the failure to decentralize, particularly the fact that party politics in Surinam have always been ethnically orientated. Many government decisions contained overtones related to party politics, and therefore to ethnic factors. As Voller states, party politicians in Paramaribo feared that these ethno-political overtones would be even more emphatically brought to light, should democratically-elected district councils become a significant political factor. The ethnic composition of a number of districts was, and continues to be, markedly one-sided. This means that a positive decision for a certain district will always be regarded as a decision in favour of a certain ethnic group. A predominantly Creole government, for example, would prefer not to be confronted with the financial and political demands of a democratically-elected district council dominated by other ethnic groups.

Furthermore, as we have already seen, the old political system was largely a matter for the party elite. This elite of course had little desire to create competing party elites at the district level. This fact meant that administrative decentralization would have to be championed by the districts themselves. In this regard, Vollers notes that a local or regional frame of reference is almost totally lacking among Surinam's population. Ties between district residents are based first and foremost on ethnic grounds. Ethnic homogeneity is further reinforced by the largely isolated residential concentrations. In the face of such a state of affairs, a regional community scarcely had a chance to take root.

The districts are governed by a district commissioner (DC), the administrative leader of the district. Since the constitutional reforms of 1948, this commissioner no longer receives his directives from the colonial governor, but from the Home Affairs Ministry. The district commissioner's tasks and powers are limited to administrative management. The DC represents the entire government, as well as each individual minister. He has charge of administrative officials from the Home Affairs Ministry, as well as of civil servants from other ministries. This latter group of civil servants often tend to lean more towards their own minister than towards the DC, which can lead to huge coordination problems. Furthermore, under the old political system, appointments to government posts were often prompted by favouritism, a fact which did little to boost the quality of district administration.

The first government to take office after the coup of 25 February 1980 immediately included the formation of district councils in its policy programme, 'in order to involve the entire population in policy-making, as well as to grant the people a say in matters which will directly influence their own lives'. Adequate administrative decentralization, however, remained virtually non-existent. It was the Department of Popular Mobilization that worked for decentralization after the coup. As we have already seen, this department was an instrument of the revolutionary movement. The activities aimed at administrative decentralization were therefore more a part of the campaign for revolutionary mobilization than any actual democratization of district administration. According to the revolutionary view, the people's committees existed primarily for the defence of the revolution (see pp. 81–9).

In 1984, the Department of Popular Mobilization was integrated into the Ministry of Home Affairs and District Administration, which was then renamed the Ministry of Home Affairs, District Administration and Popular Mobilization. This established an even stronger tie between district administration and popular mobilization. Furthermore, this ministry was placed firmly in the hands of the 25 February Movement via the ministerial appointment of Jules Wijdenbosch, who was also Chairman of the movement's Daily Executive.

Since the coup, the manner of establishment, the functioning and the powers granted to regional bodies have never been clarified. This is primarily the result of clashing ideological standpoints, with the VFB in opposition to the political parties, the trade union movement and trade and industry. The Department of Popular Mobilization and the VFB regard regional bodies primarily as grass-roots structures, which exist to provide the foundation for a centralized, revolutionary system of government. The VFB therefore opposes the direct election of district councils. According to the VFB's draft government-structure memorandum, presented to the National Assembly in November 1986, district councils were to be elected indirectly via local representative bodies. In 1984, the Surinamese trade union movement launched a joint plan for the direct election of district councils. This plan foundered in political seas.

Attempts have been made since 1980 to set up district and regional councils, but the above-mentioned lack of clarity and clash of viewpoints doomed these attempts to failure from the start. The Ministry of Home Affairs, District Administration and Popular Mobilization has itself admitted this in one of its brochures ('Orientatie op de tweede nationale vergadering van ressortbesturen', 13 July 1986). The people's committees became increasingly less active, until the majority of them 'more or less ceased to exist'. The brochure noted 'stagnation' among the district councils, and stated that the regional councils had functioned 'barely or not at all' (pages 6 to 7). The lack of democratic procedures in the composition of the local bodies undoubtedly served to reduce interest to a minimum.

Mass Organizations

Trade unions had long been active in Surinam, but they only became a politically significant factor at the end of the 1960s. A number of professional groups, such as teachers and typographers, had formed unions as early as the beginning of this century. The effectiveness of organized labour at that time was, however, fairly limited. During the 1930s, trade union activities enjoyed a brief heyday under the influence of such leaders as the left-wing nationalist Anton de Kom (see Chapter 1). The Dutch colonial government quickly extinguished this spark of unionism by the use of repressive measures. Prior to 1950, most trade union organizations were relatively short-lived phenomena and tended to disappear without a ripple (Campbell, 1977, p. 326). Exceptions to the rule were the bauxite-workers' unions, set up in the towns of Mungo and Paranam following a strike in 1942.

Two of the four trade union organizations still active today came into being around 1950. It was no accident that their establishment coincided with the rise of political parties. As mentioned earlier, the establishment of these parties was largely prompted by the social elite's need for political legitimacy. A trade union was therefore an excellent vehicle to create a constituency. As the Surinamese politician and trade union leader R. Biswamitre was to note several years later: 'Here in Suriname we have labour organizations which can be regarded as extensions of certain political parties, which have in this way been able to ensure the support of the workers' (cited by Hoppe, 1975, p. 158).

Accordingly, the Progressieve Werknemersorganisatie (PWO, Progress Employee's Organization) was set up in 1948 on the initiative of the PSV, as noted before, a party that primarily addressed itself to the Roman Catholic, Creole working class. In 1951, it was future prime minister Johan Adolf Pengel who provided the impetus for the new Moederbond trade union organization. For Pengel, the Moederbond was an important tool for winning the sympathy of the Black Creole working class. Pengel's analysis proved correct, for he ultimately succeeded in assuming the leadership of the NPS, dominated at the time by a light-skinned Creole elite. Pengel became the Moederbond's leader and was to maintain this position even during his term as prime minister. Both the PWO and the Moederbond were allied with the traditional political parties, and consequently embraced no extreme ideologies.

The Moederbond, following in the wake of the NPS, was able to become the country's largest trade union organization. It primarily consisted of unions from within private foreign firms. The PWO, on the other hand, consisted largely of unions from trading firms and the retail trade.

The Surinamese trade union movement was (and is) characterized by a decentralized organization at the level of the individual firm. The lack of trade union managers was sorely felt, particularly during the earliest period of the union's existence. Because of this, some capable trade union leaders were able to elevate themselves to the position of virtual 'trade union wholesalers' (Campbell, 1977, p. 330). The union's sole objective was to attain the greatest possible wage increases, since this was the only way in which a trade union leader could guarantee himself the continued support of his members. As a result, massive wage discrepancies arose between 'strong' and 'weak' firms, with the bauxite firms setting the extreme example. Enterprising trade union leaders could use their position within the labour movement as a springboard to a political career, because of their ability to guarantee their party a given number of votes.

An explanation for the interweaving of politics and the trade union movement can also be found in the position of organized labour in Surinam. During this initial period, no institutionalized forum existed between the trade unions and the government. Such consultation did, however, already take place on a formal basis between the government and the Verenigde Surinaamse Bedrijfsleven (VSB, United Surinamese Trade & Industry) employers' organization. In fact, an agreement had been in effect since 1955 by which all relevant draft bills were to be submitted for analysis by the VSB (Hoppe, 1975, p. 161). The trade union movement therefore needed representatives in the formal political arena in order to exert any influence at all. One cannot speak in this context of a mature system of labour relations.

The civil servants assumed a special position. It was during the Pengel/Lachmon coalition that the patronage system recieved a substantial boost, and many civil servants therefore owed their jobs to political favouritism, a fact which substantially eroded the independence of the civil servants' unions. Union membership within the civil service was relatively low and, with dozens of unions operating in this sector, dissension within the service was rife. From this it will be clear that the trade union movement at that time did not hold a position of strength within labour relations as a whole. In this regard it is perhaps also telling that the first Surinamese collective labour agreement was only signed in 1966, between the ALCOA subsidiary Suralco and the bauxite unions.

The 1960s brought a change in the trade union movement's position on the political chessboard. The political and trade union activities of the staunchly nationalistic PNR leader Eddy Bruma appear to have brought Pengel to the realization that the management of 'his' Moederbond needed reinforcement. Pengel saw that the trade union organization's old guard were unable effectively to counter the nationalists. Several promising trade unionists, including future Moederbond leader Cyrill Daal, were therefore sent to The Netherlands and the United States for leadership training. In this way Surinam received its first professional trade union leaders.

The trade union activities of the PNR nationalists greatly contributed to a growing self-awareness among the various unions. This was without a doubt the development that most served to inform the changes of the 1960s. The teachers' unions provided a major stimulus. Their preparedness for industrial action grew steadily as the government, despite price increases, continued to postpone its promised wage increases. The government itself had little financial leeway for such increases. The teachers' unions joined forces and, by 1969, their patience had run out. The move for industrial action spread to the civil servants' unions when several active union members were threatened with transfer. The action in this way took on a more political overtone, and was also aimed at autocracy within the political system. The civil servants' unions carried out sympathy strikes, and so for the first time assumed a more independent stance.

The 1969 strikes, which led as noted to Pengel's resignation, greatly influenced the position and further development of Surinam's trade union movement. The Moederbond found itself in something of a crisis. Many of its affiliated unions were disappointed with the umbrella organization's stance on the strikes, and no longer wished to be led by Pengel, with his authoritarian behaviour. On this subject, Cyrill Daal, later to lead the Moederbond himself, said: 'Pengel was the powerful ruler of the Moederbond. The rest had little to say. And anyone who dared oppose him was crushed' (J. Haakmat, 1983, p. 7). The combination of the office of prime minister with that of trade union leader was seen as particularly unacceptable. Pengel therefore resigned as chairman of the Moederbond; the organization's young leaders could now begin repairing the damage.

The aloof stance of both Moederbond and PWO led in 1970 to the setting-up of a third trade union organization, the C-47. The CLO civil servants' union was set up a year later. Both these organizations were the result of the PNR nationalists' trade union activities, and both organizations were under complete PNR control. Eddy Bruma himself was the first chairman of C-47, which took its name from the forty-seven unions that had served as the original base for the organization. The Moederbond's deplorable position was underscored by the defection of the Paranam workers' unions—representing the crucially important bauxite workers—to C-47.

With C-47 and the CLO, the 1969 strikes had produced two trade union organizations which placed greater emphasis on ideology and saw their mandate in a broader political perspective. In a speech commemorating the fifteenth anniversary of C-47, the organization's current leader, Fred Derby, described the organization's view of its task at that time as follows:

C-47 did not take a traditional approach to the interests of the worker. The organization consistently operated on the assumption that the trade union movement not only bears the responsibility for arranging collective labour agreements, but that the total social, economic and political climate must also be such that the country can develop in utter freedom by making independent decisions [speech, 11 January 1985].

The two new trade union organizations emphatically opted for a direct line with national politics. The PNR leadership was the union leadership. Following the débâcle with Pengel, the Moederbond carefully chose to maintain a greater distance from active party politics.

The Surinamese trade union movement once again demonstrated its growing self-awareness in the early 1970s. Social unrest increased during this period, owing to rising unemployment and deteriorating social conditions, as the PNP/VHP coalition government failed to attract those anticipated foreign investments needed to create jobs. The resulting frustrations were expressed not only through increased emigration to The Netherlands, but also through strikes. The four trade union organizations cooperated to a certain degree and coordinated their activities. The government narrowly avoided dissolution when the strikes were called off in the wake of a storm of emotion surrounding the killing of a strike leader by a police bullet. The strikes nevertheless had their intended effect in the form of an electoral victory for a combination platform which included the NPS and PNR parties. Leaders of the C-47 and CLO trade union federations, including Eddy Bruma and Fred Derby, were elected to parliament as PNR candidates. Bruma even went on to become Minister of Economic Affairs, and turned over the C-47 chairmanship to Derby.

The strikes during this period confirmed the continuing advance of the trade union movement. The trade union federations set up a special foundation to promote mutual cooperation, and a joint training institute was established. Yet the rivalry continued, particularly between C-47 and the Moederbond. This involved more than mere differences of political background and viewpoint. Personal rivalries between trade union leaders continue to play a role, and are expressed in the regular snatching away of unions from the rival. Campbell (1987, p. 62), points out that ideology does not constitute a hard-and-fast criterion for drawing distinctions between trade union organizations. Accordingly, the two major trade union federations, C-47 and the Moederbond, both have social-democratic overtones, although C-47 leans somewhat further to the left. Campbell (1987, p. 62) states: 'Loyalty to trade union federations is not very strong, and can be easily severed by trade union leaders choosing for another federation in the hope of having higher wage demands met.' Owing to the above-mentioned decentralized trade union structure, wage demands have indeed traditionally been ambitious and have served as vehicles for union leaders to increase their prestige.

It should be noted at this point that ethnic distinctions do not play a role in the trade union movement, as they do in national politics. Trade unions were, in fact, the first organizations in Surinam to successfully generate popular unity on a non-racial basis. None the less, the unions were much more a pragmatic collective tool for obtaining wage demands than any forum for class struggle at the grass-roots level. This pragmatism stemmed at least in part from the major role played by ethnic distinctions in national politics.

The divergent viewpoints of C-47 and the Moederbond were apparent during the 1980 coup. All four trade union organizations backed the sergeants in their conflict with the Arron government regarding the setting-up of a military union. The sergeants claimed that this was no more than a fundamental trade union right. C-47, the CLO and the PWO took the most extreme stance by threatening industrial action if the imprisoned leaders of the banned military union were not acquitted. The Moederbond, however, remained reluctant. According to Cyrill Daal, leader of the Moederbond at that time, it was important for his organization not to become involved in a 'political tug-of-war' (J. Haakmat, 1983, p. 30).

All the trade union organizations declared their support for the first post-coup government policy programme (1 May 1980), but only the 'PNR unions' emphatically allied themselves with the regime.

The trade unions were allowed to operate freely after the coup. A planning council, in which the trade unions were represented, was actually set up to advise the government on socio-economic matters. The council was short-lived, however. In the fall of 1980, after the declaration of a state of emergency and the formalization of the military's supremacy, trade union freedom was threatened with curtailment for the first time by a draft decree banning strikes. Following heavy protest, however, the proposed decree was withdrawn.

In 1981, trade union federations joined the Revolutionary Front, which included representatives from several radical parties and the military. But, as noted earlier, the Front dissolved fairly quickly, owing to lack of internal cohesion. The first frictions between the trade union movement and the military authorities arose during this same period. This resulted in the failure of the 1981 International Labour Day celebrations. Fred Derby provided the following analysis of the fiasco:

The trade union movement began mobilizing before May 1, but these activities were frustrated by the National Military Council, which wanted to summon the people itself and simply provide an opportunity for the trade union movement to have its say. Certain problems of competence were at work here [minutes of an evaluatory meeting between the military authorities and trade union leaders on 11 May 1981; noted by J. Haakmat, 1983, appendix VI].

Derby's comment provides a certain insight into the political ideas prevalent at the time among the revolutionary groups. Certain factions within the Army and the small, radical PALU and RVP parties saw total trade union freedom as a potential threat to the revolution. In the centralized executive model drafted by the Bureau of Popular Mobilization, the comment was made that trade union policies and viewpoints 'may display no discrepancies with the lines and policy of the revolution'. This model was never actually put into force, but it none the less serves to indicate an increasingly influential train of thought among certain political factions during this period.

This was illustrated again in August 1982, when members of the C-47—affiliated FAL Farmers' Federation set up blockades in Nickerie (Western Surinam) to lend weight to their demand for a higher minimum price for rice. The government's reply was to dispatch an Army unit and arrest various union leaders, and, in September of that year, members of the People's Militia occupied the office of the Moederbond. Following the December 1982 executions, which had included that of Cyrill Daal, true trade union freedom ceased to exist. The trade union leadership had felt the lash; it kept quiet and engaged in no industrial action.

So it was that the massive strikes in the bauxite sector in late 1983, described in Chapter 1, came as a total surprise. But the trade union leadership distanced itself entirely from these strikes; the C-47 leaders even made an unsuccessful attempt to call a halt to the industrial action. The bauxite strike reflected the crisis within the entire trade union movement and the gulf that had arisen between the leaders and the rank and file—a rift caused largely by the trade union leadership's passive stance. Alternative, clandestine ranks had even been drawn up within the labour movement. These alternative ranks played a major role in the strikes in the bauxite sector, which bore obvious political overtones. This series of industrial actions was characterized by a lack of leaders identifiable as such to outsiders. The formal trade union leadership hardly dared permit itself an independent role during this period.

The trade union federations began participating in the national government in 1984 (see Chapter 1). It was only with great difficulty that the trade union leadership was able to obtain approval for this participation from the rank and file. The trade union federations' position became more difficult when the federations were also given direct responsibility for government policy. The military leadership hoped in this way to make the trade union movement at least partly responsible for the much-needed reorganization of the national economy.

Beginning in 1984, however, the number of industrial actions again increased. Little credence can therefore be given to the claim that the trade union federations' participation in the government had led to greater contentment on the part of the workers. This situation was due in part to the organizational structure of Surinam's trade union movement, within which unions can operate fairly autonomously and without direct interference from the federations.

Labour conflicts arose at a number of semi-governmental institutions in particular. It is noteworthy that these actions did not centre solely around wage demands, but also involved internal policy conflicts. The regime's practice of placing political allies in positions of responsibility within these institutions, as well as attempts by the revolutionary factions to gain control of the trade unions, prompted protest. The Bruynzeel lumber concern, for example, had a trade union management consisting of RVP supporters, and a pro-regime management. The workers, however, refused to accept this situation and elected trade union leaders from among the representatives of the Moederbond federation. When the company management refused to recognize the new trade union management, the workers went on strike. Similar conflicts arose at the nationalized SAIL shrimp cannery and the SML agricultural concern in Wageningen, where PALU representatives had been parachuted into the company management.

It was primarily during and shortly after the Alibux administration that the leftist-radical groups attempted to gain influence within the labour movement. During this period, supporters of the regime—who often lacked the necessary expertise—were also appointed to managerial posts within semi-governmental concerns; but attempts to infiltrate the labour movement—such as those by the RVP during the bauxite strikes—ultimately proved futile.

Strikes in the commerce and production sectors were usually prompted by the threat of redundancies or by wage conflicts, which became more frequent because of the economic crisis. In an attempt to avoid labour unrest, the regime issued a decree in 1983 prohibiting companies from firing workers without special permission. The decree was not very effective. In 1984, the Minister of Labour spoke of 'negative developments in the working relationship between the labour movement and organized employers, both of whom have special responsibility due to their participation in the government.' The anti-redundancy decree had only limited significance in the face of the disastrous economic developments of the day. Accordingly, the government was forced to agree in 1986 to hundreds of redundancies at Suralco in order to avoid risking the complete shut-down of this economically crucial concern.

The labour movement's position was clearly undermined by the economic crisis. In May 1985 the government was therefore able to dictate a halt to all collective labour negotiations in (semi-state) institutions. Unity within the labour movement became a thing of the past. A large portion of the rank and file refused on the grounds of political principle to collaborate with the military regime. Following a ministerial conflict, C-47 resigned from the government and adopted a more critical political stance, in an apparent bid to win back the workers' confidence it had lost during the bauxite strikes.

The role of PWO Chairman Ramon Cruden and CLO Chairman Hendrik Sylvester as advisers to the authorities reinforced their unions' close ties with the military leadership. Furthermore, a number of CLO and Moederbond managers were active in the 25 February Movement. All three of these federations took part in the Supreme Council and the National Assembly. The PWO, CLO and Moederbond had in fact surrendered their independent positions as trade union federations. They also showed no hesitation in endorsing a communiqué from the Supreme Council in which their fellow federation, the C-47, was accused of 'terrorist activities' for its part in strikes and the occupation of company grounds (January 1986). The PWO and Moederbond's stance finally led to suspension by their respective international labour organizations, the World Council of Labour (WCL) and the International Confederation of Free Trade Unions (ICFTU).

The Moederbond's political stance also led to a growing exodus of its affiliated unions. On 1 May 1986, these unions combined forces to form the Organization of Cooperative Autonomous Trade Unions (OSAV). The OSAV, which has not yet assumed the official status of trade union federation, includes such major labour organizations as the Mungo mineworkers' union, the dockworkers and the national power company employees. Table 3.1 indicates the rise of the OSAV. The data also indicate that the Moederbond lost its supremacy in membership and the PWO's relegation to the role of smallest union organization.

Political Dissent

Despite the admittedly major defects of the old political system, complaints were rarely lodged against it concerning human rights violations. Very soon after the coup, however, problems arose in this sphere. Such problems existed even before the declaration of a state of emergency and the suspension of the constitution on 13 August 1980. In May of that year, a former military officer suspected of conspiracy died while in military custody. During this same period, complaints were lodged concerning the mishandling by soldiers of detained parliamentarians.

On 1 April 1981, the International Commission of Jurists (ICJ), a United Nations advisory body, published the first independent post-coup report on

Table 3.1 Trade Union Federation membership, 1986

	Private sector		(Semi-) public sector		Total	
	n.s.	%	n.s.	%	n.s.	%
C–47	10,000	53	2,000	15	12,000	38
M–Bond	5,000	27	3,000	24	8,000	25
CLO			8,000	61	8,000	25
PWO	800	4			800	2
OSAV	3,000	16			3,000	10
Total	13,900	100	18,800	100	31,800	100
Total number employed					84,000	
Membership (%)					37	

Source: Estimates based on unpublished government information.

Surinam and confirmed reports of human rights violations there. The report spoke of political arrests and the 'serious mishandling' of detainees. The ICJ report also noted limitations on press freedom by means of 'illegal and arbitrary intimidation'. The report, drafted by the American legal expert John Griffiths, also stated that: 'Without the presence of a legal authority or the possibility of appeal, civil and military authorities issue orders to the editors-in-chief of newspapers'. The Surinamese Association of Journalists had protested, with no result, against this state of affairs.

Surinam's civil rights record deteriorated in the course of what had come to be referred to as the 'revolutionary process'. The declaration of a state of emergency on 13 August 1980 meant the functional end of the old parties, which were now effectively banned from carrying out public activities. In the course of 1982, when the promised democratization failed to materialize, criticism of the military authorities from various sides was mounting. The military had, in the meantime, more firmly established its political position, and its actions had become increasingly autonomous. In July of 1982, therefore, the Military Leadership collided head-on with the legal system when it arrested two soldiers accused of conspiracy who had just been acquitted by the courts. Only after strong protests had been lodged by bodies, including the Public Prosecutor's Office and the Surinam Bar Association, were these arrests nullified. In August of that year, a number of trade union leaders were arrested by a military detachment during a demonstration by farmers, without consultation of the judicial system. Once again, protests led to a speedy release.

As we have already seen, the human rights situation in Surinam sank to an all-time low in December 1982 with the killing of fifteen prominent critics of the regime, including journalists and lawyers. The United Nations Commission on Human Rights' Special Rapporteur on summary and arbitrary executions, the Kenyan legal expert Amos Wako, concluded in his report of 12 February 1985 that 'summary and arbitrary executions took place' on the night of 8 December in the military headquarters at Fort Zeelandia. Wako's statement contradicted the official reading that the fifteen had been shot while trying to escape. Only after an initial refusal did Wako receive permission to visit Surinam in July 1984. In its annual report of 5 October 1983, the Inter-American Commission on Human Rights of the Organization of American States (OAS) went even further than Wako, concluding that high government officials were responsible for the deaths of the fifteen. A formal complaint from Amnesty International prompted the investigation by the OAS commission, which visited Surinam in June 1983.

The press was muzzled simultaneously with the execution of the fifteen critics. Military units had even destroyed several radio stations and the offices of a daily newspaper. The sole exception, the daily *De Ware Tijd*, continued to roll from the presses, but took on the function of mouthpiece for the regime. Among the broadcasting media, only the government's radio station remained on the air. A special decree of 7 May 1983 placed even further limitations on the freedom of speech. This decree banned the distribution and reproduction of information endangering national peace or security. The military's position of power made it almost impossible to demand civil rights. The 1983 OAS report spoke of an atmosphere of 'great fear'.

Following considerable international criticism, the regime made attempts to somewhat restore its tarnished image. Accordingly, several of the private media that had been closed down a year and a half earlier were allowed to resume operations as from 1 May 1984. These media were, however, bound by codes of conduct which effectively prevented any really free reporting. The prime minister himself was personally responsible for ensuring the enforcement of these codes. The media were prohibited from publishing any report potentially damaging to the country's established order. Foreign reports dealing with the Surinamese government could only be published with the prime minister's permission. Wim Udenhout, Prime Minister at the time, said: 'permission will not be given to those who, under the guise of freedom of speech, intend to hinder the achievement of our national goals by making an issue of the legitimacy of the revolution' (cited by *Surinfo*, July 1984, p. 12). Furthermore, both the National Information Service and the official Surinamese News Agency (SNA) were placed under direct military control.

The Prime Minister did indeed exercise his power in this regard. The daily *De West*, for example, was required to place an item from the National Information Service on its front page of 23 February 1985 under the headline 'Prime Minister Udenhout reprimands *De West* for non-national stance'. *De West* had enraged the regime by relegating reports of Commander-in-Chief Bouterse's visit to Colombia to its inside pages. The day after the incident, *De West* opened its front page with an eight-column report from the National Information Service: 'Colombia visit extremely successful for Surinam'.

Under the circumstances, Surinamese journalists considered it advisable to impose a considerable degree of self-censorship. Only the Church-affiliated papers continued to provide fairly open criticism of the regime. In February 1984, the priest Sebastiaan Mulder, editor-in-chief of the *Omhoog* bishopric newspaper, was detained and interrogated on several occasions after the publication of a series of articles dealing with the violent deportation of thousands of Guyanese workers and their families.

On an apparently different tack came the rescinding in August 1984 of the curfew that had been in force since the attempted coup by Surendre Rambocus on 11 March 1982. In addition, a National Institute for Human Rights was set up by decree on 10 January 1985. This institute was empowered to receive information about, to investigate and comment on human rights matters, but it could hardly be termed independent. As the Inter-American Commission for Human Rights stated in its third report on Surinam of 10 November 1986, this was an official institute 'staffed with direct links both to the government and to the military'. The virtual lack of public confidence in this body also quickly became apparent.

These measures adopted by the regime certainly did not entail the end to human rights violations. Many complaints were made in particular concerning the activities of the military police, who had taken over increasingly the tasks of the civilian police force, and whose unlimited investigative powers made monitoring extremely difficult. The second report from the above-mentioned OAS organization (October 1985) documented a number of cases of the torture and intimidation of detainees. The report also noted that a climate of intimidation and arbitrariness continued to reign, owing to the activities of the military police. The OAS report commented that no system of legal redress appeared to exist in the country with regard to national security matters. Furthermore, it stated: 'such a situation allows other abuses, damages the respect for and effectiveness of the courts and leads to the constitutionalisation of lawlessness' (OAS, 2 October 1985).

A certain degree of improvement in the field of human rights appeared to be possible through the participation by the old political parties in the government and Supreme Council. On 25 February 1986, Decree A-21 lifted the state of emergency that had been in force since August 1980. Yet the Inter-American Commission on Human Rights, which has for years monitored the situation in Surinam, said in its third report on that country:

In spite of this progress, the Commission considers that the right to freedom and opinion, expression and thought dissemination is still severely limited in Suriname ... Data gathered by the Inter-American Commission on Human Rights in 1986 allows it to take note of certain measures being taken for the return of civilian rule in Surinam but [it notes] that it still falls short of securing the effective exercise of the rights and freedoms recognized in the American Declaration of the Rights and Duties of Man.

Human rights problems have surfaced once again with the rise of guerrilla warfare in East Surinam, where the 'Jungle Commando' or Surinamese National Liberation Army is active. This guerrilla Army is based in the region populated largely by Bush Negroes, and enjoys widespread support among this ethnic group. In various raids, the National Army has removed a large number of Bush Negroes from their villages and detained them in military camps without any formal charges being pressed. In order to circumvent involvement by the legal system, the term *kazerning* (barracking) has been applied to these internal deportations. Various reports have stated that many Bush Negroes have been killed while in military detention. The national press has been prohibited from publishing any unofficial reports about the conflict in East Surinam and a state of emergency was proclaimed for this area as from 1 December 1986, allowing the Army free rein.

According to a United States State Department report published in February 1987, at least 244 civilians were killed during National Army raids in December 1986. The report stated: 'According to credible eyewitness reports non-combatant Bush Negroes, including women and children, were massacred by the military combatting the insurgency in eastern Surinam. There have also been widespread reports of military death squads operating on government instruction against Bush Negroes.'

4 The Economy of Surinam

The Colonial Period

Surinam entered the world economy as early as 1650, when the British began the permanent colonization of this section of the 'Wild coast of Guyana'. Their goal was the exploitation of the available arable land with the help of slave labour, in order to meet the growing demand for exotic foods, alcohol and tobacco on Western European markets. Yet Surinam's exploitation as a plantation economy truly came into its own after 1667, the year in which this country was conquered by the Dutch, who greatly expanded the sugar cane production begun by the British and began producing other staples for export.

The rise of sugar production in Surinam must be viewed within the context of the increasing economic importance of this production in the world economy of that day. Until the beginning of the sixteenth century, sugar was a luxury product. During this period, the price of sugar in England was so exorbitant that it 'was considered too extravagant for prudent purchase, and too much to expect from any host' (quoted in Woytinsky & Woytinsky, 1953, p. 566). The production of sugar gradually increased during the sixteenth century, and in the seventeenth century it became a mass commodity, available even to Western Europe's lowest income groups.

This growth in sugar consumption could be largely credited to the forceful increase in sugar production, with the use of African slave labour, on the new American continents and particularly in Brazil. According to Robock (1975), sugar production was the most important economic activity in Brazil in the mid-sixteenth century. With the help of slave labour, this country became the world's largest producer of sugar. The sugar production in north-eastern Brazil was controlled to a significant extent by the Dutch, who not only had the necessary capital and know-how but also controlled a large portion of the slave trade as well.

As from the second half of the seventeenth century, sugar production was transferred from north-eastern Brazil to the Caribbean region. This was due to the expulsion of the Dutch from Brazil, at the urging of the British. In return for its aid to Portugal in regaining independence from Spain in 1640,

Britain obtained extensive trading rights, formalized in treaties, for all the Portuguese colonies (Manchester, 1969, Chap. 2). An additional cause of Brazil's loss of pre-eminence as a sugar producer was the exhaustion of its soil.

With the exception of two short hiatuses, namely during the Napoleonic Wars in 1799–1802 and 1804–15, Surinam had always been part of the Dutch realm. Under the rule of the Dutch, who—as already noted—played a prominent role in the production and distribution of the crucially important production of sugar and the trade in African slaves, Surinam became a blossoming plantation economy. At the end of the seventeenth century, the country was one of the world's largest sugar producers. During the eighteenth century, Surinam was also the site for the enormous production for export of other major staples such as coffee, cacao and cotton.

The economic development of Surinam during this period was determined by the plantation owners, and it was their interests that assumed a central position. Activities related to the production of staples were largely financed by the then-flowering trading houses of Amsterdam. The enormous profits made during this period therefore also largely flowed to The Netherlands.

By as early as the end of the eighteenth century, Surinam's importance as a region of exploitation was waning. The 1773 crisis on the Amsterdam exchange is often viewed as the beginning of Surinam's decline as a profitable colony. Many planters, no longer able to receive credit, were forced to sell their plantations. This resulted in absenteeism since most of these plantations were bought up by the largely Amsterdam-based creditors who did not assume the role of planter themselves but commonly turned the plantation management over to an overseer.

Surinam's decline as a profitable plantation economy continued steadily during the nineteenth century. This was the result of structural changes in the world economy. The most important of these changes were as follows:

— the decline in the economic importance of cane sugar resulting from the greatly increased supply on the world market and particularly owing to the rise of beet sugar during the nineteenth century;
— the incorporation of Africa as a production region in the world economy, the accompanying ban on the slave trade in the first decade of the nineteenth century and the abolition of slavery in Surinam in 1863;
— the stiff competition with staple commodities from Asia, particularly owing to reduced transport costs resulting from the opening of the Suez Canal in 1869.

Attempts to continue exploiting the country as a profitable production area, by the importation of indentured labourers from China, Madeira, India and Indonesia, were not successful. Owing to Surinam's greatly decreased economic significance, The Netherlands' interest in this West Indian colony also waned. Increasing interest was shown in Indonesia, which had vast natural resources and an extensive trading market. With the exception of a 'mini goldrush' during the period 1880–1920, in which it appeared that the supply of gold was much smaller than had been hoped, and the considerable production of natural rubber during the first three decades of this century, no lucrative production activities took place in Surinam for a long time. The country became an impoverished and dependent colony, often requiring subsidies from the mother country to cover a major part of its government spending.

The Dutch government's interest in Surinam as an exploitation region had decreased so sharply that even when bauxite was discovered there in 1898 little enthusiasm was shown for its extraction or processing. Furthermore, the only know-how present in The Netherlands at that time regarding the production of non-ferrous metals was represented by the NV Billiton Company, a firm of modest size and ambitions which had concentrated its activities in Indonesia, now Holland's major exploitation region. Furthermore, the industrial use of aluminium was still limited at that time. By the time Billiton finally began prospecting for bauxite in Surinam, in 1939, the most lucrative bauxite reserves were already in the hands of the American ALCOA aluminium concern. In this context it is worth noting that it is not at all improbable that the Dutch government had approved ALCOA's 1928 bauxite agreement with Surinam (an extremely favourable agreement for the aluminium concern) in order to keep the Americans (and, notably, Standard Oil of New Jersey—now known as EXXON) out of Indonesia, and to prevent Standard Oil's participation in the exploitation of the Djambi oil reserves on Sumatra in favour of the Dutch oil company De Bataafsche Petroleum Maatschappij (currently known as Shell). Another interesting point in these considerations is that the United States Secretary of the Treasury at that time, Andrew Mellon, was also ALCOA's largest shareholder.

In view of the still limited industrial uses for aluminium, the economic significance of Surinam's bauxite reserves during this initial phase was limited. Yet the mounting demand for aluminium during the Second World War period, as a result of the burgeoning arms industry and the aviation industry in particular, once again provided Surinam's economy with new stimuli. Surinam became the major foreign supplier of bauxite for the American war effort, a relationship that resulted in the stationing of

American soldiers in Surinam. After the Second World War, aluminium was applied in an increasing number of industrial spheres. By the end of the 1940s Surinam, at 2m. tonnes per year, was the world's largest producer of bauxite (Woytinsky & Woytinsky, 1953, p. 808).

The Netherlands' renewed interest in Surinam, demonstrated as early as 1939 by Billiton's activities there, increased even further after the Second World War. This revived interest can be attributed both to the general trend of this period, in which the Third World countries were further incorporated into the world economy as suppliers of raw materials for the unprecedentedly forceful growth of production in the industrial centres, as well as to the problems between The Netherlands and Indonesia. Following a violent struggle, Indonesia won independence in 1949, and The Netherlands lost many of its economic interests in that country.

Although the promise had been made as early as 1942 that Surinam would be allowed to look after its own interests within a re-arrangement of the Dutch realm, talks on this matter only began in 1948 and it was not until December 1954 that the 'new realm' became a political fact.

The Period of the 'Koninkrijks Statutt' (Statute of the Kingdom of The Netherlands)

The Netherlands provided development aid for Surinam as from 1948, the year in which the talks concerning the internal political autonomy of Surinam and The Netherlands Antilles began. This aid began in the form of a Welfare Fund, with The Netherlands providing the sum of DG (Dutch guilders) 40m. (which equals SG (Surinam Guilders) 28.4m., or US$15.9m). This fund was to be used to set up the government institutions needed to draft and implement a long-term plan for Surinam's economic autonomy. The Welfare Fund programme also included the development of the country's agriculture, with the most important project being the reclamation of a polder for mechanized agriculture. This project, referred to as the Wageningen project, was intended to create scope for agricultural operations by Dutch immigrants, but ultimately it resulted in a large rice operation from which a number of Surinam's retail companies profited. An aerial surveying project and a number of small infrastructural and social projects were also financed from this fund. The sum allotted in the Welfare Fund, which was further reduced by the 1949 devaluation of the Dutch guilder to the equivalent of roughly US$12m. for a seven-year period, was obviously too small to initiate large-scale economic activities.

A ten-year plan and two five-year plans were subsequently implemented after the exhaustion of the Welfare Fund and during the period of the Koninkrijks Statuut. Their goals displayed great similarities, the most important of which were:

— the achievement of greater economic growth, to help close the gap with the wealthy industrialized countries and to raise the standard of living of the lowest income groups in particular;
— the combatting of massive structural unemployment;
— the reduction of economic dependence;
— the diversification of the economy.

It should be noted here that the documents for the ten-year plan placed greater emphasis on improving the standard of living of the lowest income groups than did those for the five-year plans. The objectives of the five-year plans were primarily those of economic growth, and their development strategy was based on the Harrod/Domar growth model, Rostow's stages of economic growth—in particular the requirement of a leading sector in the take-off state—and Rosenstein-Rodan's 'Big Push' concept.

It was agreed that some SG 127m. would be reserved for the implementation of the ten-year plan. The Netherlands was to provide one-third of this sum in the form of a donation and one-third in the form of a loan. The remaining one-third was to be supplied by Surinam itself. Yet it quickly became clear that Surinam's government could not meet its agreed contribution to the development fund, for the country faced a continual struggle with public spending deficits. In view of the massive structural unemployment, successive governments had continually expanded the civil service, placing permanent pressure on wage-spending for lower officials. It was therefore decided to regard those investments in the country's economic development made by Surinam's government since 1955, unrelated to the working programme of the ten-year plan, as part of Surinam's contribution to the development fund. Yet the Surinam government continued to struggle with financial problems, even after it had been agreed that the development aid received since 1964 within the framework of the EEC's development fund would also be regarded as part of Surinam's contribution to the ten-year plan.

At the end of the 1950s, per capita national income was rising at the rate of only about 1.5 per cent annually. In order to achieve higher growth, the fund for the ten-year plan was supplemented with SG 80m. and the period of the plan was extended by two years. An 'Integral Development Plan' was set up, consisting of the revision and expansion of the ten-year plan and forming the basis of the first five-year plan. The prevailing desire at that time, to greatly increase development investments in order to accelerate economic growth, is evidenced by The Netherlands' provison of DG 240m. for the first five-year plan, which began in 1967, while the Dutch contribution to the second five-year plan totalled DG 400m.

As mentioned above, Surinam was unable to make a substantial contribution from its own coffers to the development investment, and virtually all the development projects were financed by foreign development aid. To become eligible for development aid funding, each project had first to be presented to the Dutch government for approval. The Netherlands therefore also determined to a great degree Surinam's internal development policy. The aim, by means of large government investments, was to create a favourable entrepreneurial climate for attracting activities by private firms. This was in accordance with the 'industrialization by invitation' strategy applied by other countries in the Caribbean region.

Official discussions occasionally took place concerning the use of this strategy to create an optimal entrepreneurial climate, and a parliamentary protest was lodged against the provision of an inordinate number of facilities for foreign firms. Accordingly, parliamentary resistance was met in 1956 from the MPs Johan Pengel and Jaggernath Lachmon, the respective floor leaders of the NPS and VHP opposition parties, when the Unity Front government announced its plans to award a fifteen-year monopoly for the export of Surinam shrimp and fish products to the American businessman E. S. Schweig's SAIL fish-processing firm. The government had also said that it planned to grant this firm tax-free status for a period of ten years. The bill which was to make these concessions to Schweig possible was approved by the Staten (Surinam's parliament)—albeit with a majority of only one parliamentary vote (Dew, 1978, pp. 114 ff.).

Discussion concerning the excessive domination of Surinam's economy by foreign firms also assumed a central position when this same government announced its plans in 1957 to close an agreement with ALCOA for the construction of the Brokopondo Dam on the Surinam River, to provide hydroelectric power for the production of aluminium for the EC market. The Surinam government of the day first addressed an unsuccessful appeal to The Netherlands to finance this project. When it also appeared impossible to raise sufficient capital on the European market to carry out this project, the Surinam government closed an agreement with ALCOA—which was presented as a joint venture—whereby ALCOA would finance the building of the dam itself on the condition that the dam and accompanying electrical installations would remain ALCOA's property for seventy-five years, and that the government of Surinam would assume the costs of the soil and hydraulic testing, the clearing of the jungle and the resettlement costs for the inhabitants of the jungle area around the dam. Despite the fact that even the prominent coalition MP David Findlay, the most outspoken defender of the Schweig contract, expressed deep concern about the sharp reinforcement of the already dominant position of foreign concerns in general, and ALCOA in particular, the government proposal to do business with ALCOA won parliamentary approval.

The implemented policy did not prove very effective, however. Despite high infrastructural investment, it was not possible to attract enough private investment in the productive sector to achieve continuing economic development. Furthermore, all major private investments were carried out by foreign firms. Inspired by the rising nationalism of the Third World, which began in the 1950s to result in the nationalization of and/or participation by national governments in the activities of foreign firms, Surinam's government introduced the joint-venture strategy in the late 1960s. It was stated that, in view of the national industry's apparent inability to develop, the joint-venture strategy was applied as from the late 1960s. The government was to participate in foreign firms and, at a later date, offer the shares it had obtained in these companies to interested parties from Surinam, so that 'Surinamization' of the industry could be achieved. Owing to the structural government spending deficits, however, Surinam planned to finance its participation in foreign firms with development funds from The Netherlands. Since many of the firms in question were Dutch in origin, the implementation of this joint-venture strategy was a long and troublesome task. The Surinamization of industry only got into its stride from the late 1970s, when the profitability of the foreign investment in Surinam had decreased sharply as a result of the premature exhaustion of resources, obsolete production equipment owing to the failure to invest in new technologies and the excessively sharp rise in the cost of labour.

The most important private investments had taken place in the bauxite industry. During the 1960s, the ALCOA and Billiton bauxite concerns had even greatly expanded their activities in Surinam. In addition to the production of this raw material, a portion of the bauxite was also processed into alumina. Furthermore, ALCOA had built a dam on the Surinam River to generate hydroelectric power for the production of aluminium destined for the European market. Although the government did make infrastructural investments for the benefit of the bauxite firms, it can safely be stated that these private investments were clearly autonomous in nature (see Chin, 1971, p. 145ì). In addition, foreign firms—largely Dutch and American—had made considerable investments in forestry and the wood-processing industry, in agriculture and fisheries, induced by infrastructural government investments financed by foreign development aid.

Virtually no foreign investments were made in the manufacturing sector, and particularly not in the production of finished products; indeed, such investments were not stimulated to any great extent. Within the framework of the world economy, Surinam is not an attractive site for industrial production. The domestic market is too small for profitable operations by most industries. Furthermore, the country's labour costs are too high for labour-intensive, export-orientated industrial activities. The relatively high labour costs are the result of the relatively high wage level, prompted by the high wages in the bauxite industry, while the low labour productivity outside the bauxite industry is the result of the bauxite firms creaming off the best workers from the labour market. Small-scale activities by local firms directed at the domestic market have had practically no connection with industry but, with the exception of the agricultural sector, have taken place primarily in the fields of trade and other services. The only major industrial activities carried out in Surinam are several stages of the processing of the native raw materials of bauxite and wood. The advantages of these activities for the foreign firms lie primarily in the resulting lower transport costs owing to the vast reductions in volume and weight and in economies of scale in the production of alumina.

The development aid-financed government investments, which totalled an average of SG 3m. (US\$ 1.7m.) during the Welfare Fund period, increased steadily as from 1955. During the period 1955-9, the average annual investments totalled SG 9m.; in the 1960s, this rose to about SG 18m. and during the first half of the 1970s average annual government investments had reached the level of around SG 47m. It should not be forgotten in this context that considerable sums of EEC development aid were also received as from 1964. The investments financed with EEC development aid funds during the second half of the 1960s totalled SG 4m. annually, and rose to an annual average of SG 5m. during the period 1970-5. As already noted, government investments were financed almost entirely from foreign development aid. It was only during the period 1965-8, when government revenues from the bauxite industry greatly increased, that the government delved into its own coffers to make substantial investments in development projects. Yet the share of government investment financed by Surinam itself, even during this period, came to only one-fifth of the total of such investments made.

Table 4.1 shows the sectoral distribution of government investments for the period 1955-74. The item 'Others' consists primarily of investments in housing and public health and spending on the management and administra-

Table 4.1 Total accumulated development
disbursement by major sectors,
1955–1975 (percentages)

	%
Agriculture	22
Forestry	11
Mining	6
Industry	2
Transport, Public Works, Communications	32
Aerial Surveying	6
Others*	21
Total	100

* primarily consist of the management and adminis-
tration of development aid, public health and housing.
Sources: General Bureau of Statistics, Planning
Bureau of Surinam.

tion of the development aid received. If one takes into consideration that
government investments in agriculture, forestry and mining were largely of
an infrastructural nature, it is clear that virtually all investments made by the
government during this period can be termed infrastructural.

Private investments, which averaged approximately SG 20m. annually
during the 1950s, rose sharply during the 1960s to the average annual sum of
some SG 70m. This was primarily due to the extremely large investments in
the alumina and aluminium factories, and to the Brokopondo hydroelectric
project on the Surinam River for generating energy needed for industry.
During the period 1964–6, when these investments had reached their zenith,
an annual average of almost SG 110m. was invested in the private sector.
Although private investments did decrease sharply after 1966, they remained
at a level higher than that prior to 1964. At the end of the 1960s private
investments totalled more than SG 60m. annually, and an annual average of
SG 80m. was invested in the private sector during the period 1970–4. Until
the end of the 1960s, by far the largest share of private investments was made
by foreign firms. After this period local private firms gradually began
increasing their investments. However, these investments were not only

modest in scope and primarily aimed at the small domestic market, but they were also largely made within the services sector.

Despite increasing government investments within the framework of development aid, and the large private investments by foreign firms, Surinam's economic growth, with the exception of a short period in the mid-1960s, was not strong. During the period 1955–63, GNP increased by 4 to 5 per cent annually. As a result of momentum gained in the production of alumina and aluminium, real GNP showed exceptionally high growth of some 13 per cent annually during the period 1964–8. After 1968, economic growth decreased sharply. During the period 1968–70, a real growth in GNP of some 5 per cent annually was still noted, but after this period there was scarcely any economic growth to speak of. Real GNP increased by only about 1 per cent annually during the period 1971–5. Yet there was no decrease in the average standard of living during this period, owing to the concurrent and massive emigration to The Netherlands. The emigration surplus during the period 1966–75 totalled some 110,000 people, of whom 37,600 emigrated during the years 1974–5, immediately prior to the granting of independence (Central Bank of Surinam, 1974, p. 61).

The figures in Table 4.2 show not only the firm dominance of the bauxite industry, but also that activities in this sector had reached the height of their intensity during the late 1960s and the early 1970s. It should be noted in this context that the level of production activities in this sector, controlled as it is by multinational corporations, is determined to a significant extent by both the size and quality of Surinam's bauxite reserves and by the reserves available to these firms in other bauxite-producing countries throughout the world. Table 4.2 therefore shows a decrease in the bauxite industry's share in the Gross Domestic Product after 1971. This was due in part to the emergence of bauxite extraction and processing in new regions—primarily in Australia, Guinea and Brazil.

The forestry and wood processing activities, also dominated by foreign companies, had declined since the late 1960s owing to the premature exhaustion of resources. The Dutch Bruynzeel company, which controlled activities in this sector, was not required to engage in reforestation, and, despite the urging of several Dutch experts, successive governments in The Netherlands refused until the end of the 1960s to provide funds to maintain Surinam's timber supply. After this time, reforestation took place only on a modest scale.

The agricultural sector displayed a minor relative fall during the period 1955–75. Yet, in absolute terms, agricultural activities increased during this period. This is largely attributable to the activities of foreign—mostly Dutch

Table 4.2 Gross Domestic Product by sector and Gross National Product, 1955–1975

	1955	1960	1964	1968	1971	1975
Agriculture and fishery	13	12	11	11	8	10
Forestry and wood processing	4	4	4	3	3	2
Mining and bauxite processing	34	28	27	32	35	26
Industry (including water, gas, electricity and construction)	8	9	10	10	10	10
Commerce and banking	20	22	21	21	20	25
Government	17	20	22	19	19	21
Other services	4	5	5	4	5	6
GDP at current factor cost (%)	100	100	100	100	100	100
(SG m.)	112	178	227	445	538	741
Net transfer of profits (SG m.)	5	28	29	72	85	39
GNP at current factor cost (SG m.)	107	148	198	373	453	702
GNP at current market prices (SG m.)	123	176	234	422	515	911
GDP (factor cost, SG m., 1970 prices)	173	242	278	463	533	501
GNP (factor cost, SG m., 1970 prices)	165	201	242	388	450	474

US$ = SG 1.785.
  Sources: Planning Bureau of Surinam; General Bureau of Statistics, Central Bank of Surinam.

and American—export-orientated firms. The most important of these dealt in rice, palm-oil, bananas, citrus fruit and fish.

Although local enterprises were particularly active in the services sector, this sector was nevertheless largely controlled by foreign firms. Banks and insurance companies in particular were in foreign hands. Foreign firms also controlled the most important activities in the construction sector. Even the gas and electricity utilities were controlled by a foreign company, the Dutch OGEM.

In view of the construction sector's rapid growth during this period shown in Table 4.2, owing to the great increase in development aid, the table shows the significance of the truly industrial activities to have been strikingly limited. The figures in this table also indicate strong growth in the public sector. This was primarily the result of the steadily growing ranks of civil servants. This massive expansion of the government apparatus can be attributed largely to the fact that politically favoured sons at every level were regularly added to the public payroll.

The true domination of Surinam's economy by foreign firms during this period is reflected much more clearly in the export figures shown in Table 4.3. Virtually all export activities during this period were carried out by these firms. The share of the multinational bauxite companies in total exports, already at 80 per cent in 1955, rose in particular from 1964 to 91 per cent by 1971. Although the share of bauxite and its derivatives in total exports fell sharply after 1971, in the mid-1970s it was still at about the 1964 level. The remaining exports, consisting of lumber, wood products, fish and other agricultural products—mainly rice, bananas and citrus fruit—were controlled to a great extent by foreign companies.

Surinam continued in its dependence on imports of capital goods, fuels, many raw and auxiliary materials and consumer goods. It is worth noting that even many foodstuffs and simple manufactured consumer goods consistently made up a substantial part of total imports. Although the figures in Table 4.4 would indicate that the share of consumer goods in total imports decreased during the period in question, this can sooner be attributed to the rapid

Table 4.3 Exports of principal commodities, 1955–1975 (percentages)

	1955 %	1960 %	1964 %	1968 %	1971 %	1973 %	1975 %
Bauxite	80	81	82	36	28	27	26
Alumina				35	47	45	44
Aluminium				16	16	14	13
Total bauxite sector	80	81	82	87	91	86	83
Agricultural products	10	10	11	9	6	9	14
Lumber and wood products	10	8	6	4	3	4	3
Other products	1	1	1	–		1	–
Total exports (%)	100	100	100	100	100	100	100
(SG m.)*	52	83	90	219	295	320	466

* Current Surinam guilders = < 0.5%.

Sources: General Bureau of Statistics of Surinam; Central Bank of Surinam.

Table 4.4 Imports of major product groups, 1955–1975

	1955	1960	1964	1968	1971	1973	1975
Fuels	10	7	7	9	13	13	21
Raw and auxiliary materials	32	35	42	40	41	41	39
Capital goods	17	24	27	22	17	17	18
Consumer goods	41	34	24	29	29	29	22
Total imports (%)	100	100	100	100	100	100	100
(SG m.)	52	102	152	189	238	281	454

Source: General Bureau of Statistics.

relative growth of imports from the other product groups than to import substitutions of consumer goods.

Because of the dominance of the foreign companies' activities, a large share of productive value was drained from the country (see Table 4.2). During the period 1955–75, capital imports in the form of direct foreign investments totalled some Sf 460m. On the other hand, profit transferrals by foreign firms during this period totalled Sf 950m. (also, see Chin, 1971, p. 1454). This only includes official profit transfers and not any over-invoicing of imports or under-invoicing of exports.

The figures in Table 4.5 clearly show the United States and The Netherlands to be Surinam's most important trading partners. Worthy of note is the forceful decrease in the share of exports destined for the United States as from 1967, and the simultaneous relative rise in exports to European countries. This was the result of the burgeoning in Surinam of the production of alumina and aluminium for the European market. The production of alumina for export to Europe is primarily intended for Norway and The Netherlands, where further processing into aluminium can take place at low energy costs. The production of aluminium is especially aimed at export to the EC market, where Surinam, as an associated country, enjoys preferential status. In addition, exports of agricultural products to Europe, particularly to West Germany and The Netherlands, have increased.

The import figures indicate that The Netherlands' share has shown a relatively significant decrease. Imports from the United States exhibited a slight decrease, while the share of East Asian imports clearly increased. This is primarily due to a sizeable increase in imports from Japan. The large share of

Table 4.5 International trade according to major trading partners, 1957–1974 (percentages)

	Import				Export			
	1960	1968	1971	1975	1960	1968	1971	1975
United States	34	37	33	33	75	53	48	42
Netherlands	30	24	23	18	8	10	10	18
Other EEC	10	9	16	14	2	13	14	11
Scandinavia (not incl. Denmark)	–	1	–	1	–	8	7	12
Caribbean & Latin America	10	12	14	22	7	4	6	4
East Asia	5	7	10	8	2	5	4	4
Others	11*	10*	4	4	6	7	11	9
Total	100	100	100	100	100	100	100	100

* Including the United Kingdom = < 0.5%.
Source: General Bureau of Statistics.

imports from the Caribbean region in 1974 can be attributed to the considerable rise in the import value of petroleum and petroleum products as a result of the oil crisis of 1973–4. The imports of petroleum and petroleum products came largely from Trinidad and Tobago.

As we have already noted, economic growth was modest in comparison with the government investments financed by development aid, with the exception of the brief period during which alumina and aluminium came into full production. With the exception of the period 1964–8, the growth of per capita income was no greater than that in the wealthier countries. This meant that the major goal of the five-year plans in particular, namely the closing of the gap in public welfare with the wealthy, industrialized countries, was not achieved. Per capita income in Surinam did, however, rise more rapidly than in the majority of other Third World countries. With a per capita income of some US\$ 1,100 in 1975, Surinam could be ranked among the 'Middle Income Countries'.

The rise in production from the early 1950s to the mid-1970s did not create enough jobs to abate the widespread unemployment. Despite the massive emigration to The Netherlands from the early 1970s and the absorption of workers by the government apparatus, estimates of the country's unemployment on the eve of political independence range— depending on whether or not hidden unemployment in the agricultural sector in particular is taken into account—between 15 and 30 per cent of the potential labour force. The planned reduction of Surinam's massive structural unemployment, another major goal of the multi-annual plans, was therefore a decisive failure. This is largely attributable to the lack of emphasis placed by successive Surinam governments on labour-intensive production activities. Thus the bauxite sector, which contributed 26 per cent of the Gross Domestic Product in 1975, provided jobs for only 7 per cent of the country's labour force in that year, and no more than 9 per cent of that labour force worked in the industrial sector (Central Bank of Surinam, 1974/5, p. 62). Furthermore, the labour supply increased rapidly owing to migration from rural areas to the capital, Paramaribo, and the high population growth of some 3 per cent during this period.

The average welfare level rose considerably during this period, yet the lowest income groups scarcely profited from this development. These groups primarily consist of the many unemployed who, because of the virtual absence of social benefits, live at or close to the minimum subsistence level. In view of the strongly one-sided economic structure indicated by the figures on the sectoral distribution of both GDP and exports—a structure which is furthermore highly dependent on foreign economic involvement—it can be stated that, with the exception of the achievement of high economic growth during the period 1964–8, the most important goals of the multi-annual plans were not achieved.

After Independence

When the Surinam government announced after the 1973 elections that Surinam desired independence, the Dutch government of the day enthusiastically seized the opportunity to rid itself of its last-but-one colony. With far too much haste, Surinam and Dutch experts drew up a Multi-Annual Development Programme (MDP) involving gigantic investments to the tune of some SG 4.5bn. (around DG 6.7bn.). It was agreed that The Netherlands would make the sum of DG 3.5bn. available for the implementation of this plan. Yet, of this sum, DG 800m. was to be placed in reserves. Of this reserve, DG 500m. was earmarked for the provision of guarantees for loans which Surinam would take out on the international capital market for use in sound development projects, while the remaining DG 300m. was reserved for supplementary financing on the basis of strict parity with Surinam. The sum of DG 2.7bn. therefore remained for the co-financing of the MDP. In addition, once Surinam was granted independence, The Netherlands would write off its former colony's debt, which had risen as a result of development aid to around DG 500m. The commitment of this unusually large sum in development aid for a population of only around 400,000 people over a period of ten to fifteen years, as well as the remittance of the debt, played a major role in the fact that Surinam gained independence from The Netherlands as early as 25 November 1975.

The MDP's major objective was to achieve high growth through the implementation of the 'West Surinam' project. This project primarily consisted of the extraction of bauxite reserves in the Bakhuis region of western Surinam, and the on-site processing of this material into alumina and aluminium. The production of aluminium was to be made possible with the aid of hydroelectric power generated by dams to be built in the neighbouring Kabalebo-Avanavero region. Despite the fact that the MDP set as a goal the diversification of economic activities, actual policy was aimed at preserving the bauxite sector as the major sector of growth. Since no appreciable growth in this sector could be expected on the basis of the depleted bauxite reserves in central and eastern Surinam, new reserves had to be tapped. In addition, vast tracts in western Surinam would have to be cleared for the benefit of agricultural production and forestry, and high expectations were held with regard to industrial production.

Plans for tapping the bauxite reserves in western Surinam had existed even in the early 1960s. During this period, various multinational bauxite concerns had shown real interest in such activities. Following years of negotiation with various concerns, the second Pengel government signed a guideline agreement in 1968 with a consortium consisting of the Dutch Billiton concern, the French Pechiney company—which produced aluminium in The Netherlands with the help of Dutch government-guaranteed low energy prices—ALCOA and ORMET, another American concern. Since Billiton—bothered at the time by a shortage of bauxite reserves—would play a central role in these planned activities, it could be taken for granted that the necessary large infrastructural investments would be financed with Dutch development aid. The consortium planned to extract the bauxite in the Bakhuis region for export purposes. Depending on the profitability of the project, the consortium was also willing to process a portion of the bauxite on-site into alumina, as well as to cooperate at a later stage in the production of aluminium on the condition that hydroelectric power could be generated in western Surinam at sufficiently low cost.

To the great amazement of many outsiders, the next Surinam government, after the resignation of the second Pengel cabinet in 1969, had within one year signed an agreement in principle with an entirely new candidate, the American Reynolds concern, for the tapping of the Bakhuis reserves. The agreement became even more questionable when it appeared that Surinam had committed itself to building a railway from the Bakhuis range to Apoera on the Corantijn River, where a transhipment harbour was to be built. The agreement also stipulated that Surinam was to ensure that the Corantijn would remain permanently navigable. Less of a surprise was the fact that the planned extraction of the Bakhuis reserves did not take place in the following years. Reynolds had little interest in beginning activities before the Surinam government had finished all the above-mentioned infrastructural projects, and The Netherlands was unwilling to allocate large sums of development aid for the tapping of western Surinam reserves without participation by Billiton.

By 1974, when the talks with The Netherlands concerning independence and the financing of the Multi-Annual Development Plan began, no major economic activities had been carried out in western Surinam. The contract with Reynolds was quickly cancelled, which cost Surinam the sum of US$ 7m., and an agreement in principle was signed with Billiton (which had in the meantime been acquired by the SHELL concern) for a cooperative venture regarding all new developments in Surinam's bauxite sector.

Owing to the discovery of large and lucrative bauxite reserves in other parts of the world—namely in Australia, Guinea and Brazil—the economic importance of Surinam bauxite, and therefore the interest on the part of the multinational bauxite concerns, had sharply decreased since the 1960s. It is therefore not only remarkable that the dubious west Surinam project assumed a central position in the Multi-Annual Development Plan, but also regrettable that the Dutch government, on the eve of Surinam's independence, had committed itself to co-financing this plan within the framework of development aid.

Within the space of several years, massive problems had arisen in the implementation of the MDP, and it became clear that this plan would come nowhere near achieving the results suggested at the time to Surinam's people. During the period 1976-9, the government spent SG 580m. on development aid, of which some 60 per cent was spent on the development of western Surinam. Approximately SG 170m. of this 60 per cent was invested in the railway for the transportation of bauxite from the Bakhuis region to the harbour of Apoera. Yet, in 1979, when the railway was almost completed, it suddenly appeared that the bauxite concerns had no interest in tapping the Bakhuis reserves. Only then was a commission set up, consisting of representatives from Surinam's government, Billiton and ALCOA, to investigate the possibility of profitably exploiting these reserves. The commission quickly concluded that the Bakhuis bauxite could not compete on the world market, and that the processing of this bauxite into alumina at Apoera would be no profitable venture. The commission stated that the only alternative worth being examined was to transport the ore for processing to the existing ALCOA/Billiton alumina plant at Paranam.

The years immediately following independence witnessed great economic growth as a result of both the extremely large development aid-financed government investments, which increased from some SG 40m. to SG 50m. per year during the first half of the 1970s to an annual average of some SG 160m. during the period 1976-9, and the comparably sharp rise in private investments to an annual average of some SG 200m. during this period. Real GNP rose during the period 1975-8 by an annual average of more than 12 per cent. However, this explosive growth quickly stagnated, and GNP growth actually fell to 2 per cent in 1979. It then became clear that the development strategy had failed.

Before this time, it was repeatedly asserted that the government investments financed with development aid could not provide sufficient growth because of their limited scope, which prevented the implementation of a 'Big Push'. Yet, in 1979, it was shown that government investments—even when extremely large—did not automatically result in continuing economic growth, as had been imagined at the introduction of the Harrod/Domar-Rostow-Rosenstein-Rodan strategy. It also became clear that the large private investments in the alumina and aluminium industry during the mid-1960s had been autonomous ones made on the basis of a fairly concrete turnover and profit expectations. The same applied to a number of other, smaller-scale investments, such as those made in the shrimp fisheries for the benefit of export. The government investments had prompted a few private—largely foreign—investments in other primary sectors such as forestry, wood processing and agriculture (particularly with regard to the production of rice and palm-oil). However, most of these private investments, and particularly those by local enterprises, had been made in service-sector (and especially in trading) activities which did not contribute to continuing economic growth.

The high marginal (macro) capital coefficient, which in fact indicates low productivity on the part of the large development investments, comes as no surprise. As indicated in Table 4.6, the investments made during this period were also largely of an infrastructural nature. Just as before independence,

Table 4.6 Total accumulated development aid disbursement by major sectors, 1976–1979

Agriculture	13
Forestry	6
Mining	3
Industry	2
Transport, Public Works, Communications	30
Aerial surveying	4
Housing	8
Others*	34
Total (%)	100
(SG m.)	569

* Primarily consisting of the management and administration of development aid, preparatory costs of projects, public health and educational facilities.

Source: Planning Bureau of Surinam: Central Bank of Surinam.

investments in the agricultural sector, mining and forestry were largely dedicated to infrastructural projects.

Table 4.7 shows a further fall in the bauxite sector's contribution to Gross Domestic Product during the period 1975–9. A decrease is also seen in the forestry and wood processing industry's share in GDP. The same applies to the agricultural sector.

As mentioned earlier, Surinam bauxite's competitive position on the world market had been weakened by the discovery of new bauxite reserves in other parts of the world. As from the early 1970s, therefore, the multinational bauxite concerns began relocating their activities to new production areas, particularly to those in Guinea, Australia and Brazil. Surinam's most lucrative reserves, like those in the other Caribbean bauxite countries, were becoming depleted. In addition, labour costs had risen sharply owing to the ever-

Table 4.7 Gross Domestic Product by sector and
Gross National Product, 1976, 1979

	1976	1979
Agriculture and fishery	9	8
Forestry and wood processing	2	2
Mining and bauxite processing	23	19
Industry (incl. gas, electricity & water and construction)	12	15
Commerce and banking	25	28
Government	22	23
Other services	7	5
Total GDP at current factor cost (%)	100	100
(SG m.)	871	1,437
GNP at current factor cost (SG m.)	804	1,360
GNP at current market prices (SG m.)	963	1,586
GDP at factor cost (SG m., 1975 prices)	816	1,047
GNP at factor cost (SG m., 1975 prices)	753	991

Sources: General Bureau of Statistics; Planning Bureau of Surinam.

increasing wage level and the transnational bauxite concerns' failure to make sufficient investments in new technologies in view of the planned relocation of their production activities.

Despite large government investments, the growth of the forestry sector stagnated. The results of reforestation could not be counted on in the short term. The joint venture with Bruynzeel had produced few results. This can be attributed both to the failing policy of the mother company itself, which was facing a financial crisis, and to the fact that Bruynzeel Surinam, after depleting the available resources, had begun withdrawing from Surinam.

In view of the large government investments financed with development aid, the post-independence results in the agricultural sector were disappointing. Major expansions in production surface and increased yield had only been achieved in mechanized rice cultivation and the palm-oil industry. The Mechanized Agricultural Foundation was nationalized in 1976. Development investments increasingly focused on large-scale, export-orientated agricultural production, with no attention granted to local processing.

The dramatic stagnation in these productive sectors—on which Surinam's economy was based—from the early 1970s was not relieved by the extremely large investments made during the period immediately following independence. The share of these three primary sectors in GDP even showed a further sharp decline, from 34 per cent in 1975 to 29 per cent in 1979. The figures in Table 4.7 also indicate the shift in favour of the service sector and the construction industry. The sector 'industry', which comprises (primarily domestic-orientated) manufacturing activities by small local firms, showed only a slight relative increase.

As from the second half of the 1960s, a concerted effort was made to reduce Surinam's heavy economic dependence. The Multi-Annual Development Programme made a strong plea for the joint-venture strategy, which was even elevated to the level of government policy. However, apart from a certain degree of success with the nationalization of the Mechanized Agricultural Foundation, and the joint venture with HVA—which was financed with large sums of development aid—this strategy produced few tangible results. The banana-growing industry had been nationalized as early as the 1960s, yet this fact must be seen within the context of world-wide economic developments. Transnational agricultural concerns had increasingly begun shedding their risk-bearing crop-production activities and concentrating on more lucrative activities related to distribution and processing. State participation in the Dutch Bruynzeel lumber company took place only after this firm had begun suffering losses after years of depleting the valuable timber reserves and systematically neglecting investments in new technologies; moreover, nothing had yet come of Surinam's participation in the vital bauxite industry.

Within this context it should be noted that even the attempts to take over the most national of activities, namely those related to the supply of gas and electricity—which as noted earlier, were in the hands of the Dutch OGEM concern—were subject to a lengthy and difficult procedure. After years of negotiations, a joint venture was agreed upon between the Surinam government and OGEM, whereby the government received 60 per cent of the shares of the new EBS (Surinam Energy Company) utility. The management of EBS, however, remained in the hands of OGEM. The nationalization of this utility only became possible after OGEM lost interest in continuing the joint venture because of the recent and massive economic problems in Surinam.

Despite the fact that the bauxite sector's share in GDP had strikingly decreased, Surinam's exports at the end of the 1970s still primarily consisted of bauxite, alumina and aluminium. In 1979, these products still accounted for 77 per cent of the country's total export value of SG 792m. The remainder of the country's export package had also undergone no essential change, and continued to consist exclusively of agricultural products—largely rice and bananas—which accounted for 15 per cent of total exports, while shrimp, wood and wood products accounted for 6 and 2 per cent of the total export package respectively.

The structure of Surinam's import package had clearly deteriorated by 1979 in comparison with 1975. The share of consumer goods in total imports, which totalled approximately 23 per cent in 1975, had risen in 1979 to around 30 per cent. This is attributable to the strong growth in the consumption of luxuries, due primarily to the higher income levels, and the decreased growth in capital goods imports caused by stagnation in the activities of the transnational bauxite concerns.

The weak structure of Surinam's economy is also indicated by the sectoral distribution of the employed labour force shown in Table 4.8. Contrary to expectations, the decrease in the agricultural sector's share in total employment as from 1968—the year in which the economy reached its zenith—was not accompanied by relative growth in industrial employment. The flow of labour from the agricultural sector appears to have been largely absorbed by the expansion of the civil service apparatus.

A strikingly large number of Surinam nationals migrated to The Netherlands even after independence. The agreement was made during the negotiations on independence that, during a period of five years after

Table 4.8 Employed labour force according to sector, 1970 and 1980 (percentages)

	1970	1980
Agricultural sector	25	14
Forestry and wood processing	3	3
Mining and bauxite processing	7	6
Industry (incl. gas, electricity & water)	12	11
Construction	5	6
Trade, transport, banking	14	15
Government	28	40
Other services	6	5
Total	100	100

Sources: General Bureau of Statistics; Central Bank of Surinam.

independence, every Surinam national would be able to obtain a three-month residence permit in The Netherlands and, on condition that he/she be self-supporting, could obtain Dutch citizenship. Despite the massive migration to The Netherlands, which averaged more than six thousand people per year during the period 1976-8 and rose in 1979 to over eighteen thousand (Planning Bureau of Surinam, 1981, p. 29), and the fact that the ranks of civil servants had swelled from 29,400 in 1975 to 39,600 by 1979 (Central Bank of Surinam, 1980, appendix II.4), there was no fall in unemployment. According to estimates by the Surinam General Bureau of Statistics (census 1980), unemployment in 1980 had surpassed 17 per cent. This figure represents official registered unemployment, and does not take into account hidden unemployment in the agricultural and service sectors.

Although statistics concerning income distribution in Surinam are virtually unavailable, it is clear that welfare discrepancies widened sharply in the course of time—particularly during the years immediately after independence when extremely large sums of development aid were flowing into the country. Per capital national income had risen to around US$ 2,200. Yet, according to estimates by the Surinam General Statistical Office, approximately one-third of the households in Paramaribo and the urbanized portion of the former Surinam district—which jointly account for 70 per cent of the country's population—had total incomes of under SG 400 per month, a sum equated at that time with the subsistence-level minimum for a family of four. Unemployment benefits and other social provisions were virtually non-existent. The intentions expressed on the eve of independence regarding the introduction of a uniform social security system, including such facilities as unemployment benefits and a National Health Insurance, were never carried out. The National Old Age Insurance, which was actually introduced, and which provided those over 70 with benefits of SG 25 per month, remained only briefly in effect. By the end of the 1970s there was an enormous payment backlog for these benefits. Those with no income, or with an income too small to support themselves, were forced to earn money by means of various informal activities, a phenomenon referred to in Surinam as '*hosselen*'. On the other hand, the highest incomes had greatly increased, a fact made visible by the forceful expansion of the luxury estates on the periphery of Paramaribo and the rapid increase in luxury consumer goods. In view of the hopeless position of the majority of the population, primarily caused by the failure of the West Surinam project, the February 1980 coup came as a welcome change.

Economic Change During the Military Regime

The policy programme presented by the military-appointed cabinet on 1 May 1980 heralded the launch of a new socio-economic order as one of the four renewals mentioned earlier in this book. Prime Minister Chin a Sen announced their intention to implement moderate policy, the general direction of which he termed 'middle of the road'. To indicate its intention to clearly distance itself from pre-1980 policy, the policy programme stated that recent years had seen a continual widening in discrepancies of property and income, and that measures would be taken, out of solidarity with the poor, powerless and dispossessed, to begin putting an end to the inhuman situation in which many were forced to live. In addition, measures were to be taken to remove the unacceptable inequality between the sexes.

Other points in the policy programme which better indicate the character of the new government were:

— the country's economic vigour was to be increased by creating jobs, improving the living climate, effecting a more just distribution of incomes, the greatest possible regional distribution of economic activities and reductions in the country's economic dependence.
— the government saw alleviating unemployment as one of its major tasks, and would achieve this end by means which included a broadening of the production structure, import substitution and expansion of the agricultural sector.

— a new land distribution policy, based on the principle of social justice, was to guard the interests of the 'little man'.

The policy programme also stated that, although development policy was to be placed in another perspective, development aid itself remained indispensable. The private sector was to play a major role in achieving the goals proceeding from the process of renewal. To this end, the government was to implement measures to create a favourable climate for private investments. The economic ties with Caribbean countries and Latin American neighbours were to be strengthened.

The new government's planned socio-economic policy was reflected in the Urgency Programme presented together with the policy programme. This programme allocated a sum of around SG 500m. over a two-year period, during which the process of renewal was to be completed. This programme was presented to The Netherlands for financing via development aid. In addition to earlier projects from the MDP, the programme also included a number of social projects, the most important of which were:

— The construction of public housing; the razing of the slums in Paramaribo and providing credit for the purchase of private homes.
— Cutting out the delay in National Old Age Insurance benefit payments; increasing these benefits and lowering the eligible age from 70 to 65.
— The introduction of a scheme to reimburse the cost of health care for civil servants and lower income groups.
— Improving drinking-water facilities and renewing the drainage system in Paramaribo and its surroundings.

The Urgency Programme did not allocate any funds for the further development of bauxite-extracting activities in western Surinam. This was certainly not strange in view of the fact that, as mentioned earlier, the bauxite firms no longer exhibited any interest in the Bakhuis reserves. The programme did, however, maintain budgetary items for the 'bauxite line' in western Surinam and the Kabalebo hydroelectric project, to the sum of DG 100m. and 300m. respectively.

This first post-coup cabinet was not given much time to demonstrate the feasibility of its own approach to development policy. Besides the construction of the promised public housing, the reorganization of the National Old Age Insurance scheme and the reimbursement scheme for health costs, not much had changed at the socio-economic level. As mentioned before, most members of this cabinet were replaced as early as the fall of 1980 and was replaced by the second Chin a Sen government now including members of the PALU and RVP.

As noted earlier, the left-wing revolutionaries published the Manifesto of the Revolution in May 1981, in which they stated that the miserable socio-economic situation in which Surinam currently found itself could be blamed on a development process of exploitation and domination by foreign capital, due to that colonialism and neo-colonialism that had been reinforced by the complicity of 'traitorous, corrupt, opportunistic and incompetent Surinamese puppets'. But the assumption of the reins of power by 'brave and progressive' soldiers of Surinam had provided 'a definitive turning-point in the people of Surinam's battle against foreign domination and exploitation, and for improving the lot of the masses'.

A new socio-economic order was to be established, abolishing exploitation and removing other defects of the neo-colonial production order. The new socio-economic order would primarily address the needs, requirements and desires of the country's own people. This was to take place first and foremost on the basis of the country's capabilities. Sufficient domestic savings would have to be effected to prompt the country's development. The thoroughly harmonious development of all sections of the population was to be guaranteed, and the economy was to be completely controlled by Surinam itself.

In line with the Manifesto of the Revolution, the government announced in June 1981 that a change was to take place in the priorities by which Surinam applied development aid. Greater attention would now be paid to small-scale projects. The most important consequence of this policy shift was the scrapping of the Kabalebo project, and its replacement by small hydro-electric projects.

The political days of this second cabinet were also numbered. In 1981, the influence of the country's left-wing groups greatly increased. As has also been mentioned, the Manifesto of the Revolution appeared in May of that year, and in December the Revolutionary Front was formed by members of the PALU, the RVP and the trade unions. This group presented the Revolutionary Front's Minimum Programme as a guideline for future policy. The programme's premises and objectives exhibited strong similarities to those of the manifesto. Surinam's general economic and political malaise was largely blamed on the process of colonialism, neo-colonialism and imperialism, as well as the accompanying supremacy of foreign capital and its 'puppets in Surinam's traditional politics'. To summarize the most striking passage with regard to the goals and tasks proposed: a definitive end was to be put to the economic, political and cultural repression of Surinam by imperialists; all structures based on racism and serving neo-colonialism were to be destroyed, Surinam's society was to be freed from exploitation and foreign policies were to be pursued which were based on the right of every nation to rule itself and which would provide support for the people's struggle for national liberation.

The Minimum Programme was clearer than the manifesto in its description of the planned socio-economic policy. The major changes in the policy anticipated by this document were: the development of an economy independent of imperialists from any country, the reinforcement and expansion of the government sector, the implementation of economic regulatory measures and the stimulation of the formation of cooperatives. More concrete points with regard to planned socio-economic policy were:

— centralization and organization by the government of the import, distribution and export of the most essential commodities;
— majority participation in the tapping of the country's natural resources, in view of the fact that these should first and foremost be used to the benefit of the country itself;
— the reorganization of banking and the credit system, so that these institutions would serve the development of the national economy;
— the setting-up of an affordable National Health Care scheme for all Surinam nationals, in anticipation of free medical care;
— the introduction of a just fiscal system.

As mentioned before, the new government was not composed of left-wing revolutionaries, as might be expected; the military-appointed cabinet instead consisted largely of people with no clear political affiliation. However, the influence of the left-wing revolutionaries, who had come to occupy an increasing number of advisory posts and high official positions, was clearly seen in the policy programme presented by the new government on 1 May 1982. This policy programme stated the need for a struggle against those forces that would expose Surinam and other, fraternal peoples to repression and exploitation. It also stated that the February 1980 revolution had rung in a new phase in Surinam's history, and that this revolution had as its goal the combatting and elimination of all forms of colonialism, neo-colonialism and servility towards imperialism in the country.

The section of the programme dealing with the general economic and development policy stated that the Multi-Annual Development Programme was to be adapted. This adaptation was primarily to involve:

— productive investments in agriculture, forestry, cattle husbandry and fisheries, and the processing industries based on these sectors;

— the diversification of mining, as well as the implementation of smaller and medium-sized projects for the generation of energy;
— the augmentation of industrial production by government support for initiatives by both local and foreign investors, in so far as these initiatives would further the realization of national objectives.

The policy programme also stated that the government would not only strive to effect programmes within the primary sectors related to the extraction of raw materials, their industrial processing and sales at home and abroad, but that this would take place in such a way that these activities would be submitted to maximum national control. Furthermore, rising unemployment and increasing urbanization due to the disintegration of small-scale farming would be prevented by the promotion of cooperatives and the implementation of a just land-distribution policy.

In view of the composition of the new cabinet, which included no real representatives of the left-wing revolutionary factions, it could hardly be expected that the more radical objectives expressed in the policy programme would be attained. The composition of this new military-appointed cabinet already indicated that the military rulers had opted for a moderate socio-economic policy.

This government was barely to have the time to implement a clear policy. As mentioned earlier, the government resigned immediately after the executions of 8 December 1982. It was only then that both Surinam's left-wing factions, for the first time since the coup, were to form a government coalition and so, albeit with the aid of several military representatives, be given the chance to implement left-wing revolutionary policy.

On 1 May 1983, the Alibux government presented its policy programme in the form of an Action Plan for the period 1983–6. The plan included fifty points for government action. It was stated that the cabinet's task was to carry out the revolutionary mandate ('which was no easy job') by means of unity, work and struggle. The points for government action that constituted this cabinet's socio-economic policy can be classified as follows:

(a) Improving social welfare facilities by:
  — raising Old Age Insurance benefits;
  — the introduction of a national pension fund;
  — continuation of the public housing programme, with emphasis placed on distribution housing and the introduction of a rental-subsidy fund;
  — improvements in health care, including the upgrading of facilities in the large hospitals and a drastic increase in the number of health care centres outside Paramaribo;

— a thorough restructuring of general preparatory and professional education, the completion of a massive literacy campaign and related educational programmes for adults;

(b) government stimulatory measures and production activities, particularly with regard to:
— the agricultural sector, especially in the areas of rice cultivation, palm-oil production, citrus cultivation and the production of peanuts;
— cattle husbandry, particularly in the construction of a modern artificial insemination station to promote the expansion of dairy farming;
— fisheries, primarily through the establishment of both a large, modern fisheries centre aimed at production for export, and the creation of several small fisheries centres for supplying domestic needs;
— the forestry and wood processing industry, by means of substantial attention to economies within this sector and emphasis on the production of charcoal;
— energy production, namely by the expansion of onshore oil extraction by the state oil company for the domestic market, and the carrying out of small-scale hydroelectric projects;
— the manufacturing industry, with primary emphasis placed on the setting-up of a tile-manufacturing plant and the brick industry;

(c) infrastructural improvements, largely by means of:
— improvements in and expansion of the road network;
— the construction of a bridge over the Surinam River at Paramaribo;
— improvements in and expansion of Paramaribo's Zanderij Airport, as well as the country's small airports.

Also of note in the policy programme were the action points regarding the expansion of the national defence capacity and those points dealing with foreign relations, which announced more intensive participation in the movement of non-aligned nations and the reinforcement of bilateral ties with countries both within and outside Surinam's own region.

The tenor of the Action Plan was more moderate than that of the Manifesto of the Revolution and the Revolutionary Front's Minimum Programme. However, one would at least have expected that the inauguration of the Alibux government would have heralded the dawn of state control of the country's basic sectors, including banking and credit institutions. The fact that this did not take place is therefore all the more striking. In this regard it must be noted that the revolutionary government was quickly confronted with massive financial problems, especially as a result of the suspension of Dutch development aid. Furthermore, as has been noted elsewhere in this book, the regime had lost the confidence of virtually the entire population after the December 1982 executions, which were blamed at least in part on the activities of the left-wing revolutionary groups. However, it is also extremely questionable whether a radical change in Surinam's economy, including the nationalization of foreign companies as (albeit very generally) sketched in the Revolutionary Front's Minimum Programme, would have been at all feasible in a Surinam that was part and parcel of the World economic system.

Although cuts were made in development spending, remaining government expenditure rose so far that total public spending showed a drastic increase. This was due in part to the expansion and modernization of Surinam's military apparatus.

It is altogether striking that the left-wing revolutionary cabinet made repeated attempts to secure a US$ 100m. loan from the International Monetary Fund, yet their attempts failed, and even led to the demise of the Alibux government. In order to meet one of the IMF's major demands, namely the substantial reduction of Surinam's budget deficit, the Alibux government did not choose to implement economies in public spending, but rather to effect drastic tax hikes. Even the IMF delegation which visited Surinam in late October of 1983 doubted whether the rigorous tax increases proposed would ultimately produce enough results to sufficiently reduce the country's massive public spending deficit. The IMF experts favoured a combination of government spending cuts with tax increases. The IMF particularly feared that the business and investment climate would deteriorate to such an extent that investments would, in effect, be strongly discouraged and the flow of capital and trained labour to other countries would increase. Yet the government pushed ahead and announced large increases in income tax (22%), import duty (59%), motor vehicle tax (44%) and excise duties and sales tax (44%). The announcement of these taxhikes prompted strikes in the vital bauxite sector, and when the strikes threatened to spread to other sectors, the military leaders forced the resignation of the revolutionary government.

The new cabinet, composed of representatives of the military, the trade union movement and the employers' organizations, presented no socio-economic programme. It did, however, set up a Financial-Economic Advisory Group to help find solutions to the country's economic predicament. The advisory group considered the already massive public spending deficit, which it appeared would continue to rise, as one of the major problems to be dealt with. According to this group, the problem was to be approached through 'actions dealing with both spending and funding'.

The recommendations for augmenting government income covered a wide area, and varied from increases in wage tax, corporation tax, capital gains tax, property tax, excise, sales tax and import duties to levies on the purchase of foreign currency for travel purposes and increased tariffs for retail licenses. The group also made many recommendations for government spending cuts, including:

— the restructuring and reorganization of the government apparatus, including the fusion of ministries, with as a major move the dismantling of the Ministry of Civilian Mobilization and Culture which had been set up by the revolutionary government;
— a freeze on civil service promotions and on the creation of new posts, and a thorough examination of the current ministerial functions;
— economies in the foreign diplomatic service through the scrapping of certain posts;
— the scrapping of a number of facilities for civil servants.

The advisory group also noted that 'Surinam faces a national crisis with regard to its foreign currency reserves.' However, it also said that no clear conditions were present to allow for the carrying-out of the IMF recommendations for the devaluation of the Surinam guilder. The reason it gave was that the result of the lower exchange rate for the Surinam guilder would be the lack of major increases in exports 'due to the fact that the production of the most crucial export products, namely bauxite, alumina, aluminium, rice, bananas, shrimp and wood, could not be increased quickly and without large investments'. But, the advisory group said, even if the production of the main export products could be stepped up, 'customers would have to be located in the world market, which is extremely specialised for these products, and where long-term contracts are often the rule' (FEA report, 1984, p. 21). The group also expected no major import substitution to take place in the short term as a result of the higher import prices, owing to lengthy investment periods and the great dependence on raw material imports. Measures for promoting exports, including reduced levies and government subsidies (including subsidies in the form of lower tariffs) would, according to the advisory group, be more effective than a devaluation of the country's currency.

The advisory group added that the foreign currency crisis could be relieved by strict import restrictions, in addition to measures for the promotion of exports. It recommended the introduction of a system of import licensing. The recommendation was also made to 'carefully study those currency-saving measures to be taken with regard to the services and the transfer of incomes, in order to achieve a positive effect'. The group also urged that loans be applied for from the IMF and the international banks.

Surinam's financial/economic position deteriorated even further during 1984 (see Table 4.9). Despite further drastic cuts in development investments, total government spending decreased only slightly. Government income fell, on the other hand, largely owing to decreased bauxite revenues.

The import restrictions applied until now appeared insufficiently effect-

Table 4.9 Survey of government budgets, 1979–1985 (cash basis, SG m.)

	1979	1980	1981	1982	1983	1984	1985
Receipts							
Direct taxation	128	140	135	130	128	162	197
Indirect taxation	175	176	200	204	189	176	150
Net bauxite levies	88	93	96	69	68	48	31
Other	42	75	97	154	204	101	97
Total	433	484	528	557	509	487	475
Spending							
Personnel costs	245	258	265	320	355	379	410
Subsidies	60	108	88	90	127	121	147
Interest + redemption	3	6	9	10	24	27	41
Equipment and other	108	95	217	220	206	171	191
Total	416	467	579	640	712	698	789
Balance	17	17	−51	−83	−203	−211	−314
Development service							
Receipts	144	124	169	6	5	6	3
Expenditure	172	114	175	189	114	76	53
Total balance of state budget	−11	27	−57	−100	−312	−281	−364
State budget deficit as % of GDP	0.8		3.7	6.1	19.2	17.9	24.2

Sources: Socio-Economic Evaluation, 1975–80, Planning Bureau Surinam; De Surinaamsche Bank NV.

ive in combatting the steep decrease in international reserves. These reserves, which still totalled SG 425m. in 1982, had fallen by the end of 1984 to just around SG 61m., or some 10 per cent of that year's visible import value (De Surinaamsche Bank N. V., 1986, pp. 5–6). Increasing scarcity of foreign currency forced the authorities to impose more stringent measures to restrict imports. Refuge was also sought in counter-trade, a phenomenon which has continued to gain in importance in international trade. Agreements of this kind were closed or drafted with various countries, including Brazil, Italy (FIAT), Colombia, Venezuela, Taiwan, South Korea and Libya.

A new round of negotiations with the IMF concerning a US$ 100m. loan failed again, as Surinam was unwilling to meet the conditions imposed by the fund. These conditions primarily involved the devaluation of the Surinam guilder and drastic public spending cuts. The lamentable economic situation led the military to replace the government in early 1985 with a 'Government of National Unity and Reconciliation'. This government was to have a broad social base, with participation by various functional groups. By also setting up a National Assembly, charged with the drafting of a constitution, the military authorities hoped to induce The Netherlands to resume its development aid. Yet the Dutch government found these changes insufficient, and expressed its desire to see tangible steps towards a return to parliamentary democracy.

The new government presented a socio-economic and financial programme containing ten points. This programme indicated the government's intention to restore a sound internal and external value to the Surinam guilder, to take steps to achieve the resumption of Dutch development aid, to attempt to obtain development aid from such international institutions as the World Bank, the Inter American Development Bank and the European Development Bank as well as from countries other than The Netherlands, such as Belgium and the United States. It is also striking that this programme referred to Surinam's need for an 'atmosphere of confidence', including clarity concerning the government's financial and economic policies. Only then would both local and foreign private investors regain their confidence in the country. Within this context, the government was to examine which commercial government activities, for considerations of efficiency, would be better privatized. It is clear that greater distance was being established from the statements contained in the documents from the left-wing revolutionaries. The change of course in the country's socio-economic policy became even clearer when the cabinet resigned, to be replaced in June 1985 by almost the same cabinet, this time without the C 17 trade union. Slowly but surely, increasingly more left-wing revolutionaries were moving from officialdom and positions as the military's major advisers into political oblivion.

Yet the financial and economic problems continued to mount during 1985. Current government expenditure, which had not risen during 1984, once again rose sharply in 1985. As government revenues had fallen even further in this year, the state budget deficit rose to a record level of some 43 per cent of total public spending and more than 24 per cent of GNP. Table 4.9 shows how the state budget deficit, which had begun as early as 1981 to take on alarming proportions, rose sharply after the suspension of Dutch development aid in December 1982.

International reserves continued to shrink, leading to increasingly stringent measures. Service expenditures were placed under strict control, and increasing restrictions were imposed on the purchase of foreign currency for travel abroad. By 1986, Surinam had arrived at a financial and economic dead-end. GNP, which had suffered a fall of around 3 per cent in 1980 and had actually increased by almost 11 per cent in 1981, continued to fall at an annual average rate of some 2.3 per cent. As Table 4.10 shows, real GNP (factor cost) had, in 1984, been at approximately the same level as in 1980. In 1985, GNP even showed a further sharp fall of an estimated 6 per cent (IMF, 1986, p. 19). The projections for 1986 would indicate a further sharp decrease in national income.

As a result of the strict import restrictions, a parallel market has been created for imported commodities. An indication of the high prices applied on this expanding parallel market is given by the fact that the going price for American dollars and Dutch guilders in mid-1986 was approximately four times the official rate.

Table 4.10 also shows how the bauxite sector's share in GDP fell even further during the 1980s. This share, which in the early 1970s still totalled approximately one-third of total GDP, is seen to have fallen by 1984 to 17 per cent. The relocation of the transnational bauxite companies' activities from the Caribbean region to new production areas was mentioned earlier in this chapter. According to the bauxite companies, an additional factor was that the alumina produced in Surinam had, since the early 1980s, no longer been able to compete on the world market, and this production had therefore resulted in losses as from 1981. The alumina firms blamed this situation on the country's high labour costs, steep levies and the artificial, unrealistic overvaluation of the Surinam guilder.

The substantial decrease in the bauxite sector's share in GDP was, however, not compensated for by major new production activities in other sectors. The share in GDP of both the agricultural sector and forestry and wood processing decreased further. Furthermore, industrial production's share in GDP barely increased.

Work began as early as 1981 on the development of local industry. A start was made with the setting-up of the INDEX Centre for Industrial Development and Export Promotion. In addition, the government began providing more subsidies for small local ventures, and a number of state companies were set up. The limited opportunities for industrial activity in Surinam have already been noted, and these were largely due to the small domestic market, the relatively high labour costs and the firmly established trading elite. Yet, owing to the increasing import restrictions and stimulatory measures effected by the government, opportunities were created for—albeit small-

Table 4.10 Gross Domestic Product by sector and Gross National Product, 1980 and 1984

	1980	1984
Agriculture and fishery	9	8
Forestry and wood processing	2	1
Mining and bauxite processing	19	17
Industry (incl. water, gas & electricity and construction)	16	17
Commerce, transportation, banking	28	30
Government	22	24
Other services	4	3
GDP at current factor cost (%)	100	100
(SG m.)	1,530	1,955
GNP at current factor cost (SG m.)	1,499	1,953
GNP at current market prices (SG m.)	1,865	2,265
GDP at factor cost (SG m., 1980 prices)	1,530	1,516
GNP at factor cost (SG m., 1980 prices)	1,499	1,514

Sources: General Bureau of Statistics, Planning Bureau of Surinam.

scale—industrial activities aimed at the domestic market. The danger arose, however, that permanent government subsidies in particular would serve to create and entrench inefficient industrial activities.

The recent economic crisis has prompted increasing experiments with import substitution and local export-orientated industrial activities. A successful start has also been made with the extraction of the country's oil reserves for domestic use, an activity unattractive to the large multinational oil companies.

However, the greater scarcity of foreign reserves has made it increasingly difficult to import the technology and expertise needed by domestic firms. In addition, the climate for foreign investment worsened, particularly after the suspension of Dutch development aid, whereby, in addition to a lack of interest in investment in Surinam, a general tendency was noted among foreign companies to withdraw from the country. This did, however, result in the Surinam government's ability to take over at no great cost the joint ventures with HVA, as well as the perennially loss-making Bruynzeel activities. The barter deals with credit lines with various countries none the less did not result in the desired increase in the export sector's production capacity. The short-term credit arrangements were sooner spent on imports of arms and consumer goods than on capital goods.

The figures in Table 4.11 show a fall in exports as from 1980, even when expressed in terms of current prices. We see that, even after 1983, when the world economy began its recovery, alumina exports continued to fall. This table shows a further decrease in the export value of bauxite and aluminium in 1985 as well. As from 1982, the export value of wood and wood products fell sharply, while the export value of agricultural products—expressed in current Surinam guilders—was even somewhat lower than in 1979. As noted earlier, the crisis in the bauxite sector can be primarily attributed to structural changes in the world economy. With regard to the other export sectors, Surinam became trapped in a vicious circle. The country's major export products can no longer compete on the world market, largely owing to the lack of investment in either new technologies or the expansion of production capacity. This in turn resulted in a decrease in foreign currency income. The scarcity of international currency obstructed the necessary investments, weakening the competitive position of the major export products on the world market.

Table 4.12 illustrates the depressing effect of the increasingly stringent import restrictions on visible imports which, in 1984, were even slightly lower than exports. In that year there was still an SG 80m. current accounts deficit and an SG 101m. deficit in the total balance of payments. The 1985

Table 4.11 Exports according to major products and product groups (SG m. and %), 1979–1985

	1979		1980		1981		1982		1983		1984		1985	
	SG m.	%	SG m.	%	SG m.	%	SG m.	%	SG m.	%	SG m.	%	SG m.	%
Bauxite	117	15	132	14	112	13	52	7	45	7	71	11	62	11
Alumina	358	45	508	55	474	56	412	54	358	59	354	55	310	52
Aluminium	134	17	114	13	87	11	124	16	62	9	76	12	54	9
Bauxite and deriv.	609	77	754	82	673	80	588	77	492	75	501	78	426	72
Wood and wood products	20	2	21	2	19	2	21	3	12	2	10	2	6	1
Agric. products	164	21	143	16	154	18	156	20	151	23	130	20	160	27
Total exports	793	100	918	100	846	100	765	100	655	100	641	100	592	100

Sources: General Statistical Bureau; De Surinaamsche Bank NV.

balance of payments deficit was virtually cancelled out by the exhaustion of international reserves and the further tightening of currency restrictions with regard to service trade and income transferral.

International reserves, already almost exhausted by early 1985, totalled only SG 46m. at the end of the first quarter of 1986 (De Surinaamsche Bank N. V., 1986, p. 6). Counter-trade had apparently not allowed great savings in international reserves in view of the fact that, as mentioned above, those export sectors, other than bauxite, of major importance in this form of trade (namely rice, wood and wood products), encountered increasing difficulty on foreign markets and exhibited no growth. This can be attributed not only to high labour costs and the high exchange rate of the Surinam guilder, but also to the perennial lack of investment in new technologies and/or capacity expansion, mentioned earlier.

The increasing scarcity of foreign reserves and the increasingly extreme import restrictions made it more and more difficult to import those capital goods needed to maintain production levels, let alone to renew or expand production capacity in these sectors. Furthermore, scarce reserves were used to a significant extent to purchase arms and luxury goods. In 1984, consumer goods made up one-third and capital goods only 15 per cent of Surinam's total imports.

Accordingly, successive governments were unsuccessful in their attempts to reduce Surinam's massive public-spending deficits. To prevent social unrest, no rigorous tax hikes or drastic public spending cuts were implemented. On the contrary, government spending continued to mount, largely

Table 4.12 Balance of payments according to major items, 1980–1985 (cash basis, in SG m.)

	1979	1980	1981	1982	1983	1984	1985
Merchandise exports	793	−918	846	765	655	651	561
Merchandise imports	734	−900	1,014	921	804	617	543
Trade balance	59	18	−168	−156	−149	34	27
Current accounts balance	−66	−104	−218	−273	−292	−80	−44
Capital accounts balance	112	161	245	196	120	−21	35
Total balance	46	57	27	−77	−172	−101	−9

Sources: Central Bank of Surinam; De Surinaamsche Bank NV.

owing to lavish spending on the continual expansion and modernization of the country's military apparatus. Defence spending is (unofficially) estimated at 10 to 25 per cent of total public expenditure during the period 1981-6. Furthermore, as shown in Table 4.9, government revenue from the bauxite sector had continued to shrink as from 1981.

Surinam was confronted with a new problem in 1985, namely that of a skyrocketing foreign debt. Until 1982 there had been little need for foreign loans beyond the development aid from The Netherlands. Surinam's foreign debt consisted of a loan of DG 50m. for the construction of the West Surinam railroad. Furthermore, this loan was guaranteed within the framework of Dutch development cooperation. The foreign debt rose sharply after 1982, however, owing to Surinam's assumption of short-term obligations associated with trade credit lines and various bilateral and counter-trade agreements. By early 1987, Surinam was already some US$ 100m. in arrears, and its total debt had swollen to around US$ 150m.

The country's economic crisis forced the military authorities to choose between implementing drastic public-spending cuts and taking concrete steps towards a return to democratic institutions to regain Dutch development aid. It appears that the military leaders wish—albeit hesitantly—to take the latter course. According to the IMF, Surinam's authorities have admitted that such stringent economies cannot be implemented without 'firm political support', and have termed it their major task 'to build a consensus among different social groups around the required adjustment program' (IMF, 1986, p. 7).

To this end, the military authorities opened a dialogue with the old parties which they had overthrown in 1980. These talks led to the formation of a new cabinet. In addition to military representatives, this cabinet also included representatives of the three major old political parties, the trade unions and employers.

By working with the old parties, the military authorities hoped to be able to adopt the necessary austerity measures without risking social upheaval. Furthermore, the old parties were to attempt to restore development-aid ties with The Netherlands. As part of this latter effort, the government announced its plans for elections to be held in 1987.

However, the new government never implemented the anticipated drastic spending cuts. On the contrary, the country's public spending deficit soared, reaching the record level of Sf. 490m. at the end of 1986 (equal to approximately 55 per cent of total government spending). As monetary financing was consistently used to cover the government's deficit, the public debt to the Central Bank of Surinam (which totalled only Sf. 23m. in 1981) had risen to some Sf. 1.1bn. by the end of 1985. Early in 1987, this debt had risen to the record sum of almost Sf. 2bn.

The government introduced new paper currency and invalidated the old within a few days as part of what it termed a thorough monetary reorganization. In view of the fact that the official rate of the new Surinam guilder remained exactly equal to that of the old currency, it soon became clear (as was ultimately admitted by the regime) that the measure had been intended to block foreign black-market trading in the currency. In fact, this monetary reorganization was primarily intended to hinder the Dutch-based resistance from obtaining Surinamese money cheaply, and to strike a blow at the Bush Negroes as a group (because of their close association with the Jungle Commandos), and particularly those who had fled to French Guyana. The introduction of the new currency eventually proved useless, and served instead to encourage corruption and further inflate the Surinamese money supply. Irregularities have also been reported regarding the exchange of old currency for new, including the practice of accepting the old currency long after the official closure date, but at widely different exchange rates. Furthermore, The Netherlands remained unwilling to resume development aid to its former colony and stated its intention to wait until more concrete steps had been taken towards a return to democratic institutions.

The bauxite firms implemented reorganizations to compensate for their losses and to boost the international market position of Surinamese bauxite products, especially alumina. Against the government's will, and despite strong trade union protests, these concerns refused to pay the levies on bauxite and reduced their work forces by some 20 per cent. They also strongly urged the government to comply with one of the IMF's major credit demands, namely the devaluation of the Surinam guilder. Such a move would reduce these firms' overheads and cut labour costs. The Surinamese authorities have not yet complied with the IMF demand; the recent fall of the United States dollar, to which the Surinam guilder is linked, has been seen by the opponents of devaluation as a confirmation of their view.

Short-term prospects for the Surinamese economy are extremely bleak. More than eight thousand Bush Negroes fled to French Guyana after a significant number of them had been persecuted or killed by the national Army. The drain in manpower has had particularly unfavourable effects on the production and export of lumber and palm-oil, activities for which the Bush Negroes have traditionally provided menial labour. Furthermore, raids by the Jungle Commandos have resulted in the shutting-down of bauxite mining and processing operations. Since the bauxite sector constitutes the major pillar of Surinam's economy (accounting in 1986 for 75 per cent of

Surinam's total exports, which general estimates show had fallen even further in that year to around Sf. 480m.), a sharp decline in, or suspension of these activities for an indefinite time would deal a crippling blow to the country.

The ever-increasing shortage of international reserves, the flood in money supply and the fall in real production have caused prices on the black market to rise even further. In March 1987, the prices of most products on the black market were an average of 700 per cent higher than the government-controlled retail price. Furthermore, the government was forced in early 1987 to begin rationing a number of basic foodstuffs. With the expanding role of the black market and the fall in the real value of the Surinamese guilder, the country's real standard of living has significantly fallen. The official statistics published in recent years on production value and real national income therefore present a distorted image. Using these statistics, the country's true economic level has been grossly overestimated as from 1985. Moreover official registered unemployment had risen in 1986 to 25 per cent and hidden unemployment in the agricultural and service sectors, including government, was estimated at 20-30 per cent.

Surinam's authorities are currently faced with enormous economic problems which can only be solved by a far-reaching restructuring of the national economy. Account must be taken of the fact that the bauxite sector's role will diminish even further in the future. This means that economic growth must be borne by activities in the other productive sectors of Surinam's economy, namely agriculture, forestry, heavy industry and perhaps other types of mining.

Yet this restructuring process will only be possible when sufficient investments are made in expertise and new technologies. The capital needed can only be obtained from domestic reserves when drastic public spending cuts have been effected. These economies will of necessity be so far-reaching that the standard of living, which has already plummeted, will fall even further. The necessary restructuring of Surinam's economy could indeed be accomplished without such a drastic fall in the standard of living if the military authorities were to comply with The Netherlands' condition for the resumption of development aid, namely the restoration of democratic institutions. Any such reorganization would of necessity make use of the experience gained during recent years of economic crisis in locating import substitutes and export opportunities. But Surinam's economy can only be put back on a firm footing when—unlike in the past—development aid is primarily aimed at the local accumulation of technology and expertise, and when such funds are efficiently applied.

5   The Regime's Policies

Education

A 'new order in education' was the ambitious announcement in the government policy programme of 1 May 1980. This new order was to lead to a 'new Surinamese individual, an individual well aware of his own values and those of his country and people, and who has settled accounts with the burdens and traumas of the past' (Government policy programme, 1 May 1980, p. 16).

According to the programme, those burdens and traumas that the old educational system had imposed on the Surinamese were: a lack of patriotism, self-confidence, self-sacrifice and appreciation of one's own cultural values, together with the imitation of foreign values and cultural expressions, an over-appreciation of intellectual work and too little appreciation of manual labour (a 'white-collar mentality'). The form and content of education were therefore to be carefully re-examined.

The first post-coup government policy programme displayed well-justified concern about the educational system. Moreover, this concern had been noted for some time in much wider circles. In a 1968 Unesco report, Torfs said, 'it's doubtful whether the current educational system is likely to foster the creation of a specific Surinamese cultural and social pattern, because the nature of such a pattern has never been defined by the Surinamese themselves' (quoted by Mijs, 1973, p. 88). Kruijer (1973, p. 125) summarized the criticism of Surinam's educational system as follows:

By way of summary, we can state that Suriname's educational system has been cast in a Dutch mould, which serves to preserve the inequality among the various groups within the population. The people are able only, and to varying extents, to assume the culture of a foreign, yet more powerful, people. Education here also contributes to the maintenance of the status quo by convincing the Surinamese at an early age of the superiority of a system which has them in its grip.

The Dutch language has always posed great difficulties for Surinamese education. Dutch is Surinam's official language, and is therefore also used in the classroom. But the extent to which children from various ethnic groups are able to use this language differs considerably. The study by Mijs (1973, pp. 35 ff.) showed that only 15.5 per cent of the elementary school children of Indonesian origin, and only 14.3 per cent of those of East Indian origin, used

Dutch both at home and at school. Of the Creole elementary school children, however, 82.7 per cent spoke Dutch at home or at least heard it spoken often at home. It should therefore come as no surprise that the largest number of drop-outs came from the Indonesian and East Indian groups. These figures may have changed somewhat since the study was made, owing to ongoing urbanization, but they still illustrate a central problem in Surinamese education.

Furthermore, Surinamese education has also been faced with major quantitative problems. Growth was particularly rapid in the period preceding independence. During the period 1955 to 1975, the number of children attending elementary or secondary schools almost tripled, from 53,000 to 144,000. Population growth did play a certain role in this, but growing interest in education and advancing urbanization were the most significant factors. The rush to the schools took place at such a rate that participation by the potential school-going population soon compared favourably with that in other developing countries. By the late 1970s, the participation percentage for children of elementary school age had already risen to above 90 per cent. Compulsory education (for children between the ages of 7 and 12), in force in Surinam since 1876, also played a role. But the lack of qualified teachers served to severely undermine the quality of education. The rural districts were at a disadvantage, both qualitatively and quantitatively, and so were the Indonesian and East Indian groups in particular. Qualified teachers willing to work in the bush were few and far between.

One specific problem in Surinam has been the compartmentalization of education by the ecclesiastical groups. Even before education had become a public institution, the nineteenth-century Protestant Evangelische Broeder Gemeente (EBG) and the Roman Catholics were extremely active in this area. Around 1970, approximately 50 per cent of all students attended these church schools. This was largely made possible by the financial equality of private and public education, a system also applied in The Netherlands. In Surinam, this compartmentalization led to racially segregated education. Religious and ethnic lines run almost completely parallel, which has rendered the Christian schools primarily Creole institutions.

The trend towards compartmentalization, and therefore towards segregation, was even further reinforced from the early 1960s, when Hindu and Islamic communities also began setting up their own schools. This involved more of a reaction to the activities of the Christian denominations than any impulse on the part of the Hindus or Moslems to set up their own schools. The number of Hindu and Islamic schools remained limited, owing in part to the lack of professional support from the Netherlands enjoyed by the EBG and the Roman Catholic Churches. Many East Indians and Indonesians therefore attended public schools.

The Christian schools assumed an even more homogeneously Creole character during the 1960s, owing to the precedence given to children from the same (Christian) circles in the face of the increasing shortage of school places. The compartmentalization and resulting segregation were viewed with alarm. The Integral Development Plan (p. 220) of 1965 stated that, 'a multi-racial developing country cannot allow itself the luxury of all-too-pronounced compartmentalization . . . The intensification of such a system of compartmentalization will undoubtedly be accompanied by less desirable consequences for intellectual and socio-economic development, order, peace and tolerance' (cited by Mijs, 1973, p. 220). At the time it gained independence in 1975, therefore, Surinam's educational system already exhibited major defects which served to stimulate ethnic rather than national identity. The system focused more on the Dutch than the Surinamese labour market (thereby stimulating migration to The Netherlands) and reinforced social inequality.

The solution to these educational problems received encouragement shortly after independence, partly under the influence of the nationalist movement, which considered the time ripe for the development of a 'truly Surinamese' school system. This increased attention on education was reflected in the growing government spending allocation to this sector, as indicated below in Table 5.1.

Expenditures shown in Table 5.1 largely involve the salaries of school personnel and the cost of materials. The building of schools was largely financed by Dutch aid and by the European Development Fund. Educational efforts during this period resulted in a welcome rise in the number of

Table 5.1 Current spending, Ministry of Education and Popular Development, 1975–1980 (SG. m.)

	1975	1976	1977	1978	1979	1980
Educational spending as a % of	44.8	58.7	72.4	86.0	98.3	105.2
total current government spending	17.9	20.7	22.3	23.8	24.0	24.0

Sources: Ministry of Education and Popular Development; Ministry of Finance and Planning.

teachers. In 1963, for example, there was an average of thirty-five school-children to every primary school teacher. by 1979, this figure had decreased to twenty-five. The attempt made directly after independence to find lasting solutions to problems in education primarily resulted in a number of valuable studies.

Following the 1980 coup, unprecedented emphasis was placed on effecting real changes in the educational system and minimalizing Dutch influence. This in fact involved the further development of those pro-grammes set up in the late 1970s. An extremely ambitious project was begun in elementary education whereby, after tests had been conducted in schools, all textbooks were to be replaced. But a lack of experienced specialists delayed the project, while the economic crisis also presented a number of obstacles. The shortage of foreign reserves, for example, prevented the import of materials needed to print the textbooks. In 1986, however, a US$ 10m. loan from the Inter-American Development Bank saved the situation, and the project is now nearing completion.

After 1980, education continued to receive the financial priority it had enjoyed up to that time. This is clearly seen in Table 5.2, which compares current educational spending with total current government spending, in SG. millions.

Primary and secondary education never became fully imbued with the revolutionary ideology. The necessary social base for such change was lacking. In this context, it is worth noting that no attempt has ever been made to deal with the compartmentalized educational structure. According to education officials, the issue is a far too sensitive one. Table 5.3 below, which indicates the total number of pupils in primary and secondary education, illustrates the high degree of compartmentalization still characteristic of Surinam's educational system. Approximately one-half of all pupils still attend parochial schools.

Table 5.2 Current spending, Ministry of Education and Popular Develop-ment, 1981–1986 (SG. m.)

	1981	1982	1983	1984	1985	1986
Educational spending	111.4	133.8	159.2	156.9	157.5	180.2
as a % of						
total current government spending	21.7	23.3	23.5	24.2	22.7	23.6

Sources: Ministry of Education, Welfare and Culture; Ministry of Finance.

Table 5.3 Pupils in primary and secondary
education by category

	1984/5
Roman Catholic schools	29,295
EBG schools	20,066
Other Christian denominations	5,932
Sanatam Dharm (Hindu)	3,662
Arya Samaj (Hindu)	3,144
Moslem schools	2,593
Other private schools	924
Public schools	67,279

Source: Ministry of Education, Welfare and Culture.

Illiteracy continues to be a major problem in Surinam. According to official estimates, approximately 16 per cent of the population are illiterate, amounting to 35 per cent of the total labour force. A recent attempt to rapidly resolve the problem by means of a large-scale campaign can be regarded as a failure. This failure can be put down to a mixture of ideological impetuosity and a lack of experience and manpower. The ideological tone of the campaign, which began in 1984 under the name 'Alfa 84', can be attributed to the fact that the post of minister of education was held at the time by a member of the RVP party, as well as to the Ministry of Popular Mobilization's involvement in the campaign. Apparently with the idea that the group of sixty thousand illiterates constituted a grateful and untapped source of support for the revolution, a strongly propagandist instruction booklet was compiled for the campaign.

An advance edition of this booklet contains such slogans as 'One people, one organization: Stanvaste' (the popular term for the 25 February Movement), and 'Our friends are in the army, the militia and with the police' (Suriname Voorwaarts, advance edition of February 1984, Ministry of Education and Popular Development, Paramaribo). Few teachers or volunteers could be found willing to participate in such an ideological campaign.

Developments at the University of Surinam deserve special attention. The university was the sole institution of learning where an almost devastating conflict took place between revolutionary leaders on the one hand and the teaching staff and the majority of students on the other. During 1982, the university became a major centre of protest and demonstrations against the Bouterse regime. In early December 1982, student demonstrations were violently crushed by order of the military authorities. The dramatic conclusion came on 8 December 1982: among the fifteen critics of the regime executed on that date were two prominent university professors, who were regarded as part of the inspiration for the student protests.

The conflict at the university largely centred around participation in decision-making. Staff members and students made specific protests against the 'airdropping' of a revolutionary university board. The university was closed for ten months after December 1982, and was actually taken over during this period by a group of revolutionary leaders and intellectuals. A revolutionary steering committee drew up new objectives and reorganized the faculties to ensure that the university would no longer be 'a breeding ground for national lackeys' (from 'Memorandum on the Concrete Organisation of the Development University', 14 May 1983).

The university received the symbolic name of Anton de Kom, who had led resistance against Dutch colonialism in the 1930s. At the reopening of the university in October 1983, Commander-in-Chief Bouterse stated that the university's tasks would now include 'the tangible rendering of services to the government, the mass organizations, the popular bodies and to all other Surinamese people who can contribute to the struggle for national liberation'. A number of the faculty and student body had already chosen to emigrate to The Netherlands.

Cultural Policy

Herskovits (1966) sketches the problem of cultural ambivalence among Surinam's Creoles and New World Blacks in general, and notes that this is a general and far-reaching phenomenon. This cultural schizophrenia is the result of Dutch colonial policy, which aimed at isolating the Creole culture in particular, which was regarded as inferior. At the same time, however, the colonial power implemented policy aimed at assimilating those cultures present in Surinam into the Dutch culture.

The East Indians and Indonesians succeeded in maintaining their cultural identities. Their relative isolation in the agricultural regions and in non-Western religions played an obvious role in this.

Dutch (read 'Western') culture was the most prestigious in Surinam, since it offered the greatest chances for ascending the social scale—a social scale that usually led across the sea, to The Netherlands. Despite Western cultural influences, Surinam (in the words of its most prominent writer, Albert Helman) has to a great degree remained 'a cultural mosaic' (1977, p. 7 ff.). The country's cultural diversity is even more pronounced than that of comparable Caribbean nations, such as Guyana and Trinidad.

The Bush Negroes, the descendants of runaway slaves, have preserved a great deal of their native culture. When *granmans* (chiefs) of Surinamese Bush Negro groups visited the western coast of Africa (Ghana, Togo, Benin and Nigeria) in 1970, they expressed amazement at the definite presence of a common cultural tradition after centuries of separate development (De Groot, 1974). In 1982 the government of Surinam even attempted to promote cultural tourism by Black Americans, bypassing the need to go to Africa to discover their 'roots'.

Despite the increasing influence of Western culture, the three major ethnic groups (Creoles, East Indians and Indonesians) have preserved their own cultural identities. The concept of 'negritude' has become increasingly popular.

In this regard the Creole teacher J. G. A. Koenders, as early as the 1940s, had started a campaign to promote Sranan tongo, the Surinamese Creole language, and, in 1946 he published the periodical *Foetoe boi* in Sranan tongo and Dutch. During the same period the prominent Surinamese poet Henny de Ziel (Trefossa) was the first to demonstrate that high quality poetry could also be written in Sranan tongo. Their literary achievements provided an enormous impetus for Sranan tongo as a language (Voorhoeve & Lichtveld, 1975, pp. 10 ff.). Bruma's nationalist movement clearly played on this trend. The renewed importance awarded to Creole culture was primarily expressed in this group's use of its own language, Sranan tongo. Poetry enjoyed a renaissance. When speaking Sranan tongo rather than Dutch, a Creole mother will no longer tell her child not to 'act like a Negro'. And, particularly among the working-class Creoles, traditional ceremonies such as *winti* dances and the ceremonies of the *obia* man have never been abandoned. The stories about the spider Anansi (*'Anansi tori'*), which the slaves brought with them from Africa, are still told up to this day.

The renewed importance of the Creole culture prompted a defensive reaction on the part of the East Indian population. During the 1960s and 1970s the East Indians began to attach greater significance to their own cultural heritage. There was a revival of Hindi-language cultural events and Hindi studies. The ethnic-political polarization noted before independence was symptomatic of this. This did nothing, however, to halt the assimilative influence of the urbanization and increasing social mobility of the East

Indians. The use of Sarnami, a somewhat adapted Surinamese version of Hindi, has lost ground among young people in particular.

Among the Indonesians, the generation gap was expressed most clearly in the area of cultural experience. The last ships bearing Indonesian contract labourers arrived in Surinam in 1939, and some of these original immigrants are still alive today. *Gamelan* music, *wajan* puppet theatre and the *djaran kepang* dance are still practised by young people, but more to please the older generation than out of any interest on their own part. The flexible Indonesian young people have no difficulty in adopting a Western life style.

In the late 1960s, writes Albert Helman, the cultural mosaic had become more of a fluid image. This was due to the acculturation process undergone by all the ethnic groups. At the same time, however, the ethnic polarization in national politics mentioned above ensured that the stones in the mosaic still had some sharp edges. The country remained, to a large extent, a created society. It was therefore only natural that the formation of a nation was placed high on the list of priorities in the post-coup government policy programme.

The first post-coup government's programme placed cultural policy within the framework of the drive for a new order in education. An end was to be put to 'the lack of importance attached to our own cultural values and the mimicry of foreign values and cultural expressions (policy programme, May 1980, p. 16). As already noted (see pp. 158–63), this new order in education was intended to produce a 'new Surinamese individual'. The establishment of a separate Ministry of Culture (together with youth affairs and sports), which was later to merge with the Ministry of Education, indicated the priority it was felt that this field of policy deserved.

Like educational policy, however, cultural policy was more cautious than the programmes' robust rhetoric might suggest. In fact, this policy never progressed further than the ideal, propagated by the VHP, of 'unity in diversity'. Nor did the increasing influence of the radical parties in 1983 lead to a revolution in cultural ideology.

The following central concept was expressed in the official memorandum 'Policy Aspects of the Ministry of Education, Science and Culture', published in April 1986: 'Familiarity with the cultural expressions of one's countrymen generates mutual understanding and respect, and so creates the conditions needed for unity and national solidarity' (p. 23). Such a policy therefore revolves around mutual respect among ethnic groups. In fact, any alternative to this principle is scarcely imaginable, since it could only mark the beginning of cultural disintegration. Cultural diversity will therefore continue to be very much a part of Surinam.

Religion

Surinamese society, already divided along the lines of culture, language and race, receives an added dimension from religion. Religious and ethnic lines run largely parallel. The Christian denominations have always been a strong presence. Hinduism and Islam only became significant at a later stage, with the arrival of East Indian and Indonesian contract labourers. The Evangelische Broedergemeente (the Moravian Brethren of Hernhutt), and the Roman Catholic Church are by far the most important Christian denominations, with about 55,000 and 70,000 members respectively.

As was noted earlier, the first Moravian Brothers arrived in Surinam from Hernhutt as early as 1735. With the arrival of the Redemptorist Order in 1866, the Roman Catholic Church established its first permanent mission base in Surinam. The Creoles were the major ethnic group at that time, and the following of both Churches still remains largely Creole. The EBG has had an undeniably major influence on the Creole population. The EBG also took firmer root in Surinamese society because of the relatively prompt recruitment of Creole evangelists and pastors. The Roman Catholic Church continues to be represented to a great extent by the Dutch priests, although the first Surinamese bishop of Paramaribo, Monsignor A. Zichem, was appointed in 1970.

Christianity, however, was unable to disperse the central importance of such native african practices as *winti*. African cults, complete with *obia* and *loekoeman*, are still quite common, particularly among the Bush Negro population. There is also no doubt that a number of so-called 'converts' joined the Christian Churches with entirely materialist motives. This was one means, for example, by which easier access could be gained to schools and health care.

The influence of the Christian Churches involved much more than religion alone. As Van Raalte (1977, p. 301) states, Christianity opened the floodgates for Western culture and so played a 'decisive cultural role' as a missionary organization in Surinam (1977, p. 301). The EBG and Roman Catholic Churches have long been active in social affairs, of which education and health care have proved the most important. Christian parochial education has always been of great significance for the development of large sections of Surinam's population. At the same time, however, the Churches reinforced the country's social segmentation in this way. In the face of shortage of places, the Churches' own Creole followers took precedence in the schools. Vuijsje (1974, pp. 52 ff.) speaks of 'a dangerous segmentary tendency' (further, see pp. 158–63). Furthermore, separate missionary organizations existed to work with the East Indians and those of Indonesian descent. Yet the number of Christians within these ethnic groups has remained limited to only a few per cent.

Approximately 80 per cent of the East Indians are Hindu, with the majority of the remainder adhering to Islam (about seventeen thousand). The Indonesians are almost all Moslems. Approximately 80 per cent of the country's Hindus belong to the orthodox Sanatan Dharm (Eternal Law) group, while a minority belongs to the more modern Arya Samaj. Traditional Hinduism has disappeared almost entirely. Religious positions have often blurred through time, becoming marginal phenomena which serve merely to delineate group identity. The caste system has never really been of any significance in Surinam—the logical consequence of the fact that all contracted labourers, regardless of rank, were required to perform the same kind of work. Furthermore, divorce is common, even though the Sanatan Dharm does not officially recognize it. But religious self-awareness is very real among the country's Hindus. This is reinforced further by Sanatan Dharm's and Arya Samaj's other social activities, such as the schools mentioned above, as well as their care for the elderly and for orphans. The contrasts between Sanatan Dharm and Arya Samaj have also become less pronounced, as is apparent from the fact that the two organizations advance the interests of their schools from within a joint foundation.

The East Indian Moslems originally came from the Punjab. They adhered to the Hanaphatic Shar'ia, one of the four orthodox schools of religious learning. The Indonesian Surinamese were traditionally loyal to the equally orthodox Shafit movement. Pre-Islamic cultural remnants are also to be found among the Indonesians, such as spirit and ancestor worship. The reformational Ahmadiyya movement has also gained a good deal of acceptance during the past forty years among both East Indians and Indonesians. For many Moslems, the Shar'ia is something that is applied eclectically. The *hadj*, the pilgrimage to Mecca, is made only sporadically. Nevertheless, one group that can be regarded as fundamentalist does exist among the East Indian Moslems. Since the establishment of a Libyan People's Bureau in Paramaribo in 1984, Islamic denominations have received the support of several Libyan religious leaders. It appears unlikely that this support will prompt a broadly-based fundamentalist movement, because of the relative lack of motivation in this direction in Surinam as a result of its Western-orientated culture.

Although Hindus and Moslems exceed Christians in terms of numbers, the Christian Churches are the only ones to have received financial support from the government. This financial support has largely come in the form of payments to meet the cost of the salaries of EBG pastors and Roman Catholic priests. This is easily explained in a historical context by the position of power occupied by Creoles within the old political system. Vuijsje (1974, p. 48) speaks of a 'Christian mentality' within the government. Little has changed since that time. It was only in 1970 that a Hindu holiday (*Holi Phagwa*) and an Islamic holiday (*Idul Fitr*) were first officially recognized. The financial subordination of Hindu and Muslim denominations continues. The fact that no government since the 1980 coup has attempted to put an end to the financial favouritism shown towards the Christian Churches provides clear evidence of the important position that these Churches still occupy among the population.

Until just a few years ago, the religious groups hardly constituted a critical voice in Surinamese society. The EBG's religious orientation was very much a vertical one, and even exhibited traces of escapism. The Roman Catholic bishopric in Surinam only became acquainted at a late stage with the spirit of Puebla (1972 Bishops' Conference) and liberation theology, which was enjoying great popularity in Latin America. The Hindu and Islamic organizations have always had strong ties with the political parties (VHP and KTPI), and were therefore more or less unable to adopt their own independent and critical stance. Politicians from the Asiatic ethnic groups also often hold positions within the religious organizations, which, unlike the Christian Churches, do not always have their own professional leadership. Religious groups were often a means for Hindu and Moslem politicans to gain supporters.

Criticism of the government therefore only came at the end of the 1970s, and then primarily from the Committee of Christian Churches (CCK), a cooperative organization in which the EBG, Roman Catholic Church and several much smaller denominations took part. In 1978 and 1979, the CCK published two extremely critical memoranda, which can be seen as milestones in the stance of the Christian Churches in Surinam. The Churches clearly sided with the poor, who had little to expect from the Arron government of the day. The fact that the CCK did not immediately condemn the 1980 coup fitted well with this stance. In a statement presented on 27 February 1980 (two days after the coup), the CCK (27 February 1980, Paramaribo) merely called on the new authorities to exhibit great self-control and not to use their new-won power to give free rein to their 'understandable bitterness'.

In the course of the revolutionary process, the religious organizations came to adopt a more strident role as critic. In a visit to President Chin a Sen in late 1981 which almost amounted to a demonstration, these organizations showed their alliance with him in his conflict with the military authorities concerning Surinam's political course. The religious leaders, including a number of representatives from the Hindu and Islamic communities, warned against foreign ideologies creeping into Surinam, and in this way virtually echoed the president's standpoint.

In late 1982, the religious leaders made a highly explicit decision to oppose the military authorities by their alignment with the Association for Democracy. This association's letter to Commander-in-Chief Bouterse, dated 23 November 1982 (see Chapter 1) in which the military leader's view of democracy was rejected in no uncertain terms, bore the signatures of the Bishop of Paramaribo (on behalf of the CCK) and the leaders of the Hindu and Islamic organizations. This letter marked the opening of a breach between the religious organizations and the military leadership; the conflict would prove irreconcilable after the executions of 8 December 1982.

Since that time, the Christian Churches have been the clearest in their denunciation of the authorities. The ecclesiastical publications *Omhoog* (from the Roman Catholic bishopric) and *De Kerkbode* (from the EBG) have continued to be a thorn in the side of the regime. These publications often contain outright criticism of the military authorities, thereby creating an exception within the Surinamese media.

In February 1985, Father Sebastiaan Mulder, reporter for *Omhoog* and Vice-Provincial of the Redemptorist order, was brought in for questioning after a sharply critical article was printed with his by-line concerning the deportation of thousands of Guyanese workers and their families, during which several of the deportees died. The priest had accused the regime of violating human rights. The public prosecutor deemed Mulder guilty of insulting the authorities, but decided not to prosecute him 'for the sake of expediency'. This once again illustrated the authorities' fear of actually reprimanding the Churches. The regime's irritation has meanwhile risen to such heights that the CCK has on several occasions been excluded from talks between the regime and the religious organizations concerning political developments.

Relations between the state and the Christian Churches have therefore become extremely uneasy. The Hindu and Islamic organizations have always kept a somewhat lower political profile, and therefore remain on better terms with the regime. It is noteworthy in this context that the VHP and the KTPI have since become participants in the government coalition, while maintaining close relations with Hindu and Moslem religious organizations. The

NPS on the other hand, also participates in the government but has many fewer direct ties with Christian organizations.

Military Affairs

In proportion to the area of land it is intended to defend, Surinam's Army has never had more than a symbolic function. Prior to independence, the 1,100-man Army (consisting of over 700 Dutch conscripts and approximately 300 professional Surinamese non-combatants and corporals) was led by some forty Dutch officers. On gaining independence, the country became fully responsible for its own defence. On its founding day, the fledgling Surinamese Armed Forces (SKM) consisted of eight officers, 100 non-commissioned officers, 500 conscripts and 150 civilians (Fernandes Mendes, 1983, p. 146). There were originally two branches of the armed forces: the Army and the Navy. An Air Force was added after 1980.

Surinam's need for its own Army or its ability to make do with a police force were matters barely touched upon during the talks with The Netherlands at independence in 1975. The only note of criticism was raised by The Netherlands' Minister of Surinamese and Antillean Affairs, who urged that the Army in any event be 'kept small'. As far as the Surinamese government, and certainly the strongly nationalistic elements within the government, were concerned, an Army would be formed. The general opinion was that any self-respecting nation should have an Army. The protracted border conflict between Surinam and Guyana over the area between the Corantijn and Curuni rivers also played a role in this decision. Guyanese soldiers had dislodged a Surinamese Army camp from the area in 1969. Although peace had returned to the disputed area after the 1970 Chaguaramas agreement (arranged through the mediation of then-Trinidadian Prime Minister Eric Williams), the conflict remained unsettled.

The Netherlands offered Surinam any assistance it might need in forming its own Army, and formalized this offer in a treaty. An extensive Dutch military mission provided technical and organizational advice, and Surinamese soldiers were given the opportunity to receive training in The Netherlands. Yet the military budget remained very small, which resulted in a chronic shortage of military equipment. The Surinamese government wanted an Army, but not an expensive one.

As noted earlier, problems within the Army and between a large section of the Army and a hostile government concerning the demand for a military union prompted the 1980 coup (see Chapter 1). Although most of the officers sympathized with the sergeants' grievances, they did not participate in the coup itself. This impartiality can partly be traced to their thorough Dutch military training, in which heavy emphasis was placed on the subordination of the military to the legal authorities. Neither did these officers choose sides in the conflict surrounding the military union, which involved only the lower ranks. For the majority of them, there was therefore no place in the post-coup Army. After an initial period of imprisonment, the officers were dishonourably discharged by decree. Most of them emigrated to The Netherlands, placing an enormous qualitative drain on the military apparatus.

Although the problem of obsolete equipment had plagued the Surinamese Army before 1980, the post-coup 'brain-drain' brought with it additional organizational problems. The corps of officers had been reduced both quantitatively and qualitatively, while the size of the standing Army had increased. The Dutch military mission gave all possible assistance in dealing with organizational, administrative and logistic problems. But in May 1981, the Surinamese government ordered the mission to halt its activities. This development is officially referred to as the first step on the road to the 'emancipation' of Surinam's Army. It is perhaps worth noting in this context that a number of Surinamese soldiers went to Cuba for training just after the Dutch mission had been called to a halt. Surinamese soldiers received no training in The Netherlands as from December 1982, after the summary executions in that month had led The Netherlands to suspend the terms of the treaty with its former colony.

Surinamese society became increasingly militarized after the 1980 coup. The Army was no longer merely an instrument with a degree of political power: it had become the major political force in the country. This militarization has pervaded much of Surinamese life. Both the National Information Service and the Surinamese News Agency are headed by members of the military, thereby providing the regime with a near monopoly of the country's news distribution facilities. Members of the military were also appointed to cabinet posts and other government positions. One extremely significant development has been the Army's growing involvement with internal security tasks. What was once the exclusive task of the civilian police force has been increasingly taken over by the military police.

Prior to 1980, the military police only carried out the tasks ascribed to it by law, the most important of which was the maintenance of military discipline both on and off base. In 1982 the military police were empowered to carry out general investigative work: the confirmation *de jure* of the actual situation from the time of the coup. The military police, now led by one of Bouterse's close confidants, developed into a security force with almost unlimited powers. These police are also supported in their work by a national intelligence service which is in turn under direct military control. The Army itself scarcely proved a stable factor, an observation which only increased the regime's tendency towards repressive measures. Surendre Rambocus's nearly-successful coup attempt in March 1982 led to the setting-up of a people's militia. The official reading was that this militia was to symbolize the bond between the Army and the people. In actual fact, this paramilitary unit acted as informant for the regime. Furthermore, the people's militia did not shrink from intimidation—a fact which made them much feared among the population.

The people's militia never became a large unit, however. An estimated 600 to 700 civilians (including schoolchildren, who were to help form a young people's militia) received brief military training. The operative size of the militia, including only those people regularly participating in rifle drills, has never been more than 200 to 300. The militia has deliberately been kept small to ensure its reliability. The core consists of groups of several dozen leftist-revolutionary intellectuals, but is of no military importance.

The military's increasing preoccupation with its political role certainly received little support from within the Army itself, as testified to by the coup attempt of March 1982. Dissension existed even among the sixteen conspirators in Bouterse's successful coup (often referred to as 'the group of sixteen'), who were usually regarded as 'blood brothers'. One of them, Sgt. Wilfred Hawker, took part in Rambocus's coup attempt and was afterwards summarily executed. Bouterse's right-hand man, Garrison Commander Roy Horb, died under suspicious circumstances in a military prison in January 1983 (see Chapter 1). Two other members of the group, Arty Gorré and Paul Bhagwandas, were drummed out of the military leadership in 1986 for their outspoken disapproval of the dialogue with the old political parties. Both these men occupied important positions within the regime. Gorré was commander of the elite 'Echo Company' commandos and Bhagwandas was Secretary of the 25 February Movement.

A major purge was carried out as early as the first months of 1983, with the discharge of some ten officers, almost all of whom had received training in The Netherlands and had openly opposed the executions of 8 December 1982. Such purges have undoubtedly done much to reduce to a minimum the threat of a coup from within. In fact, the Army no longer contains any well-trained second-in-command who would be either served by or capable of planning a coup. Furthermore, preparations for such a coup would now almost certainly be discovered in time by the military leadership. But many of the soldiers drummed out of the corps during these purges, as well as others who left the armed forces voluntarily, have continued to pose a threat to Bouterse and his allies from the relative safety of The Netherlands. Deserters and other Surinamese exiles have in the past joined forces to plan the invasion of Surinam, either with or without the help of foreign mercenaries.

Yet the most critical threat to the military regime came in 1986, in the form of a guerrilla movement primarily active in eastern and central Surinam. This 'Jungle Commando' or 'Surinamese National Liberation Army' (SNLA) is led by Ronnie Brunswijk, one of Bouterse's former bodyguards, and is advised by the exiled officer Michiel van Rey. During the 1980 coup, Van Rey was the only commissioned officer to openly side with the sergeants, and was later appointed Minister of the Army and Police. Before long, however, his advocacy of a rapid return to barracks forced him to flee to The Netherlands.

The SNLA has been able to reinforce its ranks with deserters from the National Army, and the guerrilla forces now total at least several hundred men. The group of deserters included the new commander of the Echo Company, another illustration of the lack of cohesion within the National Army. In terms of military technique and strategy, the SNLA—with the best-trained military men among its ranks—would appear to have the advantage. The National Army's superiority is based solely on its possession of more weaponry. Motivation within the National Army, and particularly among its conscripts, is quite low. It is only the hard core, which has bound its fate to Bouterse's own and plucks the material fruits of this commitment, which appears prepared to fight to the end.

The struggle is primarily taking place in areas occupied by the country's Bush Negroes, and this has led to brutal National Army reprisals against this group by the National Army (see pp. 112–16). It is therefore little wonder that the Bush Negroes, who already harboured sympathy for the SNLA owing to their affinity with Brunswijk (himself a Bush Negro), have come to support the SNLA *en masse*. Their *granmans* (chiefs) have unanimously rejected the Bouterse regime, allowing the SNLA to exercise complete control over areas in eastern and central Surinam. The guerrilla forces largely limit themselves, after the model of the legendary Marron leader Boni, to hit-and-run tactics against such economic targets as the Suralco bauxite plants.

The struggle against the SNLA will undoubtedly require increasing funds. The National Army, including the people's militia, publishes no official figures on the size of its ranks, but experts have estimated the regime's current forces at around 2,200 men. Of these, some 120 are attached to the Navy and another 80 to the National Air Force.

The regime's arms supply has grown considerably since 1980. At first the Army possessed only nine Dutch YP-Armoured Personnel Carriers (APCs), but another twenty-one Brazilian APCs (fifteen Urutus and six Cascavels) have since been added. The Air Force has four small Defender aircraft. Since the beginning of the conflict with the SNLA, the Army has also gained access to a few helicopters. The Navy has nine patrol boats, several of which are fitted with cannons.

The military budget has risen steadily since 1980, when it totalled only Sf. 20m. By 1982, however, the official military budget totalled Sf. 51.3m. And, in 1986, official military spending had expanded to Sf. 85.1m.—equal to 11 per cent of the country's total current spending. There are clear indications, however, that actual military spending in 1986 was considerably higher in connection with the struggle against the guerrilla forces, and currently accounts for an estimated 20 to 25 per cent of the national budget in that year, placing Surinam among the ranks of the world's heavily militarized countries.

Foreign Policy

In a sense, Surinam is the cuckoo's egg in the Latin American nest. Isolated by the Dutch language and with a wealth of primarily self-centred ethnic groups, the country was scarcely orientated towards the outside world. For a long time, The Netherlands was the country's only window-on-the-world. The internal autonomy proceeding from the 1954 amendments to the Statute of the Realm changed little of this. The new relationship with the mother country actually seemed to make it more difficult for Surinam to emerge from the Dutch colonial shadow. The country's foreign policy, after all, remained a Dutch affair.

When the writer V. S. Naipaul visited Surinam in the early 1960s, he wrote: 'In Surinam Holland is Europe. Holland is the centre of the world; even America recedes. "The first thing you've got to get out of your head", an American official said to me, "is that you're in Latin America" . . . Surinam feels only like a tulip-less extension of Holland; some Surinamers call it Holland's twelfth province' (from *The Middle Passage*, 1975, p. 180).

Surinam was still not integrated into the region when it became the 144th United Nations member-state after independence in 1975. And, in the

Organization of American States (OAS), which it joined in 1977, Surinam, as a small nation, played only a passive role.

Strong ties were maintained with The Netherlands even after independence. The 1975 bilateral development-aid agreement granted Holland major influence in the economic development of its former colony (see Chapter 4). Furthermore, an additional agreement made it easier for Surinamers to emigrate to the former mother country during the five-year period following independence. In other words, a form of the old relation of both economic and psychological dependence was preserved.

The 1980 military coup at first did little to change this situation. As mentioned earlier, the Surinamese government of the day was extremely careful not to damage relations with its most important partners, the United States and The Netherlands (see Chapter 1). This caution was reflected in the government policy programme published on 1 May 1980. The programme stated that nothing more than 'shifts in accent' were to be expected with regard to the country's foreign policy. One of these 'shifts' was the decisive role in foreign policy granted to the prospects of economic benefit. The policy programme also announced plans for a more extensive Caribbean orientation and for Surinamese participation in such regional economic organizations as Caricom and Lafta.

The first post-coup government also wanted to shift the accent in the relationship with The Netherlands. One of the central foreign-policy objectives stated in the programme was 'emergence from the great economic dependence on Dutch development aid'. The decision not to initiate diplomatic ties with Cuba fitted well with the Chin a Sen government's moderate and cautious stance. Discussions on this subject had been held with Havana even before the 1980 coup, but no diplomatic steps were taken. America's sensitivity to regional politics played a major role in the Chin a Sen government's decision not to establish ties with Cuba. André Haakmat, Minister of Foreign Affairs at the time, said the following about his September 1980 meeting with American Secretary of State Edmund Muskie. Muskie clearly outlined Washington's standpoint on Surinamese–Cuban relations. 'He said official recognition of Cuba could do Surinam no good; no good at all . . . When I came back, no one in either the cabinet or the military leadership favoured diplomatic recognition of Cuba' (interview with NRC Handelsblad, 13 November 1982). But members of the revolutionary factions, especially the RVP, were already maintaining unofficial contacts with a group of Cuban political advisers who regularly visited Surinam.

The country's foreign policy was somewhat altered in 1981. A primary factor was the January 1981 appointment of Harvey Naarendorp to succeed

Haakmat. Naarendorp entertained a number of radical ideas, but his lack of an established political image at the time led Chin a Sen to consider him acceptable for a ministerial post. The March 1981 release of the left-wing soldiers reflected the revolutionary factions' increasing influence over the top military leaders (see Chapter 1). The socialist line announced at the time also had consequences for Surinam's foreign policy.

Diplomatic ties were established with Cuba within two months of the new ministerial appointment. It can rightfully be said that Harvey Naarendorp was the mastermind behind the new and far-reaching relations with Havana, and the major advocate of these relations within the cabinet. Other ministers, as well as the Prime Minister, did not reject such relations outright, but were sceptical.

The decision was finally made to accept the accreditation of a non-resident ambassador. In doing so, the government consciously opted for the Cuban ambassador in Caracas, rather than his colleague in neighbouring Guyana. According to President Chin a Sen, this would allow better monitoring of incoming and outgoing Cubans, who until that time had been able to enter Surinam more or less unnoticed by the overland route through Nickerie.

Cuba posted a full-time ambassador in Paramaribo within a few months of the Chin a Sen government's 1982 resignation. Before this, Harvey Naarendorp had set up a commission to investigate ways in which political, economic, social and cultural ties with Cuba could be expanded. The appointment of reputed political heavyweight Osvaldo Cardenas Junquera as ambassador to Paramaribo illustrated the importance Havana attached to its diplomatic post in Surinam. After Grenada, Surinam seemingly presented a second opportunity to establish a foothold in the Caribbean region. Contacts between the two countries took place largely through the RVP, the Department of People's Mobilization and a group of revolutionary intellectuals surrounding Naarendorp. Most of the information provided by the Cubans dealt with the setting-up of a revolutionary political system (see Chapter 1). Several dozen soldiers, students and press representatives also went to Havana for training.

During this same period, Surinam's relationship with the United States reached its lowest ebb. When internal unrest increased in the fall of 1982, Paramaribo accused two American diplomats, Richard Laroche and Edward Donovan, of interfering in Surinam's internal affairs. The two were expelled in early 1983. Furthermore the military authorities claimed the executions of 8 December 1982 had taken place within the context of an abortive, CIA-supported coup attempt.

The 1982 executions, and the resulting suspension of Dutch and American development aid automatically served to escalate the radicalization of the country's foreign relations. Socialist countries and groups now welcomed Surinam as an ally. The Tass and Prensa Latina press agencies reported that a 'counter-revolutionary conspiracy' had been nipped in the bud on 8 December 1982. Even the Vietnamese party daily *Nhan Dan* gave coverage to the executions, and spoke with fraternal solidarity of 'the crushing of an imperialist-abetted coup attempt in Surinam on December 8 as an important victory of the National Military Council and patriotic forces' (cited by the VNA Vietnamese News Agency).

As a member of the movement of non-aligned nations since 1979, Surinam officially kept to a policy of non-alignment but chose in actual practice the Cuban line. Overtures were also made towards Libya, in the hope of obtaining economic benefits. Commander-in-Chief Bouterse visited Libyan leader Gadaffi in March 1983, following the seventh annual conference of non-aligned nations in New Delhi. Surinam in fact made increasing use of the non-aligned movement to mobilize Third World countries against The Netherlands. Such activities were also attempted in New Delhi, but met with only limited success owing to the general awareness of The Netherlands' ready hand in distributing development aid.

Both internal and external forces, however, led in 1983 to yet another new tack in foreign policy. One internal factor was the conflict between the RVP and the PALU. The RVP, with its internationalist orientation, followed an anti-imperialistic course and saw the United States as its major opponent and Cuba as its closest ally. As a party with nationalistic overtones, the PALU was opposed only to colonialism. For this party, therefore, The Netherlands as former colonial power was the 'arch enemy', as Errol Alibux (PALU leader and prime minister at the time) expressed it. The PALU even made overtures towards the United States, partly with a view to obtaining a $100m. loan from the IMF (see Chapter 4). As noted earlier, the PALU also felt that the rival RVP would be weakened by a cooler relationship with Cuba. Even more important than this factional conflict, however, was the external pressure brought to bear by both Brazil and the United States. The results of the lightning visit to Paramaribo in April 1983 by Brazil's senior security official, General Danilo Venturini, have been described elsewhere in this book (see Chapter 1). But it was ultimately the American invasion of Grenada which prompted Bouterse to expel the Cuban ambassador and his retinue in October 1983 (see Chapter 1). Bouterse himself termed Cardenas's expulsion 'one of the consequences' of the events in Grenada (television speech, 25 October 1983).

The minutes of a private meeting between the military authorities and the revolutionary leadership on 15 December 1983 (after Venturini's visit but just before the expulsion of the Cuban ambassador) shed even more light on foreign policy during this period. These minutes show that the decision to reinforce ties with Brazil was made for primarily strategic reasons. Commander-in-Chief Bouterse said:

Everyone now knows why this relationship has been forged with Brazil. It is a strategic step. The revolution has not been sold out. We are not for sale, but we must not forget that this same Brazil, which now wants to help us, was once prepared to invade us. In other words, this strategic step must not be endangered [from minutes of meeting of 15 September 1983; conference room of the Memre Boekoek barracks, Paramaribo].

During the same meeting, one cabinet minister noted that Brazil had said it would invade Surinam if Cuban or Libyan arms deliveries entered the country. PALU leader Iwan Krolis said that consideration had been given to obtaining arms from Libya: 'The conclusion was that Libyan weapons would not be enough. The relationship with Brazil should therefore be seen as a strategic step towards consolidating the revolution'.

Relations with Brazil were strengthened only shortly after Venturini's visit to Paramaribo, which had all the earmarks of a diplomatic intervention. The prime minister at the time, Errol Alibux, subsequently paid two visits to Brasilia within a four-month period. The improved relations resulted in Brazilian economic and technical aid in such areas as agriculture, tele-communications and even military supplies (see pp. 170–4).

Relations with the United States also thawed somewhat following the expulsion of Osvaldo Cardenas. The extent of America's anxieties on this subject was reflected in American President Ronald Reagan's speech to the United Nations General Assembly in September 1983. Reagan mentioned miniscule Surinam in one breath with the world's major war zones, and referred implicitly to the December 1982 executions. The American President spoke of 'violent conflicts in the hills of Beirut, the deserts of Chad and the Western Sahara, in the mountains of El Salvador, in the streets of Surinam' (speech to the United Nations General Assembly, 26 October 1983). In talks with the Dutch Prime Minister in March of that year, American Vice-President George Bush had already expressed America's concern regarding Cuban influence and Surinam's relations with Grenada. One thing was clear: the military regime had drawn the world's attention with its internal political intrigues and related foreign policy. For the first time in its history, Surinam had become a political issue in the East–West arena.

The Americans abruptly changed their tune after the expulsion of the Cuban diplomats. Ambassador Robert Dumling said that the resumption of his country's suspended development aid to Surinam was 'not impossible'. The regime in Paramaribo also made attempts to improve relations with The Netherlands. To this end, the experienced diplomat Henk Heidweiller, a former member of the 'old guard' who succeeded in surviving the political turbulence of the entire Bouterse regime was appointed ambassador to The Hague. It was hoped that Surinam's plans for reintroducing democratic institutions would ease relations with its former mother country. Paramaribo attached great importance to the resumption of special development aid from The Netherlands. As noted earlier, this desire remained unfulfilled: Holland continued to hold out for 'concrete steps' towards democratization.

The Surinamese authorities therefore began looking for other sources of finance: an important factor in the decision to further strengthen the ties established with Libya in early 1983. A high-level delegation, including Bouterse and Prime Minister Udenhout, paid an official visit to Tripoli (Surinam's second such visit in two years) in March 1985. The Libyans underscored the importance of the visit by sending a special plane to pick up the delegation.

This time the contacts between Surinam and Libya appeared to be more than incidental. The Libyans set up a People's Bureau (embassy) in Paramaribo, and several cooperative agreements were signed on 5 March. On his return, Prime Minister Udenhout stated that these agreements dealt with fields of economics, technology, defence and culture. But the cooperative arrangement produced far less than had originally been hoped. The hope of a US$ 100m. loan remained unfulfilled.

The ties were extensive enough, however, to generate renewed American concern. Immediately after the opening of the Libyan People's Bureau, the American ambassador to Paramaribo warned Bouterse to be 'cautious' in ties with Libya. An identical warning followed in January 1986, as American planes were bombarding Tripoli. The extent of the Libyan presence in Surinam has never been made clear. The People's Bureau has only a small staff, but Libyans continue to enter and leave Surinam and are in any event active in the country's Islamic communities.

The first reports of Libyan involvement in the National Army's struggle with guerrilla forces in eastern Surinam were made in late 1986. American Assistant Secretary of State Elliott Abrams saw sufficient cause to term Libyan involvement an obstacle to good relations between the United States and Surinam (press reports, 16 December 1986).

Relations with France have also been damaged. The French have repeatedly stated their concern with developments in Surinam; such statements have become more frequent since late 1986, when thousands of Bush Negroes began fleeing to French Guyana to escape National Army reprisals against the Jungle Commandos. Furthermore, any Libyan military presence would be deeply disturbing to the French in view of the proximity of the Kourou missile base. Perhaps the ability of Surinamese guerrillas to move unchallenged through French territory is telling in this regard.

The key to Surinam's foreign policy unequivocally continues to be its relations with The Netherlands, despite all its attempts to achieve integration in the region. The fact that one-third of all Surinamers reside in the former mother country, as well as the substantial sums involved in Dutch development aid, will continue to play a major role in the foreign policy of any Surinamese government. The old political parties in particular regard good relations with The Netherlands as being of extreme importance. The political accord between these parties and the military authorities includes an implicit reference to relations with The Netherlands; this reference was included at the parties' insistence. In language rendered somewhat cryptic by the strong element of compromise in its drafting, the accord speaks of the need for 'reinforcement of the historic ties with eligible countries'.

But the potpourri of political stances at the centre of power continues to be reflected in the country's foreign policy. On 31 December 1986, for example, Surinam's Ministry of Foreign Affairs published a memorandum, addressed to the Dutch ambassador, suggesting that diplomatic relations between Surinam and The Netherlands should be reduced to a lower level. Holland was accused of providing a free base for supporters of the guerrilla movement in eastern Surinam. In January 1987, the diplomatic row culminated in the expulsion of the Dutch ambassador, who was accused of 'interfering in domestic affairs'.

Protests against the expulsion were quickly voiced by the old political parties participating in the Supreme Council. The conflict ultimately led to the resignation of Foreign Minister Henk Herrenberg. The political principle of tit-for-tat, initiated by the radical 25 February Movement in particular, prompted Prime Minister Pertab Radakishun of the old VHP to step down.

It is precisely this hodgepodge of factions within the government that has led to the tortuous course take by Surinam's foreign policy. But there can be no doubt that the outer limits of this course continue to be dictated by foreign pressure.

Concluding Remarks

A coup that was elevated to the status of a revolution but never really became one: that has been Surinam's story in recent years. It seems strangely symbolic that the soldiers who overthrew the government of Henck Arron in 1980 are now involved in regular consultation with the old political parties they so despised, but this does not mean that Surinam has come full-circle. Too many lives have been lost in a struggle (that exhibits increasing overtones of power-politics) to ever return to that point.

How could a movement that began with such apparently good intentions go so thoroughly wrong? If for no other reason than their superiority of arms, the military leaders bear the prime responsibility. The lack of experience and consequent suggestibility on the part of the young sergeants, who had no clear plans for a national development policy, certainly played a major role. The leader of the coup, Sgt. Desi Bouterse, was prepared, immediately following his successful bid for power, to accept the position of deputy minister of sports. It is a curious fact that it was precisely the civilian sector that told him that greater things were in store. After all, he had won an entire country. It was primarily those leaders of the small leftist-revolutionary groups, entirely lacking in administrative experience, who most frequently and, at first most successfully, won the ear of the new Commander-in-Chief and 'Leader of the Revolution'. They saw in him the chance to finally achieve that which had previously been impossible. And to this end they were prepared to accept a military authority with absolute power and to declare the leader of the military a 'shining example' to the revolution.

In fact, the left-wing parties remained at odds within the dominant system. Their influence, at times vehement, remains incidental and distinct from what continues to represent the mainstream, particularly after episodes which were seemingly fatal to this regime. The aloof and authoritarian stance of the leftist-revolutionary leaders has prevented them from coming close to the people. Their analyses were obsolete, over-simplified and too rigid for the complexity of Surinamese society.

Especially since the dark days of December 1982, the military leaders' struggle for power has, in a certain sense, become a struggle for self-preservation. They therefore demand guarantees for their own immunity in the course of any democratization process. In this respect, one can speak of an 'Alfonsin effect'. Surinam's military leaders cannot help but be aware that a significant number of Argentina's military junta have been prosecuted since President Alfonsin's civilian government came to power. Despite the collapse of the country's economy and increasing social unrest in Paramaribo and its surroundings, the military still appears unwilling to surrender its power.

As noted above, the military has opened negotiations with the old political parties on the steps needed to establish a 'true democracy'. The intention is to prompt The Netherlands to resume its suspended development aid and so allow the regime to implement the necessary public-spending cuts without risking bad social upheaval. By effecting such measures, the regime hopes to meet the conditions posed by the IMF for a US$100m. loan.

A power struggle has now arisen between the leftist-revolutionary groups and the old political parties over their diametrically opposite interpretations of 'true democracy'. The situation has been complicated even further by the Jungle Commandos' increasingly successful advances in areas which include western Surinam, the country's major rice-producing region. This poses a threat not only to Surinam's last significant source of income, but also to the capital city of Paramaribo itself.

It is therefore difficult to predict the short-term course of events in Surinam. On the basis of information currently available, however, several possibilities present themselves. The first is that the regime will be able, for the time being, to keep the situation under control and succeed in persuading the leaders of the old political parties to take steps towards what the military leaders and leftist-revolutionary groups regard as true democracy. This would mean that actual power would remain in the hands of the military. The result would be a further decline in the country's socio-economic situation, since The Netherlands would most probably refuse to resume its development aid under such circumstances. Social unrest and repression would mount, and the activities of the Jungle Commandos would continue. The final result would be a bloodbath, in which foreign intervention could not be ruled out.

A second possibility is that the old political parties will succeed in persuading the military leadership to take steps that would ultimately lead to free elections and a parliamentary democracy. In view of the fear of the 'Alfonsin effect', this could result in the flight of the military leaders and their advisers abroad. The old political parties would then have to establish an accord with the Jungle Commandos in order to restore national order.

The third and final alternative is a situation in which guerrilla activities will lead to even more widespread social unrest and public resistance to the regime, with increasing Army desertions. This scenario also presents the possibilities of a bloodbath, which could result in foreign intervention.

One thing, however, is certain. Dark days still lie ahead for Surinam.

Bibliography

Books and articles

Bovenkerk, F., 1981. 'Why returnees generally do not turn out to be "agents of change": the case of Suriname', in *New West Indian Guide*, **55**, pp. 154–73.
— 1983. 'De vlucht, migratie in de jaren zeventig', in Willemsen, G. (ed.), *Suriname, de schele onafhankelijkheid*. Amsterdam, Arbeiders Pers.
Brandsma, J. K., 1983. 'Afhankelijkheid en revolutie in een plantage maatschappij', in *OSO*, December, pp. 3–23.
Breeman, J., 1975. 'Beleid en Maatschappij in Suriname: de Systematiek van "hosselen" en "pinaren"', in *Beleid en Maatschappij*, **9**, September, pp. 214–26.
Campbell, E. E., 1977. 'Vakverenigingsleven in Suriname', in Helman, A. (ed.), *Cultureel Mozaiek van Suriname*. Zutphen, De Walburg Pers.
— 1987. 'Vakbeweging en arbeidsverhoudingen in Suriname', Ph.D. thesis. Brabant, The Netherlands, Catholic University.
Chin, H. E., 1971. 'Ontwikkelingshulp en economische ontwikkeling', in *Internationale Spectator*, **25**, 15, September, The Hague.
— 1985. 'Suriname: tien jaar onafhankelijkheid', in *ESB*, **70**, 3523, Rotterdam, Netherlands Economic Institute.
— 1986. 'The Need for restructuring the economy of Suriname', in Chin, H. E. (ed.), *The Caribbean Basin and the Changing World Economic Structure*. Groningen, Wolters-Noordhoff.
Choenni, C. E. S., 1982. *Hindostanen in de politiek, een vergelijkende studie van hun positie in Trinidad, Guyana en Suriname*. Rotterdam, Futile.
Derveld, F. E. R., 1981. 'Politieke mobilisatie en integratie van de Javanen in Suriname', Ph.D. thesis. Leiden, State University.
Dew, E., 1972. 'Surinam: the test of consociationalism', in *Plural Societies*, **3**, 4, Autumn, pp. 35–56.
— 1978. *The Difficult Flowering of Surinam*. The Hague, Martinus Nijhoff.
Dobru, R., 1969. *Tori Boto*. Paramaribo.
Fernandes Mendes, H. K., 1983. 'De staatsgreep in Suriname', *Nederlands Juristenblad*, No. 5, January, pp. 145–51.
Furnifall, J. S., 1944. *Netherlands India, a study of plural economy*. Cambridge, Cambridge University Press.
Geertz, C., 1963. 'The Integrative Revolution: primordial sentiments and civil politics in the new states', in Geertz, C. (ed.), *Old societies and new states: the quest for modernity in Asia and Africa*. New York, Free Press of Glencoe.
Gowricharn, R., 1983. 'Staat en accumulatie in Suriname: historische en theoretische notities', in Willemsen, G. (ed.), *Suriname en de schele onafhankelijkheid*. Amsterdam, De Arbeiders Pers.

Groot, S. W. de, 1974. *Surinaamse granmans in Afrika*. Utrecht, het Spectrum.

Haakmat, A., 1987. *De revolutie uitgegleden: politieke herinneringen*. Amsterdam, Uitgeverij Jan Mets.

Heilbron, W. & Willemsen, G., 1980. 'Goud—en Balata— exploitatie in Suriname', in *Caraibisch Forum*, January and May, Amsterdam.

Helman, A., 1977. *Cultureel Mozaiek van Suriname*. Zutphen, De Walburg Pers.

Herskovits, M. J., 1966. 'The New World Negro', in Herskovits, F. S. (ed.), *Selected papers in Afro-American Studies*. Indiana, Indiana University Press.

Hoppe, R., 1975. 'Het politiek systeem van Suriname: elite-kartel democratie', in *Acta politica*, **11**, pp. 145–77.

Janowitz, M., 1977. *Military Institutions and Coercion in Developing Nations*. Chicago, University Press of Chicago.

Keller, A. G., 1908. *Colonization: A Study of the Founding of New Societies*. Boston.

Klerk, C. J. M., De, 1953. *De immigratie der Hindostanen in Suriname*. Amsterdam, Urbi et Orbi.

Kruijer, G. J., 1973. *Suriname: Neokolonie in Rijksverband*. Meppel, Boom.

Lier, R. A. J. Van, 1950. *The Development and Nature of Society in the West Indies*, Kasinklijke Vereeniging Indisch Institut, Amsterdam, 1950.

Lier, R. A. J. Van, 1977. *Samenleving in een grensgebied*. The Hague, Martinus Nijhoff.

Lijphart, A., 1969. 'Consociational Democracy' in *World Politics*, **21**, 2, January, pp. 207–25.

—— 1971. 'Cultural Diversity and Theories of Political Integration', in *Canadian Journal of Political Science*, **4**, 1, pp. 1–14.

McPhee, A., 1926. *The Economic Revolution in British West Africa*. London, Routledge.

Manchester, A. K., 1969. *British Preeminence in Brazil, Its rise and decline*. New York, Octagon Books Inc.

Mitrasing, F. E. M., 1959. 'Tien jaar Suriname 1945–1955: van afhankelijkheid tot gerechtigheid', Ph.D. thesis. Leiden, State University.

Naipaul, V. S., 1975. *The Middle Passage: the Caribbean Revisited*. London, Penguin.

—— 1981. *The Overcrowded Barracoon and Other Articles*. London, Penguin.

Olufemi Ekundare, R., 1973. *An Economic History of Nigeria, 1860–1960*. London, Methuen.

Ooft, C. D. 1980. *Surinaams staatsrecht voor en na de omwenteling*. Paramaribo.

Panday, R. M. N., 1959. 'Agriculture in Surinam 1650–1950', Ph.D. thesis. University of Amsterdam.

Raalte, J. Van, 1977. 'De christelijke godsdiensten', in Helman, A. (ed.), *Cultureel Mozaiek van Suriname*. Zutphen, De Walburg Pers, pp. 291–303.

Rabushka, A. & Shepsle, K. A., 1972. *Politics in Plural Societies: a theory of democratic instability*. Colombia, Merill Publishing Company.

Robock, S., 1975. *Brazil, A Study in Development Progress*. London, Lexington Books.

Slagveer, J., 1980. *De nacht van de revolutie*. Paramaribo, Uitgeverij C. Kersten & Co.

Smooha, S., 1975. 'Pluralism and Conflict: a theoretical exploration', in *Plural Societies*, **6**, 3, pp. 69–89.

Voorhoeve, J. & Lichtveld, U. M., 1975. *Creole Drum, An anthology of Creole literature in Surinam*. New Haven, Yale University Press.

West, K., 1972. 'Stratification and Ethnicity in Plural New States', in *Race*, **13**, 4.

Willemsen, G., 1983. 'Koloniale politiek en transformatieprocessen in een plantage-economie, Suriname 1873–1940, Ph.D. thesis. Rotterdam, Erasmus University.

Woytinsky, E. S. & Woytinsky, E. S., 1953. *World Population and Production*. New York, The Twentieth Century Fund.

Reports, Programmes, Brochures and Other Documents

'Adviesrapport van de Denkgroep inzake te realiseren democratische structuren van duurzame aard' (Report to the Military Leader), Paramaribo, December 1984.

Associatie voor Democratie, Letter to Commander-in-Chief Desi Bouterse, Paramaribo, 23 November 1982.

Bureau of People's Mobilization, Paramaribo, 1982. 'Doel en structuur van de volkscomites'.

CCK (Committee of Christian Churches), 'Verklaring over het onwerpprogramma van de Vijfentwintig Februari Beweging', Paramaribo, 15 November 1983.

Central Bank of Surinam, various annual reports

FEA (Financial Economic Advisory) Committee Report to the Government, January 1984.

General Bureau of Statistics of Surinam, various reports and other documents

Haakmat, J., 'Cyrill Daal de vermoorde Surinaamse vakbondsleider: een historisch overzicht', Amsterdam, 1983.

IMF, Surinam, Staff Report, 20 February 1985.

—— Surinam, Staff Report, April 1986.

International Commission of Jurists (Griffiths, J.), 1980. 'Human Rights in Surinam'. 1 April, Geneva.

Keerveld, H. J., 1971. *Op weg naar een strijdend socialisme*. maart, Paramaribo.

Lachmon, J., en Arron, H., 1984. 'Basisprincipes en structuren voor de democratie in Suriname', 25 May, Paramaribo.

Lichtpunt '77, Programme van het Derde Blok, Paramaribo, 1977.

Manifest van de PALU, Paramaribo, March 1977.

Manifest van de Revolutie, Paramaribo, May 1981.

Mijs, A. A. 1973. *Onderwijs en Ontwikkeling in Suriname*. University of Amsterdam.

Ministry of Education and Popular Development, Suriname Voorwaarts, February 1984.

Ministry of Finance and Planning, various reports and other documents.

Ministry of Internal Affairs and People's Mobilization, Nota: Beleidsaspekten, April 1986.

Ministry of Trade, Transport and Industry, various documents.

Naarendorp, H. H. & Wijdenbosch, 1984. 'Structuur Vijfentwintig Februari Beweging', March.

OAS (Organization of American States), Annual Reports of the Inter-American Commission for Human Rights, Washington DC, 1983, 1985 and 1986.

Ormskirk, F., 1966. '20 Jaar NPS', Nationale Partij Suriname, Paramaribo.

Planning Bureau of Surinam, various development programmes, reports and other documents.

Politiek akkoord van VFB, VHP, NPS, KTPI, PWO, Moederbond, CLO, VSB, en ASFA, Paramaribo, 25 November 1985.

Politiek en sociaal-ekonomisch scenario voor de overgangsperiode in Suriname 1985-1986, December 1984.

Programma en statuten van de Vijfentwintig Februari Beweging, Paramaribo, 12 May 1984.

Rapport van de commissie van onderzoek: Onderzoek naar de rol van de Nederlandse militaire missie in Suriname voor, tijdens en na de staatsgreep.

Regeringsverklaring, 1980, Die vier vernieuwingen van de Surinaamse samenleving, 1 May 1980.

Regeringsverklaring, 1982-1984, 1 May 1982.

Regeringsverklaring en hoofdlijnen van het regeerprogramma 1983-1986, 1 May 1983.

Surinaamsche Bank NV, various annual reports.

SURINFO, National Information Service of the Government, July 1985.

UNCHR (United Nations Commission on Human Rights), 1985 Report by the Special Rapporteur on summary or arbitrary executions (A. Wako), 12 February 1985.

Vijfentwintig Februari Beweging, 'Structuur van de VFB', Paramaribo, March 1984.

Vollers, J. H., 1974. *Bestuurlijke structuur van Suriname*, University of Amsterdam.

Vuijsje, H., 1974. *Ontwikkelingsfuncties van religieuze organisaties in Suriname*. University of Amsterdam.

Index